Reconsidering Gender

Reconsidering Gender

Evangelical Perspectives

Edited by
MYK HABETS
and
BEULAH WOOD

PICKWICK *Publications* • Eugene, Oregon

RECONSIDERING GENDER
Evangelical Perspectives

Copyright © 2011 Wipf and Stock Publishers. All rights reserved. Except for brief quotations in critical publications or reviews, no part of this book may be reproduced in any manner without prior written permission from the publisher. Write: Permissions, Wipf and Stock Publishers, 199 W. 8th Ave., Suite 3, Eugene, OR 97401.

Pickwick Publications
An Imprint of Wipf and Stock Publishers
199 W. 8th Ave., Suite 3
Eugene, OR 97401

www.wipfandstock.com

ISBN 13: 978-1-60899-547-9

Cataloging-in-Publication data:

Reconsidering gender : evangelical perspectives / edited by Myk Habets and Beulah Wood.

xviii + 230 p. ; cm. 23 — Includes bibliographical references.

ISBN 13: 978-1-60899-547-9

1. Women in Christianity. 2. Women and Religion. 3. Feminist theology. 4. Feminism—Religious aspects—Christianity. 5. Evangelicalism. 6. Gender identity. I. Title.

BR1642 R45 2011

Manufactured in the U.S.A.

*This volume is dedicated to the many pastors—women and men—
who labor so faithfully in the Lord's vineyard to bring
God's Word to God's people in God-honouring, Bible-affirming,
and life-changing ways.*

To Christ, the head of the church, be all glory.

Contents

Foreword—Kevin Giles / *ix*

Introduction—*Myk Habets* / 1

Prologue: Gender: Divine or Human?—*Myk Habets* / 5

1. The Image of the Invisible God: (An)iconic Knowing, God, and Gender—*Tim Bulkeley* / 20
2. The Image of the Invisible God: A Response to Tim Bulkeley—*Mark Keown* / 38
3. Gender Roles in Marriage and Ministry: A Possible Relationship—*Craig Blomberg* / 48
4. Why We Still Need Feminist Theology: A Response to Craig Blomberg—*Nicola Hoggard-Creegan* / 63
5. The Gender Issue in New Zealand Evangelical History—*Peter J. Lineham* / 75
6. Is Christianity Good for Women? A Response to Peter Lineham—*Cathy Ross* / 105
7. God and Gender: The Relational Center—*Irene Alexander* / 116
8. Relationality—Getting to the Heart of It: A Response to Irene Alexander—*Joyce Carswell* / 135
9. Is There a God in This Text? Violence, Absence, and Silence in 2 Samuel 13:1–22—*Miriam Bier* / 148
10. In Whose Interests Do We Read? A Response to Miriam Bier—*Tim Meadowcroft* / 161

11 Being Masculine in My Disabled Male Body
    —*S. J. Immanuel Koks* / 171
12 Heads and Bodies: A Response to Immanuel Koks
    —*Chris Marshall* / 188
13 Divine Masculine and Feminine in Judeo-mystico:
    A Tree of Life—*Yael Klangwisan* / 196
14 Imaging the Triune God in Otherness and Encounter:
    A Response to Yael Klangwisan—*David Williams* / 213

List of Contributors / 225

Foreword

TWO THEOLOGICAL RESPONSES TO CHANGE

IN THE LAST FORTY years, one of the most momentous social changes known in human history has taken place—women's liberation. A number of factors came together in the late 1960s to open the door for this revolution. First of all, women caught up in the education stakes and then gained a small lead. Girls today do better on average at school and now over fifty percent of graduates are women. When brute strength mattered more than brainpower in the workplace, men had a big advantage. Now that brainpower has triumphed, the two sexes are more evenly matched. Then the Pill became available. Women could, from this time on, control their own fertility. They could decide when to have a family and when they did not want to get pregnant.

As a result of these two changes, women joined the work force in large numbers and soon were involved in leadership positions at all levels. Now we are not at all surprised to meet a female judge, airline pilot, bus driver, managing director, builder, prime minister or president, mining engineer or professor. What this opening up of well paid work opportunities for women has meant is that for the first time in human history women can support themselves and, if they have children, their family as well. They are no longer dependent on men. This monumental social revolution has not been easy for women to work out in theory or practice, extremely hard for men to adjust to, difficult for business to implement, and hugely challenging for Christians in general (and evangelicals in particular) to respond to theologically and biblically.

For long centuries, Christians simply reflected and endorsed the prevailing cultural norms of society, arguing that women were subordinated to men in all spheres of life—the home, the church, and every part of society. Theologians and clergy, along with everyone else until the turn of the twentieth century and often up to the 1960s, generally spoke of women as "inferior" and of men as "superior" and the Bible was interpreted to teach this. Many interpretations of key texts were demeaning to women. Tertullian interpreted Gen 3 as a reminder to women that "each of you is Eve. You are the devil's gateway: you are the first deserter of the divine law." Calvin concluded Paul taught that women "are born to obey, for all wise men have always rejected the government of women as an unnatural monstrosity." And as late as 1957 Donald Guthrie in a Tyndale evangelical commentary wrote, that 1 Tim 2:13 teaches "the superiority of men over women" and verse 14 "the greater aptitude of the weaker sex to be lead astray."

PROFOUND CULTURAL CHANGE AND THE INTERPRETATION OF THE BIBLE

In the face of this monumental social change, all Christians, including all evangelicals, were forced to rethink their teaching on women and their interpretation of the key texts that they had appealed to in the past to subordinate women. Profound changes in how people see the world always force believers to rethink their theology. When a cultural worldview changes Christians have to distinguish between what they believe as those seeking to be guided by the Bible and what they tacitly believe as those living in a given culture. This has happened many times in Christian history. When everyone thought the world was flat, theologians read the Bible to teach this. When everyone thought the sun revolved around the earth, the Bible was read to teach this. When everyone thought the world was created in seven literal days about 6000 years ago, Christians read the Bible to teach this. Changed worldviews that are compelling have always forced Christians to rethink what the Bible is teaching. Importantly, these changes in worldview did not lead to the rejection of any biblical teaching, simply to a re-reading of what it actually said.

The change in thinking on women is of this kind. It was easy for Christians until modern times to think the Bible endorsed the subordination of women because they lived in a patriarchal context where men ran the world. And because the Bible was written by those living in a taken-for-granted patriarchal context, what they wrote reflected that world. Only when the world changed did Christians see clearly for the first time that there were profound and principled statements in the Bible that spoke of the equality of the two sexes in creation and in Christ.

OPPOSING INTERPRETATIONS OF WHAT THE BIBLE SAYS ON THE SEXES

Confronted by the reality of this far-reaching and profound change in women's status and job opportunities, evangelicals developed after the 1970s two new and competing interpretations of what the Bible said on the man-woman relationship and now these two positions are firmly fixed in form and content.

Some evangelicals concluded that 1 Tim 2:11–14, supported by 1 Cor 11:3–16; 14:33–34; and Eph 5:22–23 quite clearly taught that God had given "headship" to men. The Timothy text is pivotal to this position. On this basis it is concluded that two things indicate that woman was set under man from the beginning, that woman was created second and that she was deceived by the devil in the garden of Eden. Thus male "headship" is the unchanging and unchangeable ideal that pleases God. They say Jesus endorsed this "headship of man" by appointing twelve men and no women to be the first apostles. The many references to women leaders in the Bible such as Deborah and the prophet Huldah in the Old Testament, and Priscilla and Junia in the New Testament, are explained by arguing that their leadership was of a subordinate kind under a man. Finally, appeal is made to a supposed hierarchical ordering in the Trinity where the Father commands and the Son obeys, arguing that this prescribes how men and women are to relate.

To complete this novel post-1970s reformulated reading of the Bible, three important changes were made from the way in which women's subordination had been spoken of in the past. First, new language was introduced to make this theological position sound acceptable to modern ears. Rather than speaking of women as "inferior" or subordinate, and men as "superior," as had been the case in the past, the terms "different" and "role" were used. What the Bible teaches is that men and women have "different roles" by which it is meant, men have the "headship" role, and women the subordinate "role." Second, instead of the subordination of women being universal, in the home, the church, and society—*all of creation*—as one would think if women's subordination is grounded in the created order, the assertion is made that women are only subordinated in the home and the church—*part of creation*. Third, and only from the 1990s, this reading of the Bible was called, "the complementarian position," again to sound acceptable to modern ears.

Other evangelicals developed a very different way of reading the Bible in this new social context. They insisted that the right place to begin any study of what the Bible says on the sexes is to begin where the Bible begins—the first chapter of Genesis. Here the primary and fundamental truth is revealed. God made men and women alike in his image and alike he gave them rule over creation and alike he made them responsible for procreation (Gen 1:27–28). Gen 2 and 3 are then read in the light of Gen 1. This view rejects the two suggestions that being created "second" and Eve being deceived point to the subordination of women. It bases its rejection on their incompatibility with the teaching of Gen 1:27–28, on the plain meaning of the text of Gen 2 and 3, and the fact that the subordination of women is explicitly a consequence of the fall (Gen 3:16). Rather than the subordination of women being the God-given ideal, these evangelicals conclude that it reflects what is "not good," not the ideal, something not pleasing to God and as such is to be opposed by Christians. Rather than finding Jesus supporting male headship, they argue that Jesus affirms in word and deed the equality of the two differentiated sexes.

Luke and Paul's theology of ministry, in which the Spirit's gifting trumps gender, shows that the apostles believed that in Christ there was a "new creation" (2 Cor 5:17) where social, racial, and sexual differences are transcended (Gal 3:28). The numerous examples of women leaders in the New Testament churches illustrate the apostolic theology of gift-based not gender-based ministry in practice. The three texts in which Paul *regulates* the ministry of women in some way (1 Cor 11:3–16; 14:33–34; 1 Tim 2:11–12) they take as speaking to exceptional situations where women were doing something to disrupt the life of the church. In this reading of the Bible, 1 Tim 2:11–12 is studied last because it is, when reading the Bible chronologically, the last significant text on women. When we come last to this text, what it says stands out like the proverbial sore thumb. Nothing has prepared us for this exceptional comment that is so negative about the ministry of women. The obscuring language of differing "roles" is not used by evangelicals who read the Bible in this way, and their self designation is unambiguous, "evangelical egalitarian."

After all the essays in this book were submitted the definitive exegetical study of all the texts relevant to this debate was published: Philip Payne's *Man and Woman One in Christ: An Exegetical and Theological Study of Paul's Letters* (Grand Rapids: Zondervan, 2008). His exegesis is a "must read" for those who want to know what the Bible teaches on the man-woman relationship. It stands apart and above all other books on this question.

At first the Roman Catholic Church was hostile to "women's lib," but significantly in 1987 it made an about turn. In his binding encyclical, *Mulieris Dignitatem: On the Dignity of Women,* Pope John Paul II rejected the Catholic teaching held for centuries that in creation God subordinated women to men. His statement insisted instead on their complete equality. Taking much the same interpretive approach as egalitarian evangelicals do, he maintained that in creation men and women were made "essential" equals, the subordination of women being entirely due to human sin and as such is to be opposed when possible by Christians. However on the question of leadership in the church John Paul II was not consistent. Appealing to the fact that the twelve apostles were all men, and to the traditional Catholic idea that the twelve apostles were the first priests, he argued that women therefore could not be ordained in the Catholic Church.

What this outline of the two post-1970s biblical theologies of the sexes makes plain is that this is not a debate about the authority of scripture. *It is a debate entirely about how to interpret the Bible rightly* when for the first time in human history the church has had to seriously face the fact that women are not imperfect versions of the male. They are women not men, but, like men, they are part of God's "good" creation and made alike in God's image.

NOW TO THIS BOOK

This wonderful collection of essays, *Reconsidering Gender: Evangelical Perspectives,* arising out of a conference sponsored by the two premier evangelical theological colleges in New Zealand—Carey Baptist College and Laidlaw College—gave me the impression that New Zealand evangelicals have largely endorsed the evangelical egalitarian reading of the Bible as a reflection of what the Bible actually teaches. After all, they live in a country that was the first in the world to give women the vote.

I would call almost all the writers in this symposium *post*-hierarchicalists. Most ignore the post-1970s evangelical arguments for the permanent subordination of women as outlined above. Where the exception appears in the essay by the visiting American evangelical theologian,

Craig Blomberg, what he says on the subordination of women is categorically dismissed in the following essay by Nicola Hoggard-Creegan.

For me as an Australian, and I will explain why below, this book reads like a breath of fresh air. Well researched and well written essays reveal informed conservative evangelical authors who almost take it for granted that the Bible and Christian social justice demand that Christians regard the two sexes as substantial equals with the same dignity and leadership potential. With this premise, they explore the wider issues of how the two sexes can work and minister side by side to complement and enrich one another's contributions to the cause of Christ and his kingdom.

I was particularly pleased to find that this book begins with an essay on the Trinity that, along with several other essays, predicates the case for gender co-equality on the orthodox "co-equal" doctrine of the Trinity where "none is before or after, greater or less," as the Athanasian Creed teaches. For this reason any argument for the subordination of women as the *God-given ideal* must be wrong. Please note, I say as the *God-given ideal*. Functional hierarchies are part of fallen existence and usually serve the common good. They make it possible for groups of people to get things done. In functional hierarchies people are not "born to rule" or "born to be subordinates." Leaders such as managers, captains, and generals hold their superior "role" because of competence, training, or seniority. They can be demoted and those under them promoted to lead. This is not so in classic aristocracies, or race-based slavery, or in Apartheid, or in the subordination of women in the teaching of some evangelical theologians. In the examples above, the premise is that one group is born to rule and another to obey. Training, competence, or seniority are of no significance. Upward mobility is impossible for those believed to be subordinated "by God."

Evangelicals who understand the man-woman relationship in this static hierarchical way, seldom speak of the subordination of women, preferring instead to speak of the "differing roles" of men and women. The suggestion that men and women have God-given different roles sounds acceptable to the modern ear but when unpacked we discover that this language is used to cloud the argument. The issue is not "differing roles" in the sense that any dictionary or sociological texts would suggest. The issue is "differing power relations." To them, God, in creation, appointed men to lead and women to obey, and this hierarchical ordering, because it is God-given, can never change. Women, because they are women, *are* the subordinate sex. They function subordinately because they lack what God has given only to men, the "role of headship," or in plain speech, "leadership."

The orthodox doctrine of the Trinity invalidates this immutable hierarchical ordering that sets one group over another. It tells us that such ordering cannot be *the God-given ideal* because it stands in direct contrast to what we know of God's perfect communal being in eternity. We must recognize that it is human beings who have created hierarchies and then claimed they are God-given and unchangeable. And, if human beings create them, then humans can overthrow them to make a better world.

THE WIDER WORLD

On my side of the Tasman Sea (Australia), most evangelicals argue that the Bible teaches the permanent subordination of women, or to use their preferred wording, "the differing roles" of the sexes. A *hierarchical* definition of the man-woman relationship prevails. To be an evangelical egalitarian in Australia is to have few theological friends. I see no significant change on the horizon here.

The most significant support for so-called male "headship" comes from Moore Theological College, Sydney (the largest and best funded theological college in the nation), and from its power base, the Anglican Diocese of Sydney (one of the largest, wealthiest, and most evangelistically active diocese in the world). This centre influences other evangelical churches, Bible Colleges, and organizations around the country. Nowhere is this more true than in evangelical student work. Most Australian Fellowship of Evangelical Students (AFES) groups in universities are controlled by Moore College trained men, who teach male "headship," insisting where possible that women must not lead Bible studies where men are present. Such is the power of the Sydney Anglicans and their supporters that they control much of what is published by evangelicals in Sydney and to some degree in all of Australia. What is more, the Moore College theologians put their case in absolute terms—the Bible from cover to cover teaches male "headship"; to deny this is to reject what the Bible says, and what the Bible says is what God says.

The counter opinion—that in the Bible the equality of the sexes is the creation ideal (Gen 1:27–28)—gets little if any hearing in Australian evangelical circles today. On this basis, evangelical egalitarians are denigrated by male Moore College theologians and their American counterparts, not for disagreeing over the *interpretation* of the Bible but for disobeying God himself. They are dismissed as disobedient Christians who reject what God commands.

In America things are different again. Visiting numerous evangelical seminaries and Christian Colleges in recent years, I found evangelicals split down the middle and the debate alive and vigorous. In many a staff room I was told quite openly the percentage of so called "complementarians" and egalitarians among the professors, and the percentages correlated to the social, political, and theological conservatism of the institution. What surprised me most was the bitterness of the debate. Theologians supporting male "headship" in America characteristically see their cause as a battle of cosmic proportions with the forces of light and darkness locked in battle. For them, evangelical egalitarians are crypto liberals who have embraced the destructive teaching of the "feminists" they despise and demonise.

In England there is another picture. Since the Second World War scholarly evangelicals have led the evangelical movement and this is still the case. Professor F. F. Bruce began this pattern. With such leadership, perverse readings of scripture, arguments for oppressive social ordering in any area of life, and teaching on the Trinity that directly contradicts the creeds and Reformation confessions gains little headway. What is more, F. F. Bruce and his successors such as R. T. France, I. Howard Marshall, George Carey, and Richard Bauckham, to mention four other scholarly evangelical leaders, were all outspoken supporters of "biblical equality." Alongside them have stood a number of significant evangelical women academics such as Mary Evans and Elaine Storkey, who have advanced the case for an egalitarian reading of the Bible. However, I must add that supporters of the permanent subordination of women are also well known in England, and in recent years have gained some ground, mainly through "Reform," a reactionary evangelical movement that gains support from Sydney Anglican evangelical leaders.

FINALLY

I really enjoyed reading this book and I hope you do too. What these predominantly New Zealand evangelicals have concluded is that the monumental social revolution of the late twentieth century, commonly called "women's lib," is pleasing to God. It is pleasing to God and to be endorsed in principle because it is now seen that in the Bible itself the equality of the sexes is the God-given *creation ideal,* and this high evaluation of women is what Jesus affirmed in word and deed. To be an egalitarian evangelical, they have come to see, is to be a teachable and obedient Christian.

Kevin Giles
Melbourne, Australia

Introduction

In 2007 the Centre for the Theology of Gender was established under the auspices of the Laidlaw-Carey Graduate School. A committee steers the Centre and is comprised of Dr. Nicola Hoggard-Creegan, Dr. Tim Bulkeley, Ms Jody Kilpatrick, Dr. Myk Habets, and Dr. Beulah Wood. The statement of the Centre reads:

> God created all people in the image of God, men and women alike. All have equal dignity and equal worth. In that context the Centre focuses on the theology and practice of gender from evangelical perspectives.

RATIONALE

Questions related to gender theology and practices remain insufficiently acknowledged and explored in contemporary literature. These issues form the basis of significant unresolved tensions among evangelicals, as evidenced in debates overseas over the nature of the Trinity, Bible translation, church practice, choice of language, mission leadership, decision-making in homes, and parenting, to name but a few examples. Such a critical field should not be ignored. An understanding of who we are as men and women impacts all of life. The Centre thus seeks to sponsor critical theological work on gender that will inform our living.

CORE VALUES

The Centre affirms:

a. The equality, dignity, and difference of men and women in the kingdom of God, which we seek to reflect in church, home and society.

b. The Bible as the inspired Word of God.

c. The liberating gospel of Jesus Christ given to all in our brokenness, sin, and suffering.

d. The biblical injunction to seek for truth and work for justice.

PURPOSE AND PLAN

The Centre provides a forum for dialogue, research, publication, and church resourcing, and seeks to raise awareness of a theology of gender in the church and academy. Using academic disciplines and practical observations, the Centre will face up to the current realities and discourses surrounding women and men, their person, work and interrelatedness.

COLLOQUIUM

On July 12–13, 2007, a Colloquium on God and Gender was held at Carey Baptist College at which ten papers were presented on a range of issues faced by evangelicals today on the issue of God and gender. Many of those papers appear here for the first time in print. Subsequent to the Colloquium the committee invited a number of additional contributors to submit papers and then invited each of the formal responses to the papers found in this volume. As such the present book received its initial impetus from the 2007 Colloquium but is not simply the published papers or proceedings of that event.

We appreciate all those who attended and participated in the discussions at the Colloquium and we are as equally appreciative to those contributors who presented papers and responses subsequent to the Colloquium. We trust that the presentations on aspects of gender from evangelical perspectives in this book will spur others on to further research and reflection and equip the saints for ministry more effectively.

The following chapters are not meant to provide a monolithic evangelical theology of gender, but rather to provide evangelical perspectives surrounding the topic of gender. To further this aim each paper is followed by a formal Response with an attempt at a concise and lucid perspective on the paper and pointers to further areas for investigation. Some contributors are "complementarian" while others are "egalitarian," although who is what is left to the discerning reader. The resultant unevenness in the volume is consequently just what was envisaged at the outset of the project, and is considered something of a success, reflecting as it does contemporary evangelical perspectives.

Various people are to be thanked for help in the preparation of this manuscript for publication. The contributors on the whole were timely in the preparation of their papers and Wipf and Stock has seen the work through to publication in an efficient way, as per their usual high standard. Jonathan Robinson is to be thanked for formatting the text. Dr. Beulah Wood's editorial work was superb and we thank South Asia Institute of Advanced Christian Studies (SAIACS), Bangalore, India, for allowing her the time to work on this project and for providing a context in which the final editorial work was completed by Dr. Myk Habets. Myk coordinated the Colloquium and we thank him for his efforts. LCGS is grateful for the assistance received by so many in the theological community, including the support of the Principals and staff of both Laidlaw College and Carey Baptist College, and to the many students who have graced our classrooms and taught us as much as we have taught them.

Myk Habets
Doctor Serviens Ecclesia
SAIACS, Bangalore, India

Prologue

Gender

Divine or Human?

Myk Habets

A CENTRAL FEATURE OF what it means to be human is biological gender; we are male or female (not taking into account medical exceptions) and together we represent the human race. Gender has been a much-examined aspect of theological anthropology, receiving diverse responses from theologians throughout the church age. One of the central issues confronted by a theological anthropology is that of sexual differentiation. Human identity is bound up with gender, sexuality, the body, and the socio-cultural context one inhabits.

In recent theological discourse doctrines of the Trinity have been used to illustrate the identity and roles of men and women respectively. Some of these have argued that a supposed complementarian hierarchy amongst the persons of the Trinity is a model for male-female relations, whilst others have argued that the mutual love shared and received by the three persons of the Trinity provides an egalitarian model for female-male relations. The real issue, however, seems to have been largely overlooked in these discussions; that is, that the Trinity is a model for *personhood*, not gender, and all attempts to make the Trinity a model for gender relations are misguided. Whether or not the complementarian or the egalitarian position is the best equipped to address gendered relations is not the focus of this prologue. It makes the more modest proposal that people, regardless of gender, can find in the Trinity a model for healthy interpersonal relations.

THEOLOGICAL METHOD

Feminist theologians agree that women's experience, as defined by feminists, must be the centre of their theological reflection. Tillich's method of correlation forms the larger background to feminist methodology; theology must combine the questions of contemporary culture with the answers of revelation, and the form of the answers must be determined by the cultural setting. What is determinative then for feminist methodology is the definition of what "women's experience" is. Pamela Young presents five dimensions of women's experience that differs from men's. First, as has been mentioned, all feminist theologians agree that women's experience must be the centre of theological reflection. Second, women experience their bodies differently, in that they are more closely related to the cycles of nature. Third, women have different socialised experiences, in that they are taught by culture to submit to men and to appeal to men sexually. Fourth, women now have feminist experience in which they become conscious of their gender-oppression and of unjust structures through recovery of "lost history" of women. Finally, women have different individual experiences that can be catalysts for change.[1]

In addition, feminist theologians take three distinct approaches to explicating the role of women's experience in relation to classical norms of theology. First, Elisabeth Schüssler Fiorenza typifies the approach which rejects any aspect of classical Christianity as a norm for theology, because it is so thoroughly patriarchal and therefore inimical to women. She does not consider Jesus authoritative for theology, as his life was so intrinsically interwoven with the oppressive culture of which he was a part. Fiorenza advocates Women-Church as the normative community for Christian theology.[2]

A second feminist response is represented by Rosemary Radford Ruether who asserts that what really counts as the "word of God" is what women identify, along with other women in community, as liberating for women.[3] In Ruether's opinion theology makes use of numerous sources—Scripture, non-Christian pagan religions, marginal and heretical

---

1. Pamela Dickey Young, *Feminist Theology/Christian Theology: In Search of Method* (Minneapolis: Augsburg Fortress, 1989) 53–56.

2. For representative works see: Elisabeth Schüssler Fiorenza, *Jesus: Miriam's Child, Sophia's Prophet* (New York: Continuum, 1994); Schüssler Fiorenza, *In Memory of Her: A Feminist Theological Reconstruction of Christian Origins* (New York: Crossroad, 1983).

3. Rosemary Radford Ruether, *Sexism and God-Talk: Toward a Feminist Theology* (Boston: Beacon, 1983) 18.

movements within Christianity, philosophies such as liberalism, romanticism, and Marxism, and contemporary stories of women's oppression and liberation. But the ultimate norm for interpreting what is divine revelation lies in the prophetic-liberating tradition of which Jesus was the historical paradigm. Thus in her own words: "feminist readings of the Bible can discern a norm within Biblical faith by which the Biblical texts themselves can be criticized . . . On this basis many aspects of the Bible are to be frankly set aside and rejected."[4]

In contrast to these two, and representing a third approach, is Letty Russell, who looks to the future for the theological norm. She envisions this future as a utopia of complete equality and freedom that she calls the "Household of Freedom," her metaphor for the eschatological kingdom of God. She gains this eschatological vision from Jesus' ministry and lifestyle. For Russell this future view is the norm for all theology and even Scripture must be judged by it.[5]

All these feminist theologians agree that Scripture alone (*sola scriptura*) cannot serve as the principle of authority for theology, as it is thoroughly permeated by patriarchy. They also view divine revelation as an ongoing process, such that historical events such as Jesus' life are not authoritative. They also elevate the perspective of feminist experience to be the norm for contemporary Christian theology. The key to feminist theological methodology is the primacy of women's experience defined by feminists in theological formulation.[6]

GENDER—DIVINE OR HUMAN?

In the early 1970s, American feminist theologian Mary Daly stated emotively: "If God is male, male is God."[7] With Daly many feminist theologians have sought to point out what consequences were implicit for Christian women in a theology that described God as Father who begets

---

4. Ibid., 23.

5. For representative works see: Letty Russell, *Human Liberation in a Feminist Perspective: A Theology* (Louisville: Westminster John Knox, 1995); and Russell, *Becoming Human* (Louisville: Westminster John Knox, 1982).

6. There is, of course, a new category of evangelical feminists who do take the Word of God seriously and differ substantially from the non-evangelical feminists mentioned here. Many of the feminists in the current volume fall into this category.

7. Mary Daly, *Beyond God the Father: Toward a Philosophy of Women's Liberation* (Boston: Beacon, 1973) 19.

a Son (both masculine images as you will no doubt be aware). Many suppose that the best way to approach the relation between the Trinity and gender identity is to concentrate on the gender of language about God. This may be done in several ways. The first step is to question exclusively male metaphors for God on the grounds that they do not offer women a "divine horizon" of development. The second step would be to highlight the femininity of one member of the Trinity—the Holy Spirit—as Elisabeth Moltmann-Wendel does. Alternatively, if one did not want to divide the Trinity into masculine and feminine members one could insist on the need to use feminine metaphors for all three persons of the Trinity and affirm the equivalence of feminine metaphors to male metaphors, as Elizabeth A. Johnson does in *She Who Is*.[8] The third step would be to explore what the femininity and masculinity of individual members of the Trinity or the equivalence of feminine and masculine metaphors for all members of the Trinity may mean for the construction of women's and men's identity and difference.

But does this work? In a word: No. God is not gendered. God has no sexual body. God is neither male nor female. Thus these approaches fail to really address the issue at hand. We are not here concerned with the language for God such as "Father" or "Son," although this is an important discussion in its own right, as Bulkeley and others pick up later in the present volume. Rather, in this Prologue we are interested in the gender or non-gender of God and what this has to contribute to views of human sexuality and gender. What is required is a thoroughly trinitarian account of *personhood*, applied to human beings as male and female.

WHAT ABOUT FEMINIST ANTHROPOLOGIES?

Theological anthropology is theological reflection on what it means to be human in the light of humanity's creation in the image of God. Feminist theologians criticise most traditional Christian anthropologies as focusing on men and male bodies, which are regarded as normative, while women are denied their voice in defining what it means to be human. This is what led Dorothy Sayers to declare in frustration, "are women human?"[9] Two aspects in particular are important to feminist theologi-

---

8. Elizabeth A. Johnson, *She Who Is: The Mystery of God in Feminist Theological Discourse* (New York: Crossroad, 1992).

9. Dorothy Sayers, *Are Women Human? Astute and Witty Essays on the Role of Women in Society* (Grand Rapids: Eerdmans, 1971).

cal reflections on being human: the significance of women's bodies and the idea of being human in relation.

In his 1995 encyclical *Evangelium vitae*, Pope John Paul II called for a "new feminism" which would reject the temptation to imitate models of "male domination" on the one hand and affirm the true genius of women in every aspect of life. A number of feminist scholars have taken up his challenge and are working towards a construction of a "new feminism." Michelle Schumacher is one such figure who believes the construction of such a "new feminism" must be pursued via a robust theological anthropology which is neither traditional or mainstream feminism nor patriarchal.[10]

The "new feminism" seeks to construct an anthropology in which the human person is not only relational, but also loved. Thus at the heart of the new feminism is the idea of reciprocation and mutuality between the sexes "through a sincere gift of the self." This gift of the self is motivated by the experience of love, not only love between persons but love from God to persons, love whose goal is for the self and the beloved "other." "The authentically liberated woman is, therefore, one who experiences herself as eternally loved and forgiven, and thus authentically free."[11] This "authentic freedom" is the ability to give oneself wholly to God and other persons in love without seeking her own good. Ironically, by giving herself without seeking in return she actually fulfils herself in accord with God's own manner of being and acting.

Accordingly, women do not look to men to define what it means to be women, nor do they look to other women, rather, they look to Christ to reveal it by inviting them to participate in his own mission of revealing the Father and his love.

This type of approach is extremely positive, I would suggest, for it is grounded in the Trinity and the Christian tradition, and is able to respond to contemporary challenges. It does, however, require more substantial fleshing out.

TOWARDS A TRINITARIAN ONTOLOGY

---

10. Michele M. Schumacher, ed. *Women in Christ: Toward a New Feminism* (Grand Rapids: Eerdmans, 2003).

11. Michele M. Schumacher, "An Introduction to a New Feminism," in M. Schumacher, ed. *Women in Christ*, xii.

OF PERSONS-IN-COMMUNION

The rest of this Prologue will tease out what the doctrine of the Trinity has to say to human gender and sexuality. We shall compare a few attempts at this task from Barth and Irigaray before considering a way forward suggested by Miraslov Volf.

Karl Barth and an Anthropology from Above

Barth reconceived theological anthropology on the basis of God's self-revelation in Christ. Instead of Christology being a predicate of anthropology, Barth sees anthropology as a predicate or subset of Christology. Christology alone lays the proper groundwork on which to consider the human creature. According to Barth there is no such thing as "man," rather "male" and "female." Sexuality and the male-female duality in particular, becomes an image for the difference-in-relatedness that characterises human and divine being in general. As such we should not speak of "humanity" but more precisely "co-humanity"; the human person is both irreducibly individual and constitutionally interrelated.

Covenantal relationship is the purpose of humanity and forms the structure of the relation between God and humanity. True humanity is not the isolated individual; it is what Barth terms "co-humanity," life shared with one's "fellow-man."[12] Such a covenanted relationship is itself an echo or "image" of the triune God, a "being in correspondence to God himself."[13] In terms of the covenanted relation Barth can say that:

> Entering into this relationship, [God] makes a copy of Himself. Even in His inner divine being there is relationship. To be sure, God is One in Himself. But He is not alone. There is in Him a co-existence, co-inherence and reciprocity . . . in this triunity He is the original and source of every I and Thou . . . And it is this relationship in the inner divine being which is repeated and reflected in God's eternal covenant with man as revealed and operative in time in the humanity of Jesus.[14]

Barth elaborates on the I-and-Thou analogy in terms of male and female as the ultimate expression of the I-thou encounter. For Barth, hu-

---

12. Karl Barth, *Church Dogmatics*, 4 vols. (Edinburgh: T. & T. Clark, 1956–1975) III/2, 229. Hereafter referred to as *CD*.

13. Barth, *CD* III/2, 323.

14. Ibid., 218–19.

man existence is coexistence, and this fact is paradigmatically expressed in the coexistence of man and woman.[15]

Barth makes three fundamental assertions in explaining his anthropology. First, human beings are either male or female and are called by God to affirm their particular sexual identity. Second, human beings are male and female and are called to find their human identity in mutual coordination with others who are both similar and yet also very different. Finally, human beings as male and female coexist in a definite and irreversible order.[16]

It is point three that has occasioned much debate. In his *CD* III/4, paragraph 54.1, "Man and Woman," known in shorthand as the "A and B" discussion, Barth likens men and women to the letters A and B. According to Barth, man and woman are not an A and a second A whose being and relationship can be described like the two halves of an hour glass, which are obviously two, but absolutely equal and therefore interchangeable. Man and woman are an A and a B, and cannot, therefore, be equated. In inner dignity and right A has not the slightest advantage over B nor does it suffer the slightest disadvantage. A precedes B, and B follows A. Order means succession. It means preceding and following. It means super- and sub-ordination. It does indeed reveal their inequality. But it does not do so without immediately confirming their equality.[17]

Despite his many qualifications, Barth's depiction of this irreversible order of the relationship of man and woman has been widely rejected. Contrary to Barth, argues Migliore, in the first creation story there is no mention of hierarchy, or superiority or inferiority, or an above and a below, of a first or a second in the relationship between man and woman. We are simply told that male and female together constitute the image of God. The implication is that human beings are to live in "partnership."

Critique

In his *Church Dogmatics* Barth makes the famous argument that we do not come to know what it means for God to be the Father by observing human fathers, but the other way around; we know what it means for a man to be a father by observing God the Father (*CD* I/1, 389). In this

---

15. Daniel L. Migliore, *Faith Seeking Understanding: An Introduction to Christian Theology* (Grand Rapids: Eerdmans, 1991) 126.

16. Barth, *CD* III/4, 149–81.

17. Ibid., 169–70.

Barth was consistent with his overall program and not constructing an "analogy from below" but rather an "analogy from above." I think, he was surely right. Yet as Volf and others have pointed out, Barth's theology was not entirely consistent. For Barth, God is the Father in the most original sense because he "begets" the Son in eternity and because he "begets" Jesus Christ in time. He expresses this, on one occasion, that God is "the first and true and indeed the only man" (CD III/3, 358). Indeed, Barth makes much of the eternal "humanity of God." Human males image the maleness in God; they initiate, beget, lead, and are superordinate (CD III/2, 287). The analogy goes from above—from God to human beings— but only after Barth has projected a patriarchal construction of masculinity onto God and tacitly declared it was there from the beginning! As Volf concludes, "for God to be the model of masculinity one must first project maleness into God and then use the projection to legitimize certain allegedly specifically male characteristics and activities."[18] What Barth is doing, in effect, is denying his own stated methodology. He is arguing from an *a priori* rather than *a posteriori*.

In our estimation, since God is beyond sexual difference, there is nothing in God that can correspond to the specifically fatherly relation that a man has toward his child. A human father can in no way read off his responsibilities as a father from God the Father. What a father can learn from God are his responsibilities as a human being who happens to be a father and therefore has a special relationship to his children (as well as to their mother). This applies equally to mothers. Whether we use masculine or feminine metaphors for God, God models our common humanity, our personhood to be more precise, not our gender specificity.

---

18. Miroslav Volf, *Exclusion and Embrace: A Theological Exploration of Identity, Otherness, and Reconciliation* (Nashville: Abingdon, 1996) 171. For further critique of Barth see M. D. Hampson, *Theology and Feminism* (Oxford: Blackwell, 1990); A. McElway, "Perichoretic Possibilities in Barth's Doctrine of Male and Female," *Princeton Seminary Bulletin* (1986) 231–43; E. A. Frykberg, *Karl Barth's Theological Anthropology: An Analogical Critique Regarding Gender Relations*, Studies in Reformed Theology and History 1 (Princeton, Princeton Theological Seminary, 1993); E. A. Frykberg, "The Child as Solution: The Problem of the Superordinate-Subordinate Ordering of the Male-Female Relation in Barth's Theology," *Scottish Journal of Theology* 47 (1994) 327–54; and Paul Jewett, *Man as Male and Female* (Grand Rapids: Eerdmans, 1975).

Luce Irigaray

Luce Irigaray is a French philosopher and feminist advocate, who, unlike Barth, starts from an analogy from below, projecting onto "god" feminist constructs of gender and creating "god" in that image. This is an argument from human mothers (and fathers) onto "god." Affirming the need for a projected god, she notes that in the classical doctrine of the Trinity, which speaks of the Father, the Son, and the Spirit, woman is absent; mother does not appear and the relationship between mother and daughter is lacking. Hence, she argues, there is no "horizon" in such a doctrine of the Trinity that beckons "her" to become as a woman.[19]

The problem with this approach is that there are no "horizons," either male or female, that the Trinity beckons one to become. For such gender specific horizons to exist, we would need female and male deities. And this is what, in fact, Irigaray offers. "God" for Irigaray, is a projection of the subject onto a figure of perfection, an ego-ideal specific to that subject, a mode of self-completion without finality. As the man has constructed a unique masculine god—the Father, the Son, and the Spirit—to situate himself as a finite being in relation to the infinite, Irigaray argues, so also the woman needs a woman god, a feminine trinity, a mother, daughter, spirit, which figure the perfection of her subjectivity.[20]

Critique

The most concise critique of Irigaray's position is that God models our common humanity, not our gender specificity. Irigaray's proposal raises serious objections from those committed to biblical-evangelical Christianity. The God of the Christian tradition is the God of both men and women. Irigaray (with Barth) has "ontologized" gender in God, that is, taken a particular understanding of femininity (or masculinity), projected it onto God, and then let that projection shape her social practice. In Volf's convincing estimate: "Nothing in God is specifically feminine; nothing in God is specifically masculine; therefore nothing in our notions of God entails duties or prerogatives specific to one gender; all duties and prerogatives entailed in our notions of God are duties and

---

19. Luce Irigaray, "Equal to Whom?" Trans. Robert Mazzola, in *The Essential Difference*, ed. N. Schor and E. Weed (Bloomington: Indiana University Press, 1991).

20. Luce Irigaray, *Divine Mother*, trans. S. Muecke (Sydney: Local Consumption Publications, 1986) 3–6.

prerogatives of both genders."[21] That is not to say there are no masculine or feminine attributes displayed by God. It is simply an attempt to say that while God may have masculine and feminine traits, they must not be translated into sexuality or gender with God. What God models is not gender but personhood!

SEX AND GENDER

The content of gender identity has no transcendental grounding, no divine blueprint, so what then is it rooted in? The similarity with animals in the creation narrative gives us a clue. For what humans share with animals is the sexed body—a body that carries indelible marks of belonging to either male or female sex. Men's and women's gender identities for each culture are rooted in the specificity for their distinct sexed bodies.

Notice, however, the distinction between sex and gender. Sex is a biological category (genes, hormones, external and internal genitalia, etc.). Gender is a largely social category (learned characteristics, personality traits, behavioural patterns, etc.). The distinction is useful as it helps clarify how and why notions of femininity and masculinity change over time and cultures. Gender identity is not simply biologically given. It is socially constructed. This is not to imply that sex is irrelevant to gender. The fluidity of gender is both constrained and made possible by the stability of the sexed body. Bodies are not neutral and passive with respect to the construction of gender. For instance, there is a qualitative difference between femininity lived by women and that lived by men!

SUMMARY

So far we have simply asserted that we should not seek to derive the content of gender identity by mirroring God, because any femininity or masculinity we may find in God was projected onto God; and second, the content of gendered identity is rooted in the sexed body ("nature") and forged by the history of social interaction between persons with such sexed bodies ("culture").

The question remains: what does a doctrine of God add to the question of gender and identity? As long as we are talking about the undifferentiated idea of "god," then perhaps nothing can be added. But if we are talking about the Triune God, and concentrate on the rela-

---

21. Volf, *Exclusion and Embrace*, 173.

tions between the three persons and on the construction of their identity rather than on their gender, then much ground may be gained. Thus Trinitarian identities are the path to follow.

TRINITARIAN IDENTITIES

In his work *Exclusion and Embrace*, Miroslav Volf turns to Joseph Ratzinger and Jürgen Moltmann for resources towards a Trinitarian construction of gender before offering his own proposal. Volf's critique of Ratzinger and Moltmann will not concern us here as we move straight into considering Volf's own proposals.

According to Volf, since the content of gender identity is rooted in the sexed body and negotiated in the social exchange between men and women within a given cultural context, the portrayals of God in no way provide models of what it means to be male or female. Instead, the relations between the Trinitarian persons serve as a model for how the content of "masculinity" and "femininity" ought to be negotiated in the social process.

Volf rejects any attempt to construct a theology of biblical "manhood" or "womanhood." Analyzing the biblical statements about men and women will offer many useful insights, argues Volf, and must be pursued, but not in order to construct a biblical theology of manhood or womanhood, for in the end these are not divinely sanctioned models but culturally situated examples, they are accounts of the successes and failures of men and women to live out the demands of God on their lives within specific settings. This means these stories are of limited normative value in a different cultural context since they are of necessity laden with specific cultural beliefs about gender identity and roles.

Where then must we locate normativity? For Volf the answer is in the formal features of identity and the character of relations of divine persons. He writes: "What is normative is not some 'essence' of femininity and masculinity, but the procedures, modelled on the life of the triune God, through which women and men in specific cultural settings should negotiate their mutual relations and their constructions of femininity and masculinity."[22]

Volf explores this thesis by probing three texts: Gen 1 and 2; 1 Cor 11:2–16; and Eph 5:21–33: three texts which many consider implicitly

---

22. Ibid., 182.

or explicitly subordinationist. Volf simply disregards the subordinationism as culturally conditioned and interprets the statements from within the framework of an egalitarian understanding of the Trinitarian relations, read in light of the thrust of Gal 3:28. Volf's hermeneutic is that we should let the social construction of gender play itself out guided by the vision of the identity of and relations between divine persons.

Let's look at some of his evidence. There are no generic human beings (Gen 1:28). Human beings exist in an irreducible duality of male and female. Gen 2 suggests that the duality is rooted in their sexed bodies. Adam awoke from his slumber to see Eve whom he immediately recognizes—presumably, by seeing her body—both their profound unity and their undeniable difference (Gen 2:23). Though the content of masculinity and femininity may vary from culture to culture the marks of maleness and femaleness are indelibly inscribed in human bodies. Biological (gender) difference is therefore an inalienable feature of human existence. This is the most basic lesson about femaleness and maleness Gen 1 and 2 teaches.

What then of Gal 3:28? Does this not contain a contrary lesson? In Christ, it claims, the order of creation has been transcended, so that there is no longer "male and female." Some claim that here Paul is motivated by the ideal of androgyny—something which they say comes after the eschaton. But this is not persuasive for Paul is not motivated to cancel out all differences but rather to bring all into harmony with Christ (1 Cor 10–12; Eph 4:11–18). Also Paul is not a dualist with a strict cleavage between body and spirit. Therefore Paul's claim that there is "no longer male and female" entails no eschatological denial of gender dimorphism. What has been erased in Christ is not the sexed body, but some important culturally coded norms attached to sexed bodies. Oneness in Christ is a community of people with sexed bodies and distinct gender identities, not some abstract unity of pure spirits or de-gendered "persons" (whatever they may be).

How does this relate to the Trinity? Just as in the Trinity the persons are distinct and must not be reduced to pure relations, thus collapsing each person into the other and forming an undifferentiated trinity, analogously, the one gender should neither be transformed into another (Gnosticism) nor melded into a new (androgynous) synthesis (Rosemary Radford Reuther).

Given the permanent duality of human gender, the question must be asked: Should the search for the wholeness of each take place independently of the other? While each sex at times has to legitimately concentrate on its own specific needs and solutions (whatever their merits or demerits one just needs to think of Promise Keepers, Sistas' Conference, etc.) it is mistaken as a goal in and of itself. Often an exclusive concern with one's own identity generates a pernicious ideology of superiority. Also, the turn inward misses the very character of gender identity. Men's identity is not and cannot be only men's business, just as women's identity is not and cannot only be women's business. Gender identities are essentially related and therefore the specific wholeness of each can be achieved only through the relation to the other; a relation that neither neutralizes nor synthesizes the two, but negotiates the identity of each by readjusting it to the identity of the other, or more simply, by living in genuine community. This is modelled for us in the Triunity of divine persons.

In the third text Volf considers, 1 Cor 11:2–16, he suggests, "What has been erased in Christ is not the sexed body, but some important culturally coded norms attached to sexed bodies." In this passage Paul explicates the relationship between men and women "in the Lord" and writes: "Neither is woman without [lit. not without] man nor man without [lit. not without] woman" (v. 11). Some read this as they do Gal 3:28, as an androgynous ideal existing on the level of the spirit. On this reading in the Lord men and women are identical. But this does not fit the context.

The ground for the claim that neither gender is without the other is not taken from the sphere of "the pure spirit" but from bodily creation: "For just as woman came from man so man comes through woman" (v. 12). Here many see Paul having two readings of creation: one from the perspective of the patriarchal culture, which finds hierarchy in creation (vv. 8–9), and the other from the perspective of the new life in Christ, which finds equality in creation (v. 12). Paul's second reading underscores the equality of genders but does not do so at the risk of erasing the differences between genders. In the Lord the difference of sexed bodies is not erased; to the contrary, this difference grounds the interdependence of men and women.

The "not without" clause in v. 11 is highly important. Instead of constructing gender identity on the basis of difference and opposition,

Paul and the biblical worldview constructs gender identity on the basis of a correspondence—man to woman and woman to man. It is the insight of correspondence which lends support to a trinitarian reading of gender. In the Trinity distinct persons are internally constituted by the indwelling of other persons in them (*perichoresis*). The personal identity of each is unthinkable (literally) without the presence of the others in each; because each person actually defines the other. You cannot have a "son" without a parent, in this case a "father," and the Spirit is the "Spirit of Sonship" and the "Spirit of fatherhood."

Analogously the Pauline "not without" suggests that the identity of one gender cannot be thought "without" the other. Men are not simply defined as what women are not, nor women as simply what men are not. To be a woman means to be a human being of the female sex who is "not without man": to be a man means to be a human being of the male sex who is "not without woman." As Volf states: "Unlike the idea of 'neither-one-nor-the-other,' which creates a neuter by erasing gender differences, and unlike the idea of 'both-the-one-and-the-other,' which also creates a neuter by synthesizing gender differences, the idea of 'not-without-the-other' affirms gender differences while at the same time positing one gender identity as always internal to the other. The irreducible duality is preserved and made part of a complex identity in which each, in its own way, always already contains the other."[23]

In Eph 5:21–33 Paul takes the self-giving of Christ for humanity as the model for relations between engendered persons. "Husbands, love your wives, just as Christ loved the church and gave himself up for her in order to make her holy" (vv. 25–26). While the text addresses only husbands, the larger narrative of the Bible suggests that the injunction applies to both men and women. The idea of self-giving is important. It does not mean, as it has so often been misunderstood, a loss of the self. To the contrary, both Ephesians and the doctrine of the Trinity presuppose the affirmation of the self; in the Trinity, persons are more than relations, and in Ephesians one should love the other "as" one loves oneself precisely because "no one ever hates his own body" (5:29).

What may this self-giving consist of? It means abandoning any self-absorption and moving toward the other in order to "nourish" and "tenderly care," in order to make "without blemish" and clothe in "splendour"

---

23. Ibid., 187.

(vv. 29, 27). It means an opening of the self for the other so much so that love for the other is experienced as love for the self (v. 28).

SUMMARY

In summary Volf shows that at the heart of Christianity, in the doctrine of the Trinity and of the cross, there are resources for thinking about gender identity. Human beings exist in an irreducible duality of sexual being with equal dignity. The constitution of gender identities on the basis of sexed bodies goes both ways, from men to women and from women to men. The very identity of each gender may not be "without the other"; the identity of each encompasses in its own way the identity of the other and both identities are fashioned and refashioned in relation to one another. All of this is kept in motion by self-giving love.

That is all we have space for in this Prologue. Really all we have done is cracked open what is a fascinating and important topic. I have only presented one main idea, that of Volf's Trinitarian identities. We could look at some alternative proposals and critique of this view, but that would, I think, go beyond the scope of the Prologue. I trust this has been enough to establish some parameters within an evangelical theology of gender and open up a few new possibilities for further consideration which many of the essays to follow probe and develop.

1

The Image of the Invisible God

(An)iconic Knowing, God, and Gender

TIM BULKELEY

IN DISCUSSION OF "GOD and Gender," the use of gendered imagery to speak of God plays a crucial role. Since within Christian theology and practice "Father" (and also the correlative "Son") language has had a special and central place in God-talk, the chapter will focus on this language. I start from a conviction that any Christian consideration of gendered God-language must take seriously a fundamental theological commitment that, as Thomas Aquinas put it, "*Deus non est in genere.*" God is not a member of any class.[1] A god who is part of some larger class of entities is not the God of the Bible or of the tradition, but merely an idol, a god.

However, once this is said, we are left with the problem of speaking about this unspeakable God. Again there is a long tradition of attempts to do this. They have often been broadly categorized as *via negativa* and its "opposite" *via positiva*.[2] The positive road attempts to approach God-talk through a variety of (more and less appropriate) naming, the nega-

---

1. Aquinas' slogan (among other citations: *Summa Theologiae*, prima pars quaestio III articulus 5) has been quoted very often within recent Protestant tradition, most notably by Karl Barth e.g., in *Church Dogmatics* II/1 (London: T. & T. Clark, 1957) 310.

2. This convenient terminology has a history which goes back at least to Pseudo-Dionysius (late fifth or early sixth century CE).

tive road recognizes that any talk of what God *is* fails, and so we might talk of God by speaking of what God *is not*.

Here I want to make use of a related but less sophisticated distinction.[3] Based on the biblical injunction against making images (plastic art) to represent God, I will speak of "aniconic"[4] and "iconic knowing." Aniconic knowing attempts to talk of God using verbal pictures. This approach permits us to transcend the limits of physical imagery whilst still "speaking in pictures." "Iconic knowing" by contrast desires to focus this knowing on one image (which I will argue requires first denaturing the image).

ANICONIC KNOWING: GOD BEYOND GENDER

When one draws word pictures of a God who transcends gender, then one uses language and images appropriate to both genders. Word pictures allow imagery which would be impossible or grotesque if painted or sculpted. Heb 6:19 provides an example unconnected with gender: "We have this hope, a sure and steadfast anchor of the soul, a hope that enters the inner shrine behind the curtain."

If we imagine an attempt to film this image, it would involve an anchor (representing Christ our hope) travelling through the veil of the temple, into the Holy of Holies. What is ridiculous as concrete art, communicates in words. Pictures drawn with words are, in a sense, aniconic and often do not "work" if painted, sculpted, or drawn.

Biblical faith is founded on such aniconic imagery.[5] The second commandment forbids all idols,[6] even images of the true God. In a world of gods and goddesses, both sculpted and drawn, the Bible pictures God

---

3. My concerns are in the realm of "practical theology," that is with how Christian people may speak about God in practice.

4. Aniconic, comes from the Greek word εικων/*ikon*, an image or picture. A negative prefix is added indicating an absence or opposition to such images. The Jewish and Muslim religions have obeyed the commandment against images strictly; Christianity has often understood it as only forbidding images of *other* gods! The Bible makes no such distinction, indeed it assumes the gods *are* imaged.

5. I am aware that this term is oxymoronic, yet it seems useful because it permits me to stress both, that this is "picture" language, but that such pictures work differently to those of plastic art.

6. That a פֶּסֶל/*pesel* can be an image of YHWH is seen in Judges 17–18 where Micah's mother makes a פֶּסֶל/*pesel* from the stolen silver that he returns saying, "I consecrate the silver to the LORD from my hand for my son, to make an image of cast metal."

with words alone. Yet God is person, not some abstract philosophical concept. The Old Testament reveals God's personhood at the deepest level, using God's personal name. The name of the not-to-be-pictured-God even had abbreviated versions "Yah" and "Yahu" (a nickname?), found in the exclamation "Halleluia"[7] ("Praise Yah!") and in names—like Elijah's (*Eli Yahu* in Hebrew). In a previous generation, Old Testament theology noticed that, "It is his personhood . . . which is involuntarily thought of in terms of human personality . . . not the spiritual nature of God which is the foundation of Old Testament faith."[8]

The gods and goddesses of Canaan, and of every other ancient Near Eastern culture except that portrayed in the ideology of the Bible, were imaged by statues based on human and animal forms. Such "gods" could easily be thought of as gendered. Indeed to avoid such implication is difficult for the image almost has to be either male or female. Only the Bible's aniconic God could avoid being of one sex or the other.

Deut 4 makes this connection clear and explicit, first reminding the hearers that they, "saw no form (תְּמוּנָה *temunah*) when the LORD spoke at Horeb" (v. 12), and then in verse 16 continuing, "so that you do not act corruptly by making an idol for yourselves, in the form of any figure" (פֶּסֶל *pesel* and תְּמוּנָה *temunah*). This is then expanded to make its meaning quite clear: "the likeness (סֶמֶל *semel*) of male or female." In verses 17–18 images of animals are forbidden, while verse 19 excludes also the host of heaven. However, the initial command in verse 16 mentioned and excluded explicitly, "the likeness of male or female." Since the following verses exclude all other sorts of creatures, these males and females are human. Only for human images are both genders distinguished, and *both forbidden*.

Archaeology, and the Bible's own account, shows that ancient Israel's popular religion was seldom as pure as biblical law demanded. At "high places" across Palestine, and even in Solomon's temple in Jerusalem, Yhwh was in fact worshipped alongside Asherah poles representing a goddess. Popular religion often confused the real God, Yhwh, with the Canaanite god, Ba'al (whose name means "lord," "husband," or "master"). Yet there is almost no archaeological evidence that Yahweh was ever pictured.

---

7. *Hallelu Yah*, "hallelu" being a plural imperative form of the verb "praise."
8. Walther Eichrodt, *Theology Of the Old Testament* (London: SCM, 1961) 1:211.

One drawing on an ostracon from Kuntillet Ajrud (an Israelite fortress in Sinai occupied early in the monarchic period) may portray Yhwh with a goddess. The text speaks of Yahweh and "his Asherah," and is accompanied by three stick-figures, one presumed male, one sometimes presumed female, and "behind" them, a seated (female?) figure playing a lyre. The text reads: "I bless you by Yhwh and his Ashera." Yhwh is God's name and Ashera could be the goddess. If so, and *if* the stick figures represent the text, though they are crude while the text is well written, then here is one place where an Israelite drew a picture of God. That this find is unique, and from a distant outpost, emphasises the strength of the prohibition on graven images![9]

EXAMPLES OF MOTHERLY IMAGERY FROM PATRISTIC SOURCES

The Christian theologians of the formative years (the "fathers of the church") were clear that gender categories do not apply to God. God's transcendence of human categories includes not being limited to one gender. So, Gregory of Nyssa stated, "God is neither male nor female."[10] and Jerome noted in his Isaiah commentary that "Sexual categories do not apply to the Godhead."[11] Since the Christian God was not limited by gender categories these theologians were free to picture God using both male and female imagery.

Therefore, as examples of aniconic attempts to talk of God, it is interesting to find motherly word pictures alongside fatherly ones among the early Christian theologians.

Among the feminine imagery used, maternal imagery was particularly often used of God. It focused mainly on two themes: the mother who gives birth, as we are given new birth in conversion and baptism, and the image of divine teaching as feeding, in particular as like a mother feeding the child at her breast.

---

9. See e.g., the review article by David Noel Freedman, "Yahweh of Samaria and His Asherah," *Biblical Archaeologist* 50 (1987) 241–49.

10. Migne, *PG* 44, 916B. Gregory of Nyssa, Homily VII *In Cantica Canticorum* in Greek the quotation reads: ἐπειδὴ οὔτε ἄρσεν οὔτε θῆλυ τὸ θεῖον ἐστι *epeide oute aresen oute thelu to theion esti*.

11. Jerome, *Commentariorum in Esaiam libri 1–XI* (Corpus Christianorum Series Latina 73). M. Adriaen (ed.), (Turnhout: Brepols, 1963) 459, 1.82–83, in Latin the quotation reads: *In divinitate enim nullus est sexus.*

This image of education as feeding, and particularly as breastfeeding, was a commonplace in the Hellenistic world. It occurs already in a Christian context in the New Testament. The Epistles speak of the apostles' feeding their readers with the "milk of the gospel" and extend the image to God as the source of this milk: "Like newborn infants, long for the pure, spiritual milk, so that by it you may grow into salvation … if indeed you have tasted that the Lord is good" (1 Pet 2:2-3 with a reference to the Ps 34:8; cf. 1 Cor 3:1-3; 1 Thess 2:7-8; and Heb 5:12-13). This picture was taken up enthusiastically by the "fathers" in ways that make clear that they did not picture God as male. Here are a few prominent examples.

Irenaeus (c.130-202)

Breast-feeding imagery came naturally to Irenaeus (perhaps the most influential Christian theologian of the second century). For example, discussing humanity's imperfection he writes:

> He [our Lord] might easily have come to us in His immortal glory, but in that case we could never have endured the greatness of the glory; and therefore it was that He, who was the perfect bread of the Father, offered Himself to us as milk, [because we were] as infants. He did this when He appeared as a man, that we, being nourished, as it were, from the breast of His flesh, and having, by such a course of milk nourishment, become accustomed to eat and drink the Word of God, may be able also to contain in ourselves the Bread of immortality, which is the Spirit of the Father.[12]

Irenaeus' language is poetic and rhetorical not systematic. The image's referent changes, and 1 Cor 3:2 and 1 Pet 2:2 stand alternately behind his thought. However, unlike either New Testament writer, Irenaeus applies imagery of breasts and milk directly to God, both to the Spirit and to the Son. Motherly language was not restricted to any one person of the Trinity.

---

12. Irenaeus *Against Heresies*, Book IV, Chap. XXXVIII. Translation from Alexander Roberts et al., *The Ante-Nicene Fathers Vol.I : Translations of the Writings of the Fathers Down to A.D. 325* (Grand Rapids: Eerdmans, 1989; based on the 1885 edition) 521.

Clement of Alexandria (c.150–230)

Clement uses motherly language extensively to speak of God. We will look at two instances. In the *Instructor* a section headed, "The Name Children Does Not Imply Instruction in Elementary Principles," the image of instruction is breastfeeding. Yet, Clement cannot accept at face value Paul's contrast of milk and solid food, for this would allow his heretical opponents their point. So, discussing 1 Cor 3:2, he provides a lengthy (and inevitably now out of date) presentation of the physiology and natural history of lactation, before, overcome by the wonder of God's love in the incarnation of Christ, the nurturing of the church, and of Mary, he bundles all together in a welter of exclamation and imagery:

> O mystic marvel! The universal Father is one, and one the universal Word; and the Holy Spirit is one and the same everywhere, and one is the only virgin mother. I love to call her the Church. This mother, when alone, had not milk, because alone she was not a woman. But she is at once virgin and mother—pure as a virgin, loving as a mother. And calling her children to her, she nurses them with holy milk, viz., with the Word for childhood. Therefore she had not milk; for the milk was this child fair and comely, the body of Christ, which nourishes by the Word the young brood, which the Lord Himself brought forth in throes of the flesh, which the Lord Himself swathed in His precious blood. O amazing birth! O holy swaddling bands! The Word is all to the child, both father and mother and tutor and nurse.[13]

Notice how here images of feeding, food and birthing are mixed and applied to Christ.

Clement later attempts an organised and logically persuasive presentation for those "not inclined to understand it thus, but perchance more generally." Flesh represents the Spirit; blood points to the Word, and the union of both is the Lord Jesus, who is Spirit and Word. So, the food, the Lord Jesus, the Word of God, the Spirit made flesh, "is the milk of the Father, by which alone we infants are nourished."[14] Those who believe "flee to the Word, the care-soothing breast of the Father. Who alone, as is befitting, supplies us children with the milk of love."

---

13. Clement of Alexandria *Paedogogus* I, VI translation from Alexander Roberts et al., *The Ante-Nicene Fathers Vol. II: Translations of the Writings of the Fathers Down to A.D. 325* (Grand Rapids: Eerdmans, 1989; based on the 1885 edition) 220.

14. Ibid.

That milk feeding is linked to birthing causes Clement also to say: "Wherefore the Holy Spirit in the apostle, using the voice of the Lord, says mystically, 'I have given you milk to drink.' For if we have been regenerated unto Christ, He who has regenerated us nourishes us with His own milk, the Word; for it is proper that what has procreated should forthwith supply nourishment to that which has been procreated."[15]

At the close of the work, Clement offers a "Hymn to the Tutor" (Christ), which has for its second half epithet upon epithet praising the instructing Word. It begins:

> Bridle of untamed colts,
> Wing of unwandering birds,
> Ship's sure helm,
> Shepherd of royal lambs.

This sets the tone for a hymn concerned with one who cares, guides, and protects the young, small and infant. Among pictures that recur are: shepherd, mother-bird, savior, helm, and bridle. The tone throughout is warm and affectionate. The closing reads:

> Christ Jesus,
> heavenly milk
> from the sweet breasts
> of the bride of grace,
> squeezed from your wisdom.
> The childlike,
> with tender mouths, are cherished
> filled with the dewy spirit
> of the Word's breasts,
> sing together simple praises,
> true hymns to Christ the King,
> a holy fee for life giving teaching;
> let us sing together,
> sending forth simply
> the powerful Child.
> O Christ born,
> choir of peace,
> O temperate people,
> let us celebrate together
> the God of peace.

---

15. Ibid., 221.

The prominence of motherly, and especially of breastfeeding imagery in this hymn, with which he closes the work, indicates the importance of this picture for Clement.

Eusebius (c.260–341) and Jerome (c.340–420)

In their comments on Isa 40:10–11, both Eusebius and Jerome make interesting use of the idea they find in the New Testament that the apostles are "mothers" to the churches in their care (Gal 4:19; 1 Thess 2:7–8). God is shepherd and among "his" sheep are "those that give suck"; i.e. mothers with young lambs. Eusebius and Jerome interpret these motherly ewes in God's flock similarly.[16] They quote Gal 4:19 and call them apostles.

Jerome, however, is led to further reflection. He is reminded, by the phrase from Galatians "until Christ be formed in you," of the work of the Holy Spirit. This in turn causes him to mention that in Semitic languages the Spirit is feminine. He then quotes from Ps 123:2: "As the eyes of a slave follow his master's hand / as the eyes of a slave-girl her mistress." He sees in the mistress a feminine figure of the Holy Spirit. This leads the scholarly Jerome to quote also from the, now lost, *Gospel of the Hebrews*. Here Christ speaks of the Spirit as his mother: "Even so did my mother, the Holy Spirit, take me . . ."[17] Jerome is well aware that such talk of God as motherly is unusual and may seem strange. So he points out that no one need be offended by it, for whilst in the Semitic languages the Spirit is feminine, Latin uses masculine and Greek uses neuter gender for the word Spirit. This shows that sexuality does not apply to the Godhead.

Augustine (354–430)

A little later the great Augustine extends this idea of the apostle as mother and father. He links it with Jesus' words about the mother hen, and so speaks of Christ in a motherly way. The Lord, he says, has the authority

---

16. Joseph Zeigler, *Eusebius Werke. 09, Der Jesajakommentar* (Berlin: Akademie, 1975) 252–53, Eusebius, *In Esaiam*; Jerome, *In Esaiam*. In CC, Series Latine LXXIII, 458–59. According to Michael J. Hollerich, *Eusebius of Caesarea's Commentary on Isaiah: Christian Exegesis in the Age of Constantine* (Oxford: Oxford University Press, 1999) 47, "Jerome had Origen's and Eusebius' commentary at his disposal when he wrote his own commentary."

17. Ibid., 459, 1.79.

of a father and the affection of a mother, indeed in Christ's blood we have all been called to life.[18]

Other examples of motherly thoughts about Christ in Augustine are found in his comments on John's gospel. He says that we can see that a hen is a mother because she looks worn out, so Christ wearies himself for us, his children, in the incarnation.[19] Elsewhere in this work also Augustine takes up the milk-feeding theme.

Chrysostom (354–407)

The early Christian writers loved to build up lists to illustrate the richness of Christ who is all and in all. Typical of such lists is one from the great Greek father John Chrysostom. It begins, "Father, brother, bridegroom, dwelling place, food, raiment, root, foundation," and builds again to a climax with, "brother, sister and mother." It is interesting that this list is framed and enclosed by "father" at the start and "mother" at the close.[20]

The Syriac Fathers

In the Syriac church feeding and birthing imagery were often used together, as they were in Clement (see above). In Syriac (as in Hebrew) the word for "spirit" is feminine. This seems to have encouraged the Syriac speaking church to associate the birthing imagery of baptism with the Spirit as mother to the new Christian.

The idea of the Spirit brooding is often found in connection with baptism. Aphrahat (c.280–367) writes, "From baptism we receive the Spirit of Christ, and in the same hour that the priests invoke the Spirit, 'she' opens the heavens and descends, and hovers over the waters, and those who are baptised put 'her' on. From all who are born of a body the Spirit is absent till they come to birth by water, and then receive the Holy Spirit."[21]

---

18. Augustine, *Enarrationes in Psalmos CI–CL* (Corpus Christianorum Series Latina 40). E. Dekkers, J. Fraipont (eds.) (Turnhout: Brepols, 1953) 101, 8.

19. Augustine, *In Iohannis evangelium tractatus CXXIV* (Corpus Christianorum Series Latina 36) R. Willems (ed.), (Turnhout: Brepols, 1954), on John 15:6.

20. Migne, *PG* 58, 700; Chrysostom, *Hom. in Matth.* 76,5.

21. *Dem.* VI. Translation quoted from Robert Murray, *Symbols of Church and Kingdom: A Study in Early Syriac Tradition* (London: Cambridge University Press, 1975) 143.

Ephrem (c.306–373) expresses similar pictures: "The Holy Spirit has brooded in Baptism, and mystically has given birth to eagles (virgins and prelates), and to fishes (celibates and intercessors)."[22] Here the Spirit hovering or brooding is explicitly linked to the notion of new birth. This link is natural. Baptism is new birth, spiritual as opposed to fleshly birth (John 3:4–7). So, the baptismal water is pictured as a womb, or mother. Brock gives examples from Ephrem and later writers, as well as liturgical evidence.[23] Here are two examples: "Blessed are you, Lord God, through whose great and indescribable gift this water has been sanctified by the coming of your Holy Spirit so that it has become the womb of the Spirit that gives birth to the new man out of the old."[24] "Yea, we beseech you, Father of mercies and God of all comfort, send your living Spirit and sanctify this water, and may it become the womb of the Spirit that gives rebirth anew to mankind who are baptised in it."[25] Given the linguistic encouragement of a feminine gender, it is easy to see how these early Middle Eastern Christians could speak of baptism as the "womb of the Spirit" for they were already calling her "she" and so naming her "mother."

Aphrahat in his *Demonstrations* writes: "Who is it that leaves father and mother to take a wife? The meaning is this. As long as a man has not taken a wife he loves and reveres God his father and the Holy Spirit his mother, and he has no other love."[26]

A similar idea is expressed in the Macarian homilies (though not in a related work the *Liber Graduum*), "The homilist says of men after the Fall, they did not look upon the true, heavenly Father, or on the good kind Mother, the grace of the Spirit, nor the sweet and longed-for brother, the Lord."[27]

---

22. J. H. Bernard, *The Odes of Solomon: Edited with Introduction and Notes*, Texts and Studies VIII (1912; reprinted, Eugene, OR: Wipf & Stock, 2004) 121. See also *H. Epiph.* VI, 1; *H Epiph.* VII, 16, English translation by a Mr Johnston in Gwyn (1898).

23. Sebastian P. Brock, *The Holy Spirit in Syrian Baptismal Tradition*, The Syrian Churches Series 9 (Poona: n.p., 1979) 84–87, lists the liturgy attributed to Timothy, other Syrian and Maronite liturgies, Ephrem, Theodore, Jacob of Serugh, and Severus; to these can be added others, for example *H. Epiph.* VIII:9.

24. This prayer is common to both Syrian Orthodox and Maronite services, see Brock, *The Holy Spirit*, 84.

25. The Syrian Orthodox service attributed to Timothy, quoted from ibid., 71.

26. Murray, *Symbols of Church and Kingdom*, 143.

27. Ibid., 318.

However, such language is not restricted to the Spirit, the astounding and paradoxical notion of "the womb of the Father" is also found in Syriac liturgy. It is not surprising that this phrase occurs in connection with the sending of the Spirit. Some texts of the Syrian Orthodox Baptismal service, which is usually attributed to Severus (465–536), contain the epiclesis[28]: "Have mercy on us, O God the Father almighty, and send upon us and upon this water that is being consecrated, from your dwelling that is prepared, from your infinite womb, the Paraclete, your Holy Spirit, the establisher, lord and life-giver."[29]

The Spirit is sent from the "infinite womb" of the Father. Actually, a similar picture was found in connection with the Word in the apologists (Justin, Tatian, Athenagorus, and Theophilus of Antioch). Their imagery concerning the *logos endiathetis* has been expressed like this "this internal Word lives in the womb of God, like the embryo in the womb of his mother."[30]

Clement in his only known sermon expresses the same idea in typically warm language: "Behold the mysteries of love, and then you will have a vision of the bosom of the Father, whom the only-begotten God alone declared. God's very self is love, and for love's sake he became visible to us. And while the unspeakable part of Him is Father, the part that has sympathy with us is Mother. By his loving the father became of woman's nature, a great proof of which is He whom He begat from himself; and the fruit that is born of love is love."[31]

This tradition of motherly language was still alive early in the second millennium. (Anselm provides a fine example.) However, after a well known flowering in Julian of Norwich, it seems to die out in Western Christianity. This happens at about the time when devotion for Mary the Mother of God was burgeoning. I am suggesting that the example of the

---

28. *Epiclesis* (Greek for "invocation" or "calling upon") is used as a technical term for the prayer in a sacrament which calls on God to send the Holy Spirit.

29. Brock, *The Holy Spirit*, 72.

30. A. Chollet, "Circuminsession," in *Dictionaire de Théologie Catholique* (Paris: Letouzey et Ané, 1903–1972), 11:2 col 2529 the French reads: "Ce Verbe intérieur qui vit au sein de Dieu, comme l'embryon au sein de sa mère."

31. Otto Stählin, *Clemens Alexandrinus*, 3 vols., Die Griechischen Christlichen Schriftsteller (Berlin: Akademie Verlag, 1905–1909) 183 l. 31–184 l. 4; Translation from G. W. Butterworth, *Clement of Alexandria* (Loeb Classical Library) (London: Heinemann, 1919).

early theologians is one we might usefully recover as we seek to speak of the ineffable God.

ICONIC KNOWING: JESUS AND THE FATHER

The aniconic God of the Old Testament is beyond the categories of human gender. However, the New Testament both presents Jesus (a male human) as "the image of the invisible God" and Jesus talks of God as "Father." This double imaging of the invisible God has resulted in a tendency to imagine God as male. There are however also signs within the New Testament talk of God as Father which may assist us in resisting this tendency.

Jesus was Male

Jesus' maleness has been used, often somewhat unthinkingly, to argue that God is male, or can only appropriately be represented by male "priests." Evidently the fact of Jesus' maleness is an unquestioned element of the traditions about him. But what is its theological significance? What characteristics of the human Jesus have significance as theological descriptors?

Is the maleness of the son *asarkos* (as a heavenly being, not "incarnate" or enfleshed) implied by his maleness *ensarkos* (incarnate or enfleshed)? Is a "masculine" character essential to the being of the Son or accidental to his human existence?[32]

It is clear that certain characteristics of Jesus are *not* essential, but are indeed "accident." For example, one would not, presumably, claim that the Son *asarkos* has certain genetic characteristics such as eye color or body shape as individual essence. Such characteristics are clearly accident not essential. God does not have dark curly hair, any more than a long white beard!

---

32. The distinction of accident and essence is an old one in philosophy. "Intuitively, the essential properties of an object are those properties that make the object 'what it is.' More exactly, they are the properties that the object couldn't possibly have lacked. Its accidental properties, by contrast, are those that it just happens to have but might well have lacked. Thus, the property *being a horse* is intuitively not a property that the champion racehorse Secretariat could have lacked; he couldn't have been a rabbit, say, or a stone. The property *being a horse* is thus essential to Secretariat." Christopher Menzel, "Actualism." *The Stanford Encyclopedia of Philosophy* (Summer 2002), Edward N. Zalta (ed.), online: http://setis.library.usyd.edu.au/stanford/archives/sum2002/entries/actualism/.

Yet Jesus was Jewish, descended from a long line of Semitic ancestors (Matt 1:1–17; Luke 3:23–38). If his gender applies to the Godhead, why is his ethnic inheritance not determinative of God? If his eye colour, or any other aspect of his genetic makeup are not descriptive of God, then on what grounds could his gender be so understood?

Some have argued from Jesus' maleness for an exclusively male priesthood. Does such an argument mean that "masculinity" is an essential characteristic of the Son? For example, Myers wrote, "The sexuality of Christ is no accident nor is his masculinity incidental."[33] To be fair, Myers here is using accident in the popular sense, for he continues, "This is the divine choice." If there is choice, then, in the technical sense, the sexuality (and in particular the "masculinity") of Christ *is* accident. Surely it is evident that *all* such particular genetically determined characteristics of Jesus imply nothing about the nature of God.[34]

Jesus Called God "Father"

If Jesus' maleness does not imply that the godhead is male, does his choice of Father as name for God imply more? In the debate over the ordination of women Rutler admitted, "God . . . includes in his being maleness and femaleness together," but added "God taught us to call Him . . . not Mother as the primitives liked to do, but Father."[35]

Clearly, since Rutler said "God . . . includes in his being maleness and femaleness together," the fatherhood of God cannot be understood in any literal sense. Equally, since *we* are to call him father, the intra-trinitarian Father-Son relation cannot be meant. What Rutler must mean is that Fatherhood is an analogy or metaphor of Godhead.

The Old Testament is very sparing in its use of father imagery to speak of God. It prefers language like shepherd, kinsman-redeemer,

---

33. C. Kilmer Myers, "Statement on the proposed ordination of women to the 122nd Diocesan Convention," *Journal of Ecumenical Studies* 9 (1972) 230.

34. Whether, then, it implies anything about the possibility of women priests is not an issue germane to this thesis. I suspect that to truly argue for an exclusively male priesthood one must argue that maleness (or at least masculinity) is an essential characteristic of the Son. For our purposes, it is sufficient to note, however, that Myers and others stopped short of this.

35. George William Rutler, "Speech to the Convention of the Diocese of Pennsylvania." Quoted in H. Karl Lutge, *Sexuality-Theology-Priesthood* (San Gabriel: Concerned Fellow Episcopalians, 1973) 58. The phrase "as the primitives liked to do" is sufficiently polemic to indicate the intention.

rock, and other pictures which had less dangerous echoes in polytheistic systems of thought. Interestingly, undetermined parental imagery (as in Hos 11:1ff. which mentions parental care rather than naming either parent), and imagery which mentions and so balances both parents (as in Job 38:28f.; cf. Jer 2:27) is found. Explicitly motherly language is also found in several places, most notably Isaiah 40ff. (Isa 42:14; 43:1ff.; 42:2, 21ff.; 45:8ff.; 46:3f.; 49:13–21; 50:1–3; 66:7ff.) At times the writers seem deliberately to balance motherly and fatherly pictures. The New Testament, from the gospels onward, seems to contrast with this reticence. Here father-language abounds, indeed "Father" becomes a name for God. An uncritical reading of this change may attribute it to Jesus' teaching.

Indeed German scholarship of the middle of the last century represented the father-language of the New Testament as a unique contribution of Jesus, unlike both his Jewish forebears and his early church followers. Much has also been made of Jesus' use of ἀββα / *abba* (Mark 14:36; cf. Gal 4:6; Rom 8:15), which has been portrayed as a baby-talk version of "father," and thus of the link between Jesus' special intimacy with God and his and the church's use of father-language.[36]

Before examining this argument further, however, we should ask in just what way Jesus initiates this development. Jeremias was aware of a striking feature of the Gospels' father-talk for God on the lips of Jesus.[37] This usage shows a clear pattern:[38] Mark: 3; Material common to Matthew and Luke: 4; Material special to Luke: 4; Material special to Matthew: 31; and John: 100.[39]

With the possible exception of the materials special to Luke and Matthew (whose relative order might be debated) there is a strong positive correlation between the material's distance in time from Jesus and

---

36. Jeremias is still sometimes cited in support of this claim, although he wrote: "One often reads (and I myself believed it at one time) that when Jesus spoke to his heavenly Father he took up the chatter of a small child. To assume this would be a piece of inadmissible naivety." J. Jeremias, *The Prayers of Jesus* (SBT 2/6; London: SCM, 1967) 62. Translated by John Bowen from *Abba: Studien zur neutestamentlichen Theologie und Zeitgeschichte* (Göttingen: Vandenhoeck & Ruprecht, 1966).

37. Jeremias, *The Prayers of Jesus*, 29ff..

38. These figures are taken from O. Hofius, "Father," in *New International Dictionary of New Testament Theology*, Colin Brown, ed. (Grand Rapids: Zondervan, 1986) 619–20.

39. By comparison Paul uses such language forty times only.

its use of father to identify God. The further removed from the historical Jesus the more likely a writer is to talk about God as father. Indeed, with the exception of Matthew's special material and John, the figures are not strikingly greater than we might expect in sections of the Old Testament.

It has long been recognised that such use of "Father," and especially of expressions like "Father in heaven," were becoming more common in Palestinian Judaism around this time, and that such language was beginning to be used with respect to individuals (and not exclusively in relation to the nation or community as a whole as in the Old Testament).[40] So it would seem that the earliest witnesses to Jesus' speech remember him as using such expressions in ways which would not seem abnormal in a Jewish teacher of his time and place.

Later traditions, however, remember his usage as much more frequent, to the extent that in the New Testament as a whole, Father becomes a name for God, and one which is especially associated with Jesus as Son. The phrase "the God and Father of our Lord Jesus Christ" (Rom 15:6; 2 Cor 1:3; Eph 1:3; 1 Pet 1:3) is a good illustration of this thinking.

In drawing attention to this development, one is led to wonder why the tradition increasingly remembered Jesus to have used this language.[41] In this connection it is interesting to notice that by contrast the earliest strands of the New Testament, and in particular Paul seem to make use of the figure of Wisdom to understand Jesus in relation to God. "What pre-Christian Judaism said of Wisdom, and Philo also of the Logos, Paul and the others say of Jesus. The role that Proverbs, ben Sira, etc. ascribe to Wisdom, these earliest Christians ascribe to Jesus."[42] However, no matter how close the association of personified Wisdom in these text with God, she was not God. Increasingly therefore "Son" became the dominant

---

40. Jeremias, *The Prayers of Jesus*, 15–29; Alon Goshen-Gottstein, "God the Father in Rabbinic Judaism and Christianity: Transformed Background or Common Ground?" *Journal of Ecumenical Studies* 38 (Fall 2001) 470–504 (for a more recent and critical Jewish perspective).

41. I am unconvinced by Jeremias' claim that since it is used in Jesus' prayers it was necessarily his own usage, since Jesus' prayers like his other speech comes to us remembered by others, whose own patterns of prayer may influence the wording they remember. We know that this usage was common in the earliest church.

42. James D. G. Dunn, *Christology in the Making: A New Testament Inquiry into the Origins of the Doctrine of the Incarnation* (Grand Rapids: Eerdmans, 1996) 167.

metaphor for understanding the person of Christ, and therefore "Father" is reinforced as a name for God.

Pointing out that use of Father as a name for God was probably remembered in Jesus' speech more often than he in fact used such language, does not deny that Jesus spoke of God as a "father" or even used Father as a name for God. However, it should caution us from making too much of the origin of this language in Jesus.

A Motherly Father in Jesus Parables

It is also interesting to examine how God is pictured as father in Jesus' words. What did he mean by calling God "father"? Authority and discipline (especially with respect to sons) was a strong and frequent overtone of father-language in the ancient world. Pilch neatly summarises the cultural stereotypes of the biblical world: "Clearly, the father is viewed as severe, stern, and authoritarian; the mother is viewed as loving and compassionate. Children respect and fear the father but love the mother affectionately even after they are married."[43]

Such an understanding of the stern authoritarianism is almost absent[44] from father-talk in the Gospels. Here fathers are responsible for feeding their children (Luke 11:13) and perhaps the best loved parable describing God by any image is the story of the two sons (Luke 15:11ff.). Considered in the light of cultural stereotypes (ancient or modern) this parable "works" because the father breaks the stereotype. If the story were told substituting "mother" for "father" (whether or not a substitution of "daughter" for "son" was also made) the tale would be unremarkable. This parable operates, and has captured the imaginations of generations of Gospel readers precisely because the father acts like a stereotypical mother!

RICOEUR AND AN ANICONIC FATHER

The commandment not to image God protects the divine from the human tendency to reduce things to our level. An imaged god is the divine reduced to a thing we can understand and to whom we can apply the meaningful "techniques" of religion. The biblical God refuses such

---

43. John J. Pilch, "Parenting," in John J. Pilch and Bruce J. Malina, eds., *Handbook of Biblical Social Values* (Peabody: Hendrickson, 1998) 147.

44. Matt 21:30–31; John 14:28 may be exceptions.

imaging. In the Old Testament even verbal images are often used of God with care. For example in Isa 40:10f. the image of God as a victorious general or king (v. 10) is paired with the contrasting image of God as a tender shepherd who cares for the weak (v. 11). Such use of language enables a form of imaging which resists the idolatrous tendency inherent in imagining the ineffable. In a world of gods and goddesses who either give birth or impregnate, parental pictures are potentially idolatrous. Thus, when parenthood is invoked to describe God the usage may not specify which parent is intended (e.g., Hos 11:1ff.), or both parents may be invoked in the same passage (Job 38:28–29), or their roles may both be suggested through careful wording (Deut 32:18; cf. 6).

These usages are supple and flexible linguistic responses to the need to speak of God, while acknowledging that whatever we say is inevitably inadequate. Ricoeur in his exploration of this theme[45] ties this reticence to the revelation of the divine name in Exodus. "For the revelation of the name is the dissolution of all anthropomorphisms, of all figures and figurations, including that of the father. The name against the idol."[46] He then talks of how, in order to make use of father language, "father" must first be "reinterpreted on the basis of this relation of similitude." So father language is understood in dependence on other images (in view of the date of his work it is perhaps less strange that he does not mention "mother" here). Finally one arrives at "the zero degree of the figure."[47] That is, as I have understood him, according to Ricoeur we may only accurately call God "father" if we first reduce the concept "father" to its degree zero, by stripping it of the distinguishing features (such as maleness or engendering) that give "father" its specific character. Indeed it is here that Ricoeur does go on to mention "mother." In the movement from the "exteriorizing" of story to the "interiorizing" of faith: "I take the word 'interiorize' in the sense of *Erinnerung*, which is both memory and interiority-recollection. Entry into *Erinnerung* is at the same time entry into feeling; the affective connotations are, moreover, extremely complex, ranging from sovereign authority to tenderness and pity, as if the father were also the mother."[48]

---

45. Paul Ricoeur, "Fatherhood: From Phantasm to Symbol," in *The Conflict of Interpretations* (Evanston: Northwestern University Press, 1974) 468–97.

46. Ibid., 486.

47. Ibid., 487.

48. Ibid., 487–88.

CONCLUSION

A central thread of biblical understanding of God is that, by contrast with the gods of human ideologies, God is aniconic. The prohibition of plastic images for God provides a powerful protection against the worst forms of idolatry. It allowed the biblical writers great freedom to talk about God, for we can talk about what we cannot image, at least by combining distinct even opposite images (as the poet does in Isa 40:10–11). Yet to forbid plastic images is not sufficient in the end to protect humans against our idolatrous tendency. For, of course, we desire a god we can control, and understand. (See the discussions in the poetry of Job!) Therefore in the end we must add another warning, God is ineffable. Not only can the true God not be truly represented in plastic images, but verbal images too fail to express the full truth of God.

As Thomas Aquinas (quoted often, among others by Karl Barth) put it. "*Deus non est in genre*."[49] God is not a member of any class. God, then *is* not a father, any more than God is a rock. But father is a good and frequently used verbal image which points towards what God is like. However, to use the image of father alone is to turn our backs on Scripture and tradition (for Scripture and at least a millennium of orthodox Christian tradition also images God as mother).

It is said that a great theologian and preacher was once introduced as the man who could "know the unknowable, unscrew the inscrutable and eff the ineffable." The desire to do these things lies deep in the human psyche. Yet, unless the image of father is first reduced to its degree zero, to use it alone to "eff the ineffable"[50] is merely to deceive ourselves. In practical everyday use of language about God, talk in "degree zero" is not possible. In such contexts we need to follow the biblical model and speak of God as both victorious general and tender shepherd, both father and mother whose powerful tender love exceeds those of even the best of human parents.

---

49. E.g., Karl Barth, *Church Dogmatics* II/1 (Edinburgh: T. & T. Clark, 1957) 310, quotes Aquinas' slogan from *Summa Theologiae*, prima pars quaestio III articulus 5; though Aquinas (like Barth) repeated the theme in other places as a central element of his thought.

50. In recent scholarly discussion the phrase "to eff the ineffable" is usually attributed to the character Arsene in Samuel Beckett's *Watt* (New York: Grove, 1994) 62. Though the word play evidently predates the playwright's use of it in 1953!

2

The Image of the Invisible God

A Response to Tim Bulkeley

Mark Keown

TIM BULKELEY IS TO be congratulated for his most interesting contribution to the important and on-going discussion concerning the gender of God and its relationship to human gender issues.

He rightly begins with the working assumption, restated at the conclusion, that "God is not a member of any class." Due to God's transcendence we certainly are limited in our ability to use language to define God and doing so is a precarious business. In this regard, the distinction he makes between aniconic (using verbal pictures) and iconic (one image) knowing is a helpful perspective other than the more traditional mode of speaking of God *via negativa* and *via positiva*.

The survey of the historical material is fascinating revealing that a number of early church thinkers were not restrained by the masculine gender when talking about God, and in particular Christ. Rather, they were prepared to utilize feminine metaphor in terms of God and the relationship between divinity and humanity. That these writers were doing so in a strongly patriarchal context indicates that, while God is primarily understood as "father," this does not indicate that he is to these writers, male.

Furthermore, they utilized motherly language while being faithful to images in the New Testament. The force of these texts cannot be underestimated. In Matt 23:37, Jesus laments the historical rejection of those sent by God including the prophets and himself (cf. Luke 13:34). Jesus states, "How often have I desired to gather your children together as a hen gathers her brood under her wings, and you were not willing!" (NRSV) This is a vivid picture of Jesus in motherly terms. As Blomberg notes, "Jesus' words betray great tenderness and employ maternal imagery. God transcends gender and displays attributes that humans often associate with women, as well as those commonly associated with men. Here Jesus wishes he could gather all the recalcitrant 'children' of Israel, to love, protect, and nurture them like a mother hen does with her baby chickens."[1]

Paul too, was unafraid of using motherly metaphor in terms of his own ministry (1 Cor 3:2; Gal 4:19; 1 Thess 2:7–8 cf. 1 Pet 2:2) despite understanding himself as the "father" of his churches (1 Cor 4:15). Thus for Paul, the notion of "father" in terms of his ministry which was a reflection of Christ's ministry (cf. 1 Cor 11:1), encompassed feminine cultural notions of gentleness and nurture (cf. Eph 5:24—6:4 [below]). Of significance is the claim that it was at the time that reverence for Mary as the mother of God flourished, that the motherly notion recedes. All this is a timely reminder that exclusively masculine talk concerning God is out of keeping with the tradition of the church, even in its evangelical expression.

The discussion of Jesus and the notion of "Father" is also helpful in clarifying what Jesus and the New Testament authors meant by "Father" language and the dangers of applying this uncritically, without regard for the wider testimony of Scripture and Church tradition. Bulkeley rightly notes that the picture of "Father" in the "Lost Son" Parable does not conform to the cultural stereotype of the time and one of the keys to its power is the manner in which the father embraces a fatherhood that could easily be replaced with a mother-image. However, that being said, the parable *requires* a "father" image in its historical, social, and religious setting to embrace the power of the parable fully. His warning that just as graven images fail to express the full truth of God, verbal images also have similar limitations, is an important point.

I especially resonate with his recognition that the maleness of God is not essential[2] any more than his eye-color, Jewishness, or right or left

---

1. Craig Blomberg, *Matthew*, New American Commentary 22 (Nashville: Broadman & Holman, 1992) 350.

2. Having said that, I consider that the term "accident" is unhelpful in terms of the modern uses of the term and prefer "non-essential."

handedness. As such, Bulkeley rightly notes that Jesus' maleness should not lead us to assume that all Christian leaders must be male any more than Jewish. Indeed such dimensions of Jesus' personhood tell us little if anything about the nature of God and even less about the gender of church leaders. In a similar way, the gender of the twelve apostles does not necessarily lead to the conclusion that all Christian leaders must be male anymore than they must be Jewish. Neither does Jesus' maleness tell us that God is male anymore than his Jewishness tells us God is a Jew. While every aspect of the historical Jesus is of value, such dimensions of Jesus are indeed non-essential in terms of God-talk.

A truly incarnate God had to be either male or female, and Jewish or non-Jewish. He/she could not encompass both genders even with modern medical procedures! It is entirely logical to me that in a broader world where sexuality within the pantheon was normative and where society was highly patriarchal, Jesus came as male rather than female. Certainly the latter would have emphasized the reversal of the kingdom and caused great shock in a world anticipating a male Messianic descendant of David coming in power and triumph. However, his maleness granted him serious audience among his people, access to the synagogue,[3] continuity with the religious tradition of his people and ultimately the avoidance of misunderstanding concerning sexuality within the Godhead. It is indeed contentious that the non-essential elements of Jesus' personhood say anything about the gender, race, or otherwise of church leaders.

Having noted a general degree of affirmation for Bulkeley's work, from my reading of the chapter, there are two main areas I consider worthy of response.

REFLECTION ON HUMANITY IN GOD'S IMAGE

I was surprised that at points where the notion of "image-bearing" and images are mentioned in regard to representing God, that Bulkeley does not develop this idea in the direction of the notion of humanity created in God's image.

---

3. The importance of the synagogue as a centre for Jesus' ministry to the Jewish people cannot be underestimated: see Matt 4:23 ("Jesus went throughout Galilee, teaching in *their synagogues*"; Matt 9:35 ("Jesus went through *all* the towns and villages, teaching in *their synagogues*"); cf. Matt 12:9; 13:35; Mark 1:21–28, 39; 3:1; 6:2; Luke 4:15, 16–28; 4:44; 6:6; 13:10–14; John 6:59; 18:20.

In many ways, Gen 1:27–28 sets the agenda for discussion on the gender or lack thereof of God. In these verses it is clear that both the male and female human image God in the world, another reason that there is a complete renunciation of using graven images to represent God.[4] Using Bulkeley's essential distinction of aniconic and iconic knowing, this is a form of iconic knowing. While there is a complete denunciation of all forms of idolatry and imaging of God through graven images in the biblical witness, *humanity* images God within God's world. Just as humanity's imaging is not limited to male or female, neither is it limited to Jew or Greek, slave nor free, or any other category.

Thus, while Jesus was the incarnate God and was male, the creation narrative indicates from the gender balance of God's image bearers, that God's gender is decidedly not male; rather he is genderless or retains within himself in his oneness both the dimensions feminine and masculine. Consequently, to call God "father" uncritically and to load on him (her) "maleness," as opposed to "femaleness" is theologically imbalanced.

That humanity is made in God's image both male and female, also suggests that critical reflection on the nature of humanity's image bearing will give us grounds for reflection on the nature of God. There are dangers here which illustrate how, through the history of Christian thought, we have been led up some false cul-de-sacs. However such error must not deter us from continuing to explore this area. It is important that we reflect back to God language based on reflection of humanity in God's image; and indeed, if we are to say anything about God, limited as we are to our created image bearing humanness, I would say this is unavoidable.[5]

That the Scriptures, at such a foundation point in the creation narrative, note that humanity male and female were *both* created in God's image, guards me against "fatherising" God and limiting God in gender terms. This thought does not contradict or weaken Bulkeley's presentation, but would further strengthen his overall point.

Further, that "father" language dominates the biblical witness is eminently logical in a patriarchal world where the autonomy and au-

---

4. At no point however does the biblical witness suggest that humanity become the object of worship.

5. See for example passages like 1 John 4:8–21 and Eph 5:1–2 where our understanding of love and relationality are based on and derive from God's love.

thority of the *paterfamilias* is so dominant.⁶ The notion retains that of sovereignty and power whereas "mother" suggests *in that context*, submission, a severely limited sovereignty and "weakness" (cf. 1 Pet 3:7). To have utilized mother language of God in the main would have perhaps enhanced the subversive and counter-cultural dynamic of the kingdom, but would have potentially seen the power of God misunderstood. A crucified male Messiah was barely palatable to a few Jews (cf. 1 Cor 1:22); one wonders how a female Messiah would have been viewed in the Jewish or Greco-Roman worlds. Yet Jesus, while male, was not averse to expressing "feminine" (in cultural terms) character,⁷ suggesting that even in his maleness, he expressed a masculinity that was both "strong" and "soft."⁸

While working within the patriarchal social structures of his day, Paul is utterly countercultural in his appeal for husbands to love your wives (Eph 5:25–33) and for fathers "not to provoke to anger your children (Eph 6:9); instead, bring them up in the training and instruction of the Lord."⁹ Whereas the appeals to the "weaker" partners in the *Haustafel*

---

6. As C. C. Kroeger, "Head," in *Dictionary of Paul and His Letters*, edited by G. F. Hawthorne, R. P. Martin and D. G. Reid (Downers Grove, IL: InterVarsity, 1993) 376 notes: "[a]ccording to Roman *patria potestas*, the oldest living male (*paterfamilias*)—whether father, grandfather, or great-grandfather—controlled all the other members of the family, regardless of age or political importance. Only the *paterfamilias* was recognized as a full person in the eyes of Roman law and society. As such, he held the power of life and death over other family members and assumed accountability for their behavior."

7. See above on Matt 23:37 (cf. Luke 13:34). See also Luke 19:41 and John 11:33–35, where Jesus is deeply moved and weeps.

8. I am not at all wishing to demean women at this point; rather, to reflect a first century cultural perspective; see for example (from A. Oepke, 'Women in Judaism,' in *TDNT*, 1.781–82): *b.Qidd.* 82b: "happy is he whose children are males, and woe to him whose children are females"; *Gen. Rab.*, 45 on 16:5; *b. Šabb.*, 33b: where women were seen as "greedy, inquisitive, lazy, vain and frivolous"; *b. Qidd.* 49b: "Ten qab of empty-headedness have come upon the world, nine having been received by women and one by the rest of the world"; Hillel, in *m. Aboth* 2:7: "many women, much witchcraft"; *y. Sotah* 10a, 8: "May the words of the Torah be burned, they should not be handed over to women"; *m. Sotah* 3:4: "The man who teaches his daughter the Torah teaches her extravagance"; Philo, *Opif.*, 165: "in us the attitude of man is informed by reason (*nous*), of woman by sensuality"; Josephus *C. Ap.*, 2.201: "for, says the Scripture, 'A woman is inferior to her husband in all things.' Let her, therefore, be obedient to him; not so, that he should abuse her, but that she may acknowledge her duty to her husband; for God hath given the authority to the husband."

9. William Arndt, Frederick W. Danker, and Walter Bauer, *A Greek-English Lexicon*

would have met with approval within the social order of the day, the rhetorical force of Eph 5:19—6:10 is found in the radical appeals to the "weaker" members of the social order.[10] The picture of loving husbands, child-raising fathers, and servant slave masters[11] is astonishing and challenges strongly "masculinised" views of fatherhood and leadership.

A strong doctrine of the Spirit here is also helpful. The terms for Spirit in Scripture are feminine in the OT (*ruach*) and neuter in the NT (*pneuma*). The absence of the masculine here brings balance to the notion of God's gender. This Spirit indwells humanity and so knows intimately and relationally our gender and participates in it. Again, this leads us to an understanding of God that transcends gender, knows gender and importantly, participates in gender.

THE ARGUMENT THAT THE DEVELOPMENT OF FATHER LANGUAGE IS LINEAR

I am not convinced by Bulkeley's claim that in the New Testament there is a historically temporal linear development in the use of "Father-talk" based on the Gospels. It *can be* argued that across the Gospel-tradition, there is an increasing use as Bulkeley (utilizing Jeremias) notes. However, the writings of Paul, and complications in ordering the Gospel material, cause difficulties for this notion.

It is generally agreed that most if not all of Paul's letters are the earliest writings in the NT.[12] In the undisputed Paulines there are twenty-three references spanning the earliest of Paul's letters (Galatians)[13] to the

---

of the New Testament and Other Early Christian Literature, 3rd ed. (Chicago: University of Chicago Press, 2000) 311 notes that ἐκτρέφω (*ektrephō*) indicates "to provide food, nourish" or "to bring up from childhood," "rear, bring up." Hence it involves nourishing a child in its growth, a decidedly feminine image.

10. The appeals to women to "(submit) to their husbands"; to children to "obey your parents"; to slaves to "obey your earthly masters" are non-controversial and fit the social order. However, the appeals to the "stronger" partners are sensationally counter cultural and radical; thus the rhetorical force applies to the appeals to the "stronger" partners.

11. The appeal for master to treat their slaves in the "same way" calls for the humility and servanthood expected of the slaves; the seeds of the end of slavery.

12. Only James in the NT can be argued to precede the earliest Paulines, cf. D. A. Carson & D. Moo, *An Introduction to the New Testament* (Grand Rapids: Zondervan, 2005) 627, who date it before the Jerusalem Council, the early and mid-forties. See note 29 for others who hold this view. *Patēr* is found in James, of God, 3x (1:17, 27; 3:9).

13. Some would argue that 1 Thessalonians is the earliest of the Paulines. If so, the point still stands.

latest (Philippians).[14] There are also eighteen in the disputed Paulines for a total of forty-one references.[15] Significantly, the Aramaic *Abba* is used by Paul in both Gal 4:6 which, if the earliest of Paul's letters, would date around AD 48[16] and Rom 8:15 (c. AD 56).[17] Interestingly, if we argue that the Pastorals are late in date after Paul's death, as many do, there are only three references to God as "Father" in these later documents (1 Tim 1:2; 2 Tim 1:2; Tit 1:4).

Moreover, Bulkeley's analysis of "father" language across the strands by my reckoning is debatable. First, there are problems with the assessments of frequency. By my analysis there are four references in Mark to God as "father" (*patēr*) not three.[18] "Father," of God, is found in the material common to Matthew and Luke nine times rather than four.[19] It is found five times and not four in the Lukan unique material.[20] By my estimation, "Father" is used of God eighteen times in the unique Matthean material rather than thirty-one times, a significant difference.[21] However, Matthew also includes "Father" in the material common to Luke where Luke does not use the term on five other occasions.[22] John on the other hand uses it more frequently than Bulkeley claims, 117 rather than 100.[23]

---

14. The references are: Rom 1:7; 6:4; 8:15; 15:6; 1 Cor 1:3; 8:6; 15:24; 2 Cor 1:2, 3; 6:18; 11:31; Gal 1:1, 3, 4; 4:6; Phil 1:2; 2:11; 4:20; 2 Thess 1:1, 3; 3:11, 13; Phlm 3.

15. In the disputed Paulines there are another eighteen references for a total of forty-one (cf. Bulkeley's forty): Eph 1:2, 3, 17; 2:18; 3:14; 4:6; 5:20; 6:23; Col 1:2, 3, 12; 3:17; 2 Thess 1:1, 2; 2:16; 1 Tim 1:2; 2 Tim 1:2; Tit 1:4.

16. On the earlier date, which I prefer, see R. Longenecker, *Galatians*, WBC 41 (Dallas: Word, 1990) lxxii–lxxxviii. Others since J. B. Lightfoot, *St Paul's Epistle to the Galatians*, Libronix CD Rom, 35–55 date it closer to Romans and 2 Corinthians, i.e. the mid fifties.

17. J. D. G. Dunn, *Romans 1–8*, WBC 38a (Waco: Word, 1988), xliii notes Romans was probably written "in the middle 50s, and most probably late 55/early 56, or late 56/early 57."

18. Mark 4x: 8:38; 11:25; 13:32; 14:36.

19. Common: Matt 5:48/Luke 6:36; Matt 11:25, 26, 27 (3x)/Luke 11:21–22 [5x]; Matt 6:9/Luke 11:2; Matt 7:11/Luke 11:13; Matt 6:32/Luke 12:30.

20. See Luke 2:49; 22:29; 23:34, 46, 49.

21. See Matt 5:16; 6:1, 4, 6, 8, 14, 15, 18; 13:43; 15:13; 16:17; 18:10 (possibly); 18:19, 35; 23:9; 25:34; 26:53; 28:19.

22. Matt 5:45 cf. Luke 6:35; Matt 6:26; cf. Luke 12:24; Matt 7:21; cf. Luke 6:46–47; Matt 10:29; cf. Luke 12:6; Matt 18:14; cf. Luke 15:7.

23. See John 1:14, 18; 2:16; 3:35; 4:21, 23 (2x); 5:17, 18, 19 (2x), 20, 21, 22, 23 (2x), 26, 36 (2x), 37, 43, 45; 6:27, 32, 37, 40, 44, 45, 46 (2x), 57 (2x), 65; 8:16, 18, 19 (2x), 27, 28, 38,

Interestingly, across the remainder of the NT its use is consistent and it is John who uses this term most frequently. This suggests not that there is a clear increase across time in a linear sense, but rather that it was a favorite term of John.[24] If we date Luke early as some do (c. 61–62),[25] perhaps a trend can be argued. However, many date Luke at a time similar to Matthew, and consider Paul precedes all the Gospels. As such, it is a tenuous historical argument.

Moreover, the existence, date, and nature of Q are also highly disputed.[26] Our only genuine evidence of its existence (either written, oral, or some combination of forms) comes from Matthew and Luke, which means at the earliest the early 60's, and possibly later (i.e., the 70s–80s). This is at the earliest after most of Paul's letters were completed or at the latest, after them all. By this time, "father" language was commonly being used. Thus to track a linear development through Mark, Q, the unique material of Luke and Matthew to John is speculative.

It seems to me then that the term "Father" (*patēr*) for God is etched into the tradition early as noted in Paul. So, aside from John and arguably Matthew, there is not "a strong positive correlation between the material's distance in time from Jesus and its use of father to identify God." These writers may be reflecting their theological preferences not a trend across the early church.[27]

Similarly the claim that this led to "Father" becoming a name for God across the NT in relation to this historical reconstruction such as "the God and Father of our Lord Jesus Christ" (Rom 15:6; 2 Cor 1:3; Eph

---

41, 42, 49, 54; 10:15 (2x), 17, 18, 25, 29 (2x), 30, 32, 36, 37, 38 (2x); 11:41; 12:26, 27, 28, 49, 50; 13:1, 3; 14:2, 6, 7, 8, 9 (2x), 10 (3x), 11 (2x), 12, 13, 16, 20, 21, 23, 24, 26, 28 (2x), 31 (2x); 15:1, 8, 9, 10, 15, 16, 23, 24, 26 (2x); 16:3, 10, 15, 17, 23, 25, 26, 27, 28 (2x), 32; 17:1, 5, 11, 21, 24, 25; 18:11; 20:17 (3x); 20:21.

24. Across the remainder of the NT it is used Acts (3x): 1:4, 7; 2:33; Hebrews (3x): 1:5 (2x); 12:9; 1 Peter (3x): 1:2, 3, 17; 2 Pet (1x): 1:17; 1 John (11x): 1:2, 3; 2:1, 14, 15, 16, 22, 23, 24; 3:1; 4:14; 2 John (3x): 3, 4, 9; Jude (1x) 1; Rev (5x) 1:6; 2:28; 3:5, 21; 14:1.

25. See for example D. Bock, *Luke 1:1—9:50*, BECNT (Grand Rapids: Baker, 1994), 16–18 among a number of others.

26. See for example the discussion of G. N. Stanton, "Q," in *Dictionary of Jesus and the Gospels*, edited by J. B. Green, S. McKnight and I. H. Marshall. (Downers Grove, IL: IVP, 1992) 643–50.

27. Interestingly a similar pattern is noted in terms of the use of "Son" (*huios*) as applied to Jesus as God's son: Mark 8x; Matthew 17x (5x M; 5x Q; 10x Markan material [2x adding it in]); Luke 12x (2x L; 5x Q; 5x Mark); John 26x; Paul 18x (16x in the undisputed; 2x in the disputed).

1:3; 1 Pet 1:3) is tenuous. Romans and 2 Corinthians can be dated confidently in the mid 50s (56),[28] and, while the authorship of Ephesians and 1 Peter is disputed, good arguments can be made for these documents being co-terminus or earlier than the first Gospels.[29] I would argue on this basis that this is not a strong argument to deal with this issue. It would seem that "Father" language for God is found very early in the tradition. Indeed, if we date Galatians in the late 40s as many (though not all) do, we have the term *Abba* utilized very early indeed. However, having noted this weakness in Bulkeley's case, this critique is not fatal to the overall thrust of his argument.

CONCLUSION

Having noted these minor issues in Bulkeley's work, an additional argument (humanity as image-bearers) and a critique (the Gospel linear development argument), I concur with his overall conclusions. Much as it causes consternation to some conservatives, the term "father" as applied to God does not define God in terms of gender and so "father" is not an exclusive term for naming God. On the basis of humans both male and female being made in the image of God, arguing that God can only be known as Father and never Mother limits our understanding of God and reinforces false understandings of God in gender terms. In addition, it can lead to the false bolstering of arguments that Christian leadership must be male.

Having said this, I would argue that "Father" remains an appropriate term to be utilized as *a* dominant term to define God for these reasons. First, it retains the notion of God as "person" which is difficult to achieve through neutral terms. Second, while some cultures are increasingly egalitarian in gender terms, the world remains patriarchal to a large degree. As such, using "mother" as equal to or as the dominant term for God may affect mission in that this God may appear less powerful and weaker than other claimants; "father" retains the power of God. Third, having a neuter New Testament term for Spirit and both God and

---

28. On the date of Romans see above (cf. AD 56). M. J. Harris, *The Second Epistle to the Corinthians: A Commentary on the Greek Text* (Grand Rapids: Eerdmans, 2005) 67 notes that "2 Corinthians dates from the fall of 56."

29. See Peter T. O'Brien, *The Letter to the Ephesians* (Grand Rapids: Eerdmans, 1999) 5 notes "around AD 61–62 is most likely"; Carson & Moo, *Introduction*, 645–47, argue it "was written in AD 63–63."

the Son defined in male terms reduces the likelihood of a polytheistic syncretism which leads to sexuality in the godhead. While this is less likely in the west, it remains an issue in other people groups.

Having noted this, I believe that our use of "Father" must be clearly defined to ensure that we avoid leading believers to consider God male, to image him as male, and falsely apply his supposed "maleness" to leadership.

Further, the subversive element of the gospel including feminine images for God must not be suppressed. Where Christians are mature and have a fuller understanding of God, "mother" language alongside "father" language may be appropriate. As the gospel breaks into new cultures, the feminine dimension and naming of God can be gently and pastorally presented so that it is understood and apprehended. This will further the liberation of both genders in kingdom terms (cf. Gal 3:28). For this, as Bulkeley argues, we need to use aniconic language and imagery to define God, ensuring that God's full nature in regards to gender is perceived.

3

Gender Roles in Marriage and Ministry
A Possible Relationship

CRAIG BLOMBERG

INTRODUCTION

I WOULD LIKE TO be an egalitarian. I was raised in a liberal parish of the old Lutheran Church in America, with my teenage years spanning the turbulent late 1960s and early 1970s. Before it ever became popular elsewhere, we had a young husband and wife with a hyphenated last name do their internships together in our church just prior to their ordination during those years. As far as I knew, the congregation strongly supported them both. At home, my mother played a lot of the roles I later came to learn were often associated with fathers, most notably handling all the finances for the family, not least because mathematics had always been my dad's least favorite subject. He was a brilliant high school Spanish teacher but remarkably slow with his multiplication tables, and pocket calculators were yet to be invented!

My true conversion came through a Campus Life/Youth for Christ club in high school, however, when I was introduced for the first time to the concept of following Jesus as Lord on a daily basis in a way that made a difference how I lived in between Sunday mornings. My college years found me gaining my greatest Christian nurture through a chapter of Campus Crusade for Christ. Both organizations had staff and student leadership of both genders. Occasionally, the topic would turn to gender roles and I was vaguely aware that conservative churches excluded women from certain leadership roles. However I did not attend a church from which I ever derived my primary Christian fellowship and instruction until I became active in the Evangelical Free Church where I met my wife-to-be while we were both attending Trinity Evangelical Divinity School. Even then it was more from traditionalist or hierarchicalist professors at seminary (the word complementarian had not yet been deployed) than at my church that I learned just how restrictive many evangelicals had been and still were regarding women in ministry, and what their models for ideal family life looked like. But those were also the days when Trinity had several leading biblical feminist professors (the term of choice before egalitarian became more common), including the academic dean, Kenneth Kantzer, and the Old Testament professor who would succeed him in that role, Walter Kaiser. So we heard cogent, representative cases for a healthy variety of perspectives.

During my doctoral studies in Aberdeen, I became acutely aware that, while my seminary training had well prepared me for teaching at an elementary undergraduate level, where I would most likely begin my professional career, if I wanted a well-rounded, in-depth education, I would have to supplement my British research degree with independent study on my own in areas of academic weakness. Otherwise, I might come out as one of the world's experts on "the tradition history of the parables peculiar to Luke's central section"[1] and still not yet know what I believed about baptism, church polity, or gender roles—three areas I had assiduously avoided taking stands on up to that point because I did not want to upset my family if I decided to change any of the views I had been raised to believe. A group of us New Testament PhD students, all recognizing these kinds of gaps in our educational backgrounds, formed an *ad hoc* study group, which chose a series of topics for in-depth study and discussion when we were not working on our theses. One of the topics that almost all of us agreed we had not yet settled was gender roles in home and church. So we read widely, conversed vigorously, formed provisional opinions, and then moved on to another topic. A few of the men (and we were a small group of all married men) were reinforced in their more tentative beliefs or shifted modestly from them; I was the only one, though, who changed from cautiously feminist to moderately hierarchi-

---

1. The title of my PhD thesis, submitted to the University of Aberdeen and successfully defended in 1982.

calist. It was not because I wanted to do so; I just found the weight of the Scriptural evidence and the arguments in the most persuasive secondary literature compelling me to move in that direction.[2]

Over the years, I have moderated even my moderate complementarianism (to use the current term of choice), to the point that Bill Webb has dubbed me an "ultra-soft patriarchalist."[3] I know what he means and the compliment he intends, but I do not like either part of the label. Other than in contexts like descriptions of toilet paper or tissues, I don't know that "ultra-soft" generates much respect from anyone, while "patriarchalist" sounds like the harshest and most antiquated of all the titles anyone has thought up for non-egalitarians. My former colleague Alice Mathews says I am pushing hard on the wall that separates the two "camps," but that I'm still on the complementarian side of the wall. My former colleague Jim Beck thinks I have forged a third, mediating position, but he could not convince Zondervan to accept that claim.[4] Most of the time I just feel like I'm sitting on an uncomfortable fence, getting shot at from both sides!

Why do I begin with these somewhat lengthy autobiographical data? It has come to be somewhat customary in writings on topics like this for authors to be transparent about their backgrounds, preunderstandings, social locations, and the like.[5] Many egalitarians have assumed that no one would ever come to a complementarian view, however mild, unless he or she was raised in and with it, and it is certainly true that it is more common to hear of those who have broken from such backgrounds in favor of egalitarian positions. But the charge of just holding, even if tempering a little, the views with which I was raised simply does not apply

---

2. Particularly influential at that time were James B. Hurley, *Man and Woman in Biblical Perspective* (Grand Rapids: Zondervan, 1981); and Stephen B. Clark, *Man and Woman in Christ* (Ann Arbor, MI: Servant, 1981).

3. William J. Webb, *Slaves, Women, and Homosexuals: Exploring the Hermeneutics of Cultural Analysis* (Downers Grove, IL: InterVarsity, 2001) 242–43.

4. Hence, even the revised version of our book, *Two Views on Women in Ministry* (edited by James R. Beck. Grand Rapids: Zondervan, 2005) preserved the "two views" title, even though now my chapter replaced Ann Bowman's from the first edition in which Jim and I were co-editors.

5. Rightly so, in view of the nearly universal acknowledgment that presuppositionless exegesis is impossible, but that our best safeguard is to acknowledge our "interpretive locations" whenever possible. See, e.g., Jeannine K. Brown, *Scripture as Communication: Introducing Biblical Hermeneutics* (Grand Rapids: Baker, 2007) 121–24.

to me. So this should help filter the rest of what I say through the grid of my own experiences.

What I would like to do is explore an issue of which I have been aware for years but have never confronted head on. It is well-known that the pairing of forms of the Greek words *anēr* and *gunē* in the same context usually implies a focus on a man (or men) and a woman (or women) in their gendered identities as male and female or in their marital roles as husband and wife.[6] No scholar, to my knowledge, seriously argues today that the terms as they are used in Col 3:19–20, Eph 5:22–33, or 1 Pet 3:1–7 mean anything broader than husbands and wives. These pericopae form domestic codes in which the contexts make the appropriate translations of the terms patently obvious. Nevertheless, when we turn to the three most famous "problem passages" in the New Testament concerning gender roles and ministry (1 Cor 11:2–16; 14:33b–38; 1 Tim 2:8–15), most translations and commentators utilize the broader renderings of "men" and "women." Still, it is also nearly universally agreed that the early church modeled itself after the home, with Jewish and/or Greco-Roman domestic structures,[7] and there have always been dissenting translations that have opted to retain "husbands" and "wives" in one or more of these passages.[8] Are there reasons why this little-held minority position should command more attention than it has thus far?

ANĒR AND *GUNĒ* IN THREE TEXTS: MAN AND WOMAN OR HUSBAND AND WIFE?

1 Cor 11:2–16

The context of our (chronologically) first passage (11:2—14:40) is a collection of problems with the Corinthian congregation's worship. Here

---

6. Cf. *BDAG*, 79–80, 208–9; Louw and Nida, 1:107–9, 119.

7. See esp. Carolyn Osiek and Margaret Y. Mitchell, *A Woman's Place: House Churches in Early Christianity* (Minneapolis: Fortress, 2006).

8. The TNIV notes the option in a footnote at 1 Cor 11:3 and 1 Tim 2:12, while employing "husbands" as the translation of choice in 1 Cor 14:35. Translations that opt for "husband" and/or "wife" in 1 Cor 11:3 include The Bible in Current French, ESV, God's Word to the Nations, LBP, NAB, and NRSV. Most all translations opt for "husbands" in 1 Cor 14:35 but do not follow through consistently by using "wife" anywhere in this context. Exceptions include the Catalán Bible, TCNT and Tyndale Bible. Translations that choose "wives" and/or "husbands" in 1 Tim 2:11–12 include the Catalán Bible, the Italian *Bibbia Nouva Riveduta* and Williams' Translation.

it involves what certain men and certain women are or are not putting on their heads. The text begins broadly enough. After commending the whole congregation for holding to his teachings (on the freedom and equality found in the gospel?[9]), Paul declares, "But I want you to know that the Christ is the head of every *andros*, but the *anēr* is head of a *gunaikos*, and God is the head of the Christ" (v. 3).[10]

Nothing thus far would suggest the notion that Jesus is head only of husbands, but the context of addressing Christians does make it clear that Paul is not calling Christ the acknowledged head over every male human but over *Christian* men.[11] So it would not be surprising if there were some implicit limitations in the men referred to in the second clause as well. Does every woman have a male head? Some have appealed to the ancient custom that a woman was under a father's authority until she married and then her husband substituted for her father in that role. But even though never-married women were far less common in the ancient Mediterranean world than in western cultures today, substantially shorter life spans left plenty of widows, and easy divorce created still more adult women who were single again, many of whom would not have a father alive any longer to whom they could return.[12] It would not be unnatural, therefore, to understand *anēr* as narrowing its scope in its second appearance here, yielding "the husband is head of a wife."[13]

Most of the rest of the passage, in fact, supports this understanding. True, the requirement for every *anēr* to pray with his literal head uncovered so as not to dishonor his spiritual head, Christ (v. 4), probably does refer to every Christian man, analogous to the way verse 3 begins. But for every *gunē* to cover her literal head so as not to dishonor her spiritual head (v. 5) is again much more naturally understood as the wife not dishonoring her husband.[14] While a bewildering array of suggestions have been made for what cultural signals would have been sent to Jews,

9. Gail P. Corrington, "The 'Headless Woman': Paul and the Language of the Body in 1 Cor 11:2–16," *PRS* 18 (1991) 225.

10. All translations of New Testament passages are my own.

11. Mary Evans, *Woman in the Bible*, 2nd ed. (Carlisle, UK: Paternoster, 1998) 85.

12. Cf. Bruce W. Winter, *Roman Wives, Roman Widows: The Appearance of New Women and the Pauline Communities* (Grand Rapids: Eerdmans, 2003) 124–25.

13. Cf. esp. Jason D. BeDuhn, "'Because of the Angels': Unveiling Paul's Anthropology in 1 Corinthians 11," *JBL* 118 (1999) 300–301.

14. Craig S. Keener, *1-2 Corinthians*, NCBC (Cambridge: Cambridge University Press, 2005) 92–93.

Greeks, and Romans by men and women violating these restrictions—both if the head covering in view were long hair and if it were some external covering like a veil or shawl—all of them boil down to not wanting to look as if they were sexually and/or religiously unfaithful.[15] Given the number of forms of head coverings or hairstyles that were required in those cultures particularly of married women,[16] it makes good sense to see Paul concerned that wives not dishonor their husbands.[17] Indeed, in a patriarchal culture of honor and shame (thus the use of *aischron* in v. 6, "disgraceful" or "shameful"), we would be surprised if such claims were *not* made. But one man's wife was most assuredly not the glory of any other man, so Paul must be referring only to husbands and wives in verse 7, not to all women being the glory of all men in general.[18]

Verses 8–9 and 11–12 do remain intelligible if Paul has all men and all women in view. Indeed, the implicit allusions to Adam and Eve and to creation and new creation in these verses could tip the scales in favor of this interpretation, since the first human pair were progenitors of the whole race. But Adam and Eve were also the first husband and wife, so they can just as easily illustrate timeless principles applicable to all married couples. We need not jettison our approach that has been emerging from the passage thus far. Verse 10 will then mean that a wife has the ability to control what is on her head,[19] so that she continues to honor her husband.

On this interpretation, verses 13–16 continue to refer solely to husbands and wives because, at least by this juncture in the passage, Paul is clearly centering his attention on hair*styles*. Like various traditional cultures in today's world, children and young single adults could

---

15. See Craig L. Blomberg, *1 Corinthians*, NIVAC (Grand Rapids: Zondervan, 1994) 210–11, 215.

16. A good, concise survey appears in Craig S. Keener, "Head Coverings," in *Dictionary of New Testament Background*, edited by Craig A. Evans and Stanley E. Porter (Downers Grove, IL: InterVarsity, 2000) 442–47.

17. Walter L. Liefeld, "Women, Submission and ministry in 1 Corinthians," in *Women, Authority, and the Bible*, edited by Alvera Mickelsen (Downers Grove, IL: InterVarsity, 1986) 143–47.

18. Raymond F. Collins, *First Corinthians*, SacPag 7 (Collegeville, MN: Liturgical, 1999) 410.

19. See Craig L. Blomberg, "Women in Ministry: A Complementarian Perspective," in *Two Views on Women in Ministry*, edited by James R. Beck, 2nd ed. (Grand Rapids: Zondervan, 2005) 159.

grow their hair in most any way their parents would permit. Only when a girl got married were certain styles either taboo or required, demonstrating that she was no longer "available,"[20] a rough equivalent to today's wedding ring. Only when a boy reached puberty did he have to worry, in at least certain circles, that overly long hair could connote homosexuality.[21] The rationales in these four verses are all strictly cultural, suggesting that the timeless principle of the passage involves honoring rather than dishonoring one's spiritual head through external appearance in worship.[22] What specific forms this takes will vary from one culture or era to the next.

1 Cor 14:33b–38

Paul's silencing of women in worship appears in the same multi-chapter section of 1 Corinthians as our last passage. In its immediate context, it interrupts the otherwise very precise flow of thought of chapter 14. After giving his most fundamental reason for preferring prophecy to tongues—it is more immediately intelligible—in verses 1–25, Paul turns to criteria for how everyone can share their gifts in a church service, including especially for prophecy and tongues (vv. 26–40). Each apparent manifestation of these gifts must also be evaluated. This is precisely the point (vv. 32–33a) at which Paul seems to digress, with his commands to women in verses 33b–38, only to returning to his original topic with his concluding remarks in verses 39–40. One can see why a few, very late manuscripts, therefore, moved verses 34–35 to the end of the chapter to remove the appearance of a disjointed text.

This scribal editing scarcely provides adequate grounds for surmising that Paul never wrote those verses to begin with, as too many have

---

20. Cf. David W. J. Gill, "The Importance of Roman Portraiture for Head-Coverings in 1 Corinthians 11:2–16." *TynB* 41 (1990) 258.

21. Bruce W. Winter, *After Paul Left Corinth: The Influence of Secular Ethics and Social Change* (Grand Rapids: Eerdmans, 2001) 131–32.

22. Granted, Paul's references to *phusis* (normally "nature," but here probably deeply-entrenched "custom") in v. 14 and "no other practice" in the churches in v. 16 could sound stronger than this. But Paul would have known of at least one very godly form of long-haired man, the Nazirite, so he cannot mean this to be a timeless absolute. Anthony C. Thiselton, *The First Epistle to the Corinthians*, NIGTC (Carlisle, UK: Paternoster, 2000) 844–46 opts for "the ordering of how things are" for *phusis* here, as a *via media* between the timeless sense of "nature" and the very temporary sense of "custom."

argued.²³ But it does provide a good clue as to the meaning of those verses. Paul cannot be silencing all women, or even just all wives, throughout every church service, since he has just taught about their proper decorum for praying (usually done aloud in ancient services) and prophesying (always done aloud) in those same services. But if he is telling them not to participate in the evaluation of prophecy, at least at the highest level of leadership on whom a final decision would ultimately have devolved, then the location of these verses makes perfect sense.²⁴ Here is where the common, current complementarian approach makes best sense.

But how then does Paul's injunction fit when he insists that women wanting to learn must ask their questions of "their own men at home" (v. 35)? Fathers are not elsewhere called women's "own men"; this must refer to a wife asking her husband. Eph 5:22 and 1 Pet 3:1 and 5 both employ the identical expression to refer unambiguously to husbands in similar contexts of instruction on submission.

Of several egalitarian views, by far the most sensible here is the one that recognizes the comparatively rare opportunities in antiquity for women to receive religious education and the likelihood that wives' questions would disrupt the flow of proceedings and require a more basic kind of instruction than time in the middle of the worship service permitted.²⁵ But this cannot be the entire solution. There always were some women, particularly among the more well-to-do, who had access to education and leadership experience in their pre-Christian lives. And there were plenty of men who did not have access to either, who would have needed every bit as basic a level of instruction. It is actually the egalitarian view here, if left unmodified, which becomes, as D. A. Carson phrases it, "unbearably sexist."²⁶

Perhaps we are meant to combine the views. If *anēr* and *gunē* here mean strictly husband and wife, then Paul could be saying that wives are not to interrupt the proceedings of evaluating prophecies lest they

---

23. For details, see Craig L. Blomberg, "Neither Hierarchicalist nor Egalitarian: Gender Roles in Paul," in *Paul and His Theology*, edited by Stanley E. Porter, Pauline Studies 3 (Leiden: Brill, 2006) 302–3.

24. E.g., Thiselton, *First Corinthians*, 1150–58.

25. E.g., Craig S. Keener, "Women in Ministry: Another Egalitarian Perspective," in Beck, ed., *Two Views on Women in Ministry*, 229–30.

26. D. A. Carson, "'Silent in the Churches': On the Role of Women in 1 Cor-inthians 14:33b–36," in *Recovering Biblical Manhood and Womanhood*, edited by John Piper and Wayne Grudem (Wheaton, IL: Crossway, 1991) 147.

usurp the authority or challenge the leadership of their husbands, either in what their husbands have pronounced, potentially under the Spirit's leading, as a prophecy, tongue, or interpretation of a tongue, or in what their husbands have publicly stated, if they are leaders, in their evaluation of a prophecy or of the interpretation of a tongue.[27] Again, in a culture of honor and shame, this could prove particularly disgraceful to those husbands. Unmarried adult women, however, would not be under the same restrictions because they would have no husbands present whom they could potentially dishonor.[28]

1 Tim 2:8-15

At first glance, this would appear the least promising of our three texts for the narrower interpretations of *anēr* and *gunē*. Surely Paul intends for all men, not just husbands, to lift up holy hands in prayer without anger or quarrelling (v. 8). Surely all women, not just wives, should adorn themselves with godly behavior rather than costly, ostentatious apparel (vv. 9-10). Indeed, it is hard to imagine Paul disapproving of the extension of his commands here to both genders, as if women *could* pray while angry and divisive or men *could* flaunt extravagant clothing and ignore righteous living! Fair enough. But verse 11 begins without any connective to the preceding verses, suggesting that verses 11-15 form a separate subsection of this chapter's flow of thought.

Once we discover how much the vocabulary in verses 11-12 repeats key terminology from our last two passages, we may be justified in translating *gunē* in its three occurrences in verses 11, 12, and 14 as "wife."[29] "Submission" (v. 11) and "silence" (v. 12) recall forms of the same root words in 1 Cor 14:34, while "learn" (v. 11) reuses the identical verb as in 1 Cor 14:35. The reference to the order of creation in v. 13 reminds

---

27. Cf. David E. Garland, *1 Corinthians*, BECNT (Grand Rapids: Baker, 2003) 668-69; Anthony C. Thiselton, *1 Corinthians: A Shorter Exegetical and Pastoral Commentary* (Grand Rapids: Eerdmans, 2006) 251.

28. Cf. further E. Earle Ellis, "The Silenced Wives of Corinth (1 Cor. 14:34-5)," in *New Testament Textual Criticism*, edited by Eldon J. Epp and Gordon D. Fee (Oxford: Clarendon, 1981) 213-20.

29. Cf. Sharon H. Gritz, *Paul, Women Teachers, and the Mother Goddess at Ephesus: A Study of 1 Timothy 2:9-15 in Light of the Religious and Cultural Milieu of the First Century* (Lanham, MD: University Press of American, 1991) 125; Jerome D. Quinn and William C. Wacker, *The First and Second Letters to Timothy*, ECC (Grand Rapids: Eerdmans, 2000) 199-200.

us of 1 Cor 11:8–9, with its comparable discussion of Adam and Eve, even if not by name.

While Paul, like almost everyone in his day, would probably have agreed that every student should exhibit a submissive spirit and calm demeanor in most all educational settings, verse 11 now takes on particular poignancy. Why should *wives* especially learn in this fashion? Because their instructors *in church* might well be their husbands! Lest this not be clear, Paul immediately adds in verse 12 that a wife should not hold the authoritative teaching position[30] over her *husband*. After all, in Eph 5:22b–24 and 25b–27 he has already likened the role relationship between husbands and wives to that of Christ with the church.

Whatever we make of Paul appealing to "creation ordinances" in order to support his restrictions on women in ministry, he makes crystal clear that domestic relationships must apply *new* creation principles.[31] It is harder to imagine a more forceful way of disclosing the timeless nature of a biblical mandate. And since the false teaching which Timothy has to combat in Ephesus promotes celibacy (1 Tim 4:3), Paul has to argue again for the importance of marriage and childbearing (2:15).[32] In this larger context, then, an interpretation of *anēr* and *gunē* as "husband" and "wife" may well fit better than the broader connotations of all men and all women.

IMPLICATIONS

Does this alternative exegesis gain us anything? By all means. One of the most persuasive egalitarian arguments against traditional complementarianism is that it forbids women from playing certain roles or holding certain offices in the church strictly on the basis of a factor they have no control over—their gender. Pathological cases aside, then, women are consigned for life to be barred from the very ministries for which they may be gifted and to which they may feel called.[33] But on our in-

---

30. For the exegetical decisions made for this understanding of *didaskein oude authentein*, see Blomberg, "Neither Hierarchicalist nor Egalitarian," 315–18.

31. See esp. throughout Stephen F. Miletic, *"One Flesh": Ephesians 5.22–24, 5.31: Marriage and the New Creation*, AnBib 115 (Rome: Pontifical Biblical Institute, 1988).

32. On which, see esp. William D. Mounce, *Pastoral Epistles*, WBC 46 (Nashville: Nelson, 2000) 146–47.

33. See throughout Rebecca M. Groothuis, *Good News for Women: A Biblical Picture of Gender Equality* (Grand Rapids: Baker, 1997) esp. 41–89.

terpretations, this objection no longer applies. There would now be no role or office from which all women are automatically barred, only those that would place a wife in a position of authoritatively teaching God's word to her husband. I have elsewhere argued that what this most likely meant for Paul was that she should not be an elder or overseer in a given congregation but that for us today the functional equivalent of this usually means only that she should not be the senior (or sole) pastor of a congregationally structured church.[34] (In churches with Presbyterian or Episcopal ecclesiologies the role of the highest teaching authority may reside with one or more individuals in a denominational hierarchy outside and above the local parish, allowing women to be senior or sole local pastors as well, if one grants the legitimacy of the larger ecclesiology.)

To put it bluntly, some women, not least for the sake of avoiding the navigation of these churning waters, may choose to remain single, in which case they should be free to pursue any role for which they are gifted and called that a man may pursue. If they marry, do they automatically restrict themselves from certain teaching or pastoral positions? I suspect that the answer for today is "not necessarily." While structures of first-century churches remain shrouded in substantial obscurity, it seems most likely that once Christianity in a given community outgrew its first house church, additional home congregations developed, with one elder/overseer per home forming the "authoritative teaching leadership" role for that group of about thirty-five to fifty people. Occasionally all the Christians in a given city may have come together out-of-doors for larger services or activities but these would not have been the norm. The collection of elders of the various house churches probably gathered periodically for discussion but we know little more than this.[35]

Given the tightly knit nature of families, clans, and neighborhoods, it might well have been unthinkable for a husband and wife not to attend the same home congregation. Particularly if the husband were the elder, his wife would be expected to join him in the local "parish." Given the frequent correlation between those wealthy enough to have sufficiently large homes to host house churches, those who had been patrons in their pre-Christian lives and those who would have thus become the elders

---

34. Blomberg, "Women in Ministry," 169–70, 181–83.

35. Cf. esp. Bradley Blue, "Acts and the House Church," in *The Book of Acts in Its Graeco-Roman Setting*, edited by David W. J. Gill and Conrad Gempf (Carlisle: Paternoster, 1994) 119–222.

of the churches that met in their own homes, many elders' wives would have doubled as hostesses, with all the domestic responsibilities for entertaining fellow Christians as they shared a common meal together.[36] Thus to prohibit a wife from exercising the teaching authority of an elder over her own husband for all intents and purposes probably prevented her from being an elder in any context.

Today, however, for a whole host of reasons, it is perfectly possible for a husband and wife to each pastor their own congregations. It is possible for one of the two to be the lead elder in one congregation while the other worships in and submits to the authority of an entirely different church nearby. When times of services in the two congregations vary sufficiently, such dual allegiances need not prevent one or both partners from also attending the congregation in which the other has "membership" in an act of support for their spouse. One can certainly debate the merits of such arrangements, but they are by no means impossible or unheard of. Thus a married woman who feels led to become a senior pastor may have opportunities to do so without violating Paul's principles for the role relationships within a marriage.

WHY NOT FULLY EGALITARIAN?

By this time my egalitarian readers may well be thinking, "Good heavens, what casuistry! Why doesn't he just give up, take the last tiny step across the threshold and become a full-fledged egalitarian?" Perhaps some day I will; I don't know. But, as I said before, it will have to be because I can become convinced by the best possible exegesis and application of Scripture. When I see that husbands' and wives' relationships are buttressed by new covenant rationales in ways that injunctions about gender roles in ministry are not, I have a harder time setting aside the domestic design as merely situation-specific.

That is not, however, to say that I have adopted the position one occasionally finds of a scholar arguing for complementarianism in the home and egalitarianism in church.[37] Because I see the two as inextricably intertwined, I would still find it hard to accept a wife exercising ultimate

---

36. See esp. throughout Andrew D. Clarke, *Serve the Community of the Church: Christians as Leaders and Ministers* (Grand Rapids: Eerdmans, 2000).

37. E.g., Richard M. Davidson, "Headship, Submission, and Equality in Scripture," in *Women in Ministry: Biblical and Historical Perspectives*, edited by Nancy Vyhmeister (Berrien Springs, MI: Andrews University Press, 1998) 259–95.

teaching authority over her husband in doctrinal matters (and I say that, even with a wife who could be viewed as fully capable of doing so, as she is nearing completion of her doctorate in missiology). But the model I am tracing out here still allows her to exercise such authority over *other* Christians, as well as to preach, teach, and lead in penultimately authoritative contexts over groups of which her husband is a part.

In addition to this fundamental, Scriptural reason, however, I will add a variety of historical and anecdotal evidence, fully aware of the limitations of remarks that fall under either heading. But I also know how readily social-scientific evidence is abused, or ignored, and how frequently, claims as to what the social sciences have or have not demonstrated about human behavior, personality, and makeup change dramatically.[38] So rather than aiming for stronger empirical support that might seem valid today but be overthrown tomorrow, I opt for some more modest observations with which I confess I am not terribly sure what to do.

Historically, we are now in a better position than ever to see all the exceptional things women have done in ministry throughout the world and across the ages.[39] But the adjective "exceptional" offers a deliberate play on words. There has never been an epoch, to my knowledge, or denomination, or revival, or other Christian movement, in which women have remained over a substantial period of time as the primary highest authoritative teachers of Scripture. For good or ill, charismatic authority gives way to institutionalization; specially called and gifted figures move or pass on, and supernaturally inflamed movements calm down as routine and respectability set in.

Even in those denominations which were among the first and most aggressive in encouraging the ordination of women in the mid-twentieth century, the majority of pastors remain male, especially at the levels of senior or sole pastors, even when administrative hierarchies and attendant parachurch organizations have attained full parity.[40] Is this all just

---

38. Mary S. van Leeuwen, "Opposite Sexes or Neighboring Sexes: What Do the Social Sciences Really Tell Us?" In *Women, Ministry and the Gospels: Exploring New Paradigms*, edited by Mark Husbands and Timothy Larsen (Downers Grove, IL: InterVarsity, 2007) 171–99.

39. See esp. Ruth Tucker and Walter L. Liefeld, *Daughters of the Church: Women and Ministry from New Testament Times to the Present* (Grand Rapids: Zondervan, 1987).

40. Trends from 1977–2000 in the Episcopal Church of America and the Presbyterian Church USA actually showed slight *declines* in numbers for women. See D. Paul Sullins,

accident of history or do the patterns mean something else? At least one answer is that a large percentage of women still get married and a large percentage of those women raise children, and there is only so much one human being can do! But is there more?

The emergence of the initial stages of what may turn out to be twenty-first century trends also intrigues me. Many observers have commented on a more resurgence of traditional role relationships among contemporary Christian young adults than my generation would ever have anticipated when we were their age, given all the social trends that had begun and, indeed, that have persisted.[41] Other religions are almost uniformly *more* conservative than contemporary Christianity in these areas. The irreligious, of course, may be found experimenting with virtually any model for relationships but it remains surprising, to me at least, how conventional secular courting and marriage patterns remain. Sexual relations may have become almost universal apart from marriage in ways they have not been historically, but men and women alike, with notable exceptions, still appear to want men to take the lead in numerous caring, selfless ways throughout their relationships. They take it for granted that women will (or should) have equal opportunity at any educational, professional, or public task they choose to tackle, but that by no means guarantee that they want to avail themselves of these opportunities. Sherwood Lingenfelter notes two "nearly universal characteristic[s]" of human society: (1) "the male public authority/female domestic authority dichotomy" and "the centrality of marriage in the definition of gender roles."[42]

Is this a testimony to something in our God-ordained natures, rather than just nurtured by our surroundings? Does marriage permit and even encourage the disclosure of aspects of gender differentiation we may have to suppress in other contexts? I have had high-profile, powerful egalitarian women take me aside privately and say "off the record" that something like what I am suggesting here they suspect is true, and

---

"The Stained Glass Ceiling: Career Attainment for Women Clergy," *Sociology of Religion* 61 (2000) 243–66.

41. See, e.g., Margaret K. Peterson, "Identity and Ministry in Light of the Gospel: A View from the Kitchen," in *Women, Ministry and the Gospel*, edited by Mark Husbands and Timothy Larsen (Downers Grove, IL: InterVarsity, 2007) 161–62.

42. Sherwood Lingenfelter, "Gender Roles and Authority: A Comparative Socio-Cultural Perspective," in *Women and Men in Ministry: A Complementary Perspective*, edited by Robert L. Saucy and Judith K. TenElshof (Chicago: Moody, 2001) 273.

that if the evangelical church would on any broad scale accept the very minimalist kind of complementarianism that I support, they would be more than content. But because they realize that one never gets all for which one lobbies, they lobby for everything, in the hopes that they will get as many opportunities for teaching ministry and leadership as possible.

CONCLUSION

I offer all these remarks tentatively, aware of the strength of the arguments against them. If there is any merit to them, then I have taken even one more step closer to the fully egalitarian position that, affectively speaking, I would like to be able to endorse. Maybe that makes me a hyper-ultra-soft patriarchalist! At any rate, I welcome response and interaction. May we all continue to labor together to understand and apply the Bible in the most accurate and most pastorally sensitive ways possible. Let us agree to disagree with one another in love where we must, but give each other as fellow evangelicals the benefit of the doubt when we are all trying to understand God's will as best as possible on this topic and, once we have understood it, to follow it faithfully.

4

Why We Still Need Feminist Theology

A Response to Craig Blomberg

NICOLA HOGGARD-CREEGAN

MY PARTICULAR THANKS AND apologies must go to Craig Blomberg, with deep respect. You have helped to crystallize in my mind why we still need feminist theology.

I remember the first time I heard a detailed exposition of the thesis that women were not equal to men. I was sitting in a theology class at Gordon Conwell Theological Seminary in Massachusetts. The lecturer did end up saying that in Christ men and women were equal, but along the way we heard all the reasons why, from every other point of view, women were considered to be less than men. Thus the conclusion appeared weak. I felt the shame of being "on trial." Women, the lecturer argued, always want to dominate men. This was the meaning of the Hebrew word for "desire" in Gen 3:16. A part of me doubted that very much. One does not open the newspaper every morning to find new stories of women who have dominated men; instead the papers tell more often of yet another tragic domestic death of a woman at the hands of a man. I remember weeping because although in some sort of way the lecturer had argued for equality the charge of inequality still lingered, as did the charge of always wanting to dominate men. Nothing in my upbringing in Catholicism, or my secular university education had prepared me for this type of accusation. At another level, acquiescing to the powerful male voices around me, I internalized the charge of inequality, with resultant confusion and pain.

I am no longer tempted to internalize those particular charges, but I react in very similar ways when I read Craig's conclusions—mild and balanced, and well intentioned though they are. One manner of looking at these arguments is to say; yes Craig is almost an egalitarian. His is very, very ultra soft patriarchalism. Perhaps one should not push too far. Perhaps he goes far enough, or is an egalitarian at heart. There is, however, another way of seeing these arguments. Craig is saying that at the heart of marriage, the most intimate and deep and vulnerable relationship in human experience, there is order, and hierarchy, and priority under God. Being a good woman or a good Christian requires one to act out hierarchical priorities in that relationship when involved in the most important part of one's life—talking about God. Precisely *because* the arguments are made about the relationship between husbands and wives they are most damaging.

Craig's arguments at one level are so out of sync with the contemporary world, and so hedged about with caveats that they make sense only in the context of an ongoing suspicion of women in leadership, and a deep seated fear that women are teaching out of turn. As Christine Pohl and I said in our book, there is a fear that "if evangelical egalitarians are wrong, then evangelicals and feminists are in danger of disrupting deep rooted gender roles and idolatrously re-imaging God in human image."[1] With arguments as weak as those offered by Craig, and in the context of a wealth of arguments on the egalitarian side, one might expect the whole issue to be less charged. The case for women's inequality can only be as strong as say, the case that Paul was right about remaining single (1 Cor 7:8), yet that argument is not taken very seriously in the evangelical community. Discourse about gender is taken seriously in evangelical circles because so much seems to be at stake, and the default position in conservative Christian circles is to start with some degree of gender inequality.

True, Craig's conclusions almost don't restrict women's practical exercise of ministry, but they do get under the skin, affecting a woman's sense of her being before God. They also emphasize all the latent powerful signs in ecclesial life that God is ontologically male. Moreover, and perhaps more importantly, Craig's conclusions do nothing to critique the harmful effects of the various degrees of patriarchalism, and less

---

1. Nicola Hoggard Creegan and Christine Pohl, *Living on the Boundaries* (Downers Grove, IL: InterVarsity, 2005) 129.

than soft complementarianism around. Only egalitarianism can do that. In the rest of this response, then, I address these questions of power and argue for why we still need feminist theology today.

SCRIPTURE

Beginning with Scripture, I argue that numerous arguments have been made from Scripture for hundreds of years in the defence of equality.

First, biblical language is complex. There is a fluidity and intuitiveness to many biblical arguments. There are deep resonances and irony that we are in danger of missing because language commonly functions in such a propositional and functional and pragmatic way for us. Rikki Watts, for instance, talks about the way in which images of creation and new creation are preset in texts which do not specifically relate back to earlier events except in very indirect ways.[2] In many cases, then, I think we have to say that the particular utterance of the moment is now unclear, and perhaps was never meant to be worked in the pedantic way we sometimes do today. The depth of Scripture is also sometimes the obscurity of Scripture. We cannot say to every text at its surface value that "this is the Word of the Lord."

Second, and following from the first point, there are obvious and much charted contradictions between these odd problematic texts and Paul's practice. There are also unproblematic texts. In Gal 3: 28, "there is no male nor female." Why do we need to go further than that?

Third, there is the whole spirit of freedom, and the freedom-trajectory of Scripture. The problematic passages are used by one lot of people to argue that they should have authority over another set of people, even if in Craig's case it is very few people have authority over very few, or even one. Surely, this is not in the spirit of Jesus of the Gospels, nor in the spirit of the whole Old Testament emphasis upon exodus and freedom. Jesus' repeated question to his disciples, "Are you so dull . . . Don't you see?" (Mark 7:18) assumed that there was a moral value in reading text and context in the Spirit of love and truth.

Fourth, Paul himself, said; "But even if we or an angel from heaven should preach a gospel other than the one we preached to you, let that person be under God's curse!" (Gal 1:8). One can, of course, argue about

---

2. Rikk Watts, "The New Exodus/New Creational Restoration of the Image of God," in *What Does It Mean to Be Saved?*, edited by John G. Stackhouse (Grand Rapids: Baker Academic, 2002) 16.

what constitutes the gospel, but I would maintain that adding religious burdens is not a part of the gospel. The character of the restrictions on women, as Craig and others ague them, are so much at odds with the other "grammars" of the gospel, that the first shall be last, that the worker arriving at the eleventh hour will be paid, that the poor will inherit the earth. Always the weak and those dishonored by humanity are the ones honored in the kingdom of God. In the contemporary evangelical church this is often the women.

Fifth, there are the promptings of the Spirit. Women are convinced and convicted of the need to preach and to lead. Surely we must not be a church which assigns all such inner calls to the status of deception—if women's husbands are around. Didn't Jesus say that the Spirit would teach you things? Should we refuse to listen to this wisdom?

Sixth, it was Jesus whom Paul served who showed how relative is the law of the day. He healed on a Sabbath, he ate with sinners, and he affirmed the woman who lavished him with oil.

Seventh, there are the prophetic passages and practices. There are the old men and the young women in Joel 2, and Acts 2 who prophecy and pray. There is Mary the mother of Jesus who trained and loved and taught Jesus himself.

And so I would say to Craig and to any other non-egalitarians, aren't these enough to outweigh the slight patriarchal gloss you wish to find on a few utterances in the Pauline letters? Is it worth risking the potential harm that is done by opting for anything less than equality? *Keeping these arguments alive, then, is one reason why we still need feminist theology today.*

The Historical Arguments

Craig ends his chapter with these words, and this ending, more than any of his other arguments, suggests that there is indeed some inner intuition that really fuels the whole debate: "There has never been an epoch . . . in which women have remained over a substantial period of time as the primary highest authoritative teachers of Scripture. For good or ill, charismatic authority gives way to institutionalization, specially called and gifted figures move or pass on, and supernaturally inflamed movements calm down as routine and respectability set in." Craig then quotes a high profile egalitarian woman who says that "privately" and "off the record," something like the mild complementarianism he is advocating does reflect our God given gender natures.

And I would say, yes it has always been this way, but *why*? Craig himself considers but dismisses the idea that this is a result of the contingencies of history. There are indeed two possibilities. One is that this is how men and women are meant to be. The other is that there are natural human tendencies which are ubiquitous but wrong. There are obvious examples of such ubiquitous-but-wrong tendencies—the making of war, for instance. There never has been a time of sustained peace. There is an enthusiasm for war that has persisted through human history, at least since our ancestors made their way to the ends of the earth in the second African Diaspora. Is war then a part of the natural God-given order? I would hope not.

I would argue that this has been the fate of women for reasons which are interconnected, and all related to the basic human frailty this species has inherited and exacerbated. One is a natural tendency on the part of women to acquiesce to the status quo because women value, at least for a while, community, family, and intimacy, and if this is the price one must pay most women will pay willingly. The other reason is that arguments in this sphere seem to carry no weight, and these deeper natural tendencies have a habit of reappearing whenever the revival is over and life has returned to normal. The third cluster of reasons is associated with the complexities of self-sacrifice, and the depth and hiddenness of prejudice in human life, which I will examine in another section.

I will look first at the way in which arguments seem to carry very little weight in this controversy, and will then look at why it seems women will acquiesce to these less than acceptable arrangements.

Good enough arguments for the equality of women have been made over and over again throughout the history of the modern church, yet the fortunes of women have waxed and waned. One could begin, for example, in 1666 or thereabouts. In that year Margaret Fell, a Quaker woman, published an essay called: *Women's Speaking Justified, Proved, and Allowed of by the Scriptures, All such as speak by the Spirit and Power of the Lord Jesus. And how Women were the first that Preached the Tidings of the Resurrection of Jesus, and were sent by Christ's own Command, before he Ascended to the Father, John 20.17.*[3] This is an exhaustive study of

---

3. Margaret Fell, *Women's Speaking Justified*. Online: http://www.qhpress.org/texts/fell.html.

the reasons why women can and even should preach, taken from many angles. Women were present at the resurrection. Women are weak, and are therefore called upon to overcome the strong. Women are a part of the collective, the church, and are thus called upon to speak. Troublesome passages are dealt to, new insights are pointed out.

If arguments were all that were needed this should have put an end to the question of women's oppression and exclusion, not to mention the charges of witchcraft. In the 1660s however, three Quaker women were hanged for the sin of antinomianism in the town of Boston. At the end of the same century, in 1692, in the Massachusetts town of Salem, nineteen women were hanged for witchcraft. Six men, most of them defending the women, were included in this list. The madness of the charges of witchery reveals the subterranean territory which I believe is still ready to emerge, like the volcanoes around us, in gender life and practice. The popularity and relevance of *The Crucible*, recently screened in Auckland, suggest better than any argument that this episode is not yet "over" in terms of the dynamics it reveals. For this reason alone we still need feminist theology, to keep watch for impending ruptures in our social and ecclesial life.

The ecclesial fortunes of women were to ebb and flow a great deal more.[4] Margaret Fell's were only the first of many arguments, many more of which appeared throughout the eighteenth and nineteenth centuries. Phoebe Palmer and Catherine Booth published similar treatises in nineteenth century America. Oberlin College was a haven for women and blacks seeking an education, and knowledge of Greek.[5]

As we know, gender gains were slow and backlashes common.[6] Relatively large numbers of women were preaching in the nonconformist churches by the end of the nineteenth century in the USA. By early twentieth century the gains had been eroded. Women were much more successful in their campaigns against slavery than they were in the area of gender. Not until the 1970s did most of the mainline churches in the West begin the process of ordaining women.[7]

---

4. For examples of gains and losses, see Margaret Lamberts Bendroth, *Fundamentalism and Gender, 1875 to the Present* (New Haven: Yale University Press, 1993).

5. Gerda Lerner, *The Grimke Sisters from South Carolina: Pioneers for Women's Rights and Abolition* (Raleigh: University of North Carolina Press, 2008).

6. Bendroth, *Fundamentalism and Gender*.

7. Ibid.

Nevertheless we cannot take progress in this area for granted. In an article entitle *Once There Was a Camelot*, Tisa Lewis and Susan Shaw spoke of the golden years from 1982 to 1992 in Southern Baptist Seminaries.[8] What followed? The Southern Baptist Convention was taken over by fundamentalists. Throughout the 1990s most women and women affirming men were sacked from these seminaries which have become polarized, fundamentalist, and unrelentingly conservative in a way that has gender hierarchy at its core. I was living in the American South during this time, and witnessed this change at first hand.

The arguments are made in theology, in biblical studies, in hermeneutics. Why does each generation have to start anew? In the past, arguments about slavery, also centring on hermeneutical issues and deep seated human habits, once made, were readily accepted. The whole British Empire faced ruin if slavery was undermined. The American South has not recovered to this day, but we do not rehearse those arguments, though prejudice and oppression still continue along racial lines of course. Why is it so different with women?

I think the reason is an inbuilt patriarchy, in which both women and men participate, that, and the fact that male/female relationships are amongst the most intimate and the most passionate in the human repertoire. Women will "make do," at least for a time, for family and for peace. Women need men in a way that African Americans or Maori do not need whites or pakeha. Yet this "making do" has a toll. The willingness to compromise does not mean that this is an ideal state of affairs.

We know from primate studies and paleoanthropology that species have a tendency to certain patterns of gender affiliation and dominance. Humans have a natural tendency to be patriarchal and aggressive. Bonobos, our cousins, are naturally, it would appear so far, matriarchal and peaceful. Chimps are more like us. Yet these natural tendencies have enabled our greatness and our depravity. The reasons and explanations cut deep to the heart of who we are.

As I have argued elsewhere then, I find some comfort in Gen 3, which readily predicts this situation: "I will make your pains in childbearing very severe; with pain you will give birth to children. Your de-

---

8. Susan M. Shaw and Tisa Lewis, "'Once There Was a Camelot': Women Doctoral Graduates of the Southern Baptist Theological Seminary, 1982–1992, Talk About the Seminary, the Fundamentalist Takeover, and Their Lives since S.B.T.S," *Review and Expositor* 95 (1998) 397–423.

sire will be for your husband, and he will rule over you." If taken more generally this text speaks not to the desire of women to dominate men, but to the puzzling acquiescence of women to male domination through history. You see it everywhere in the women who are beaten and then go back and begin again and again. Why? There is inevitability about it, predicted, right there in the text. This is the story one hears today in every women's shelter. Part of the price humanity has paid for unloving dominion over the earth is in the lives of women. This acquiescence to unbalanced gender relationships is anticipated at the heart of the foundational story of origins.

I argue then, that feminism is like farming. Farming of course is good. But Gen 3:17–19 speaks of a different curse, on the ground which will grow thorns and thistles. Yet nobody ever suggests we should leave the thistles there because they were predicted in Genesis. (Well, people now are arguing against the agricultural experiment in human history, but that is another story.) Christians do not suggest that because land has never in and of itself produced food and sustenance without trouble, that we should just leave it as it is. Men have always thought it right and proper that both men and women, sometimes especially women, should work to keep the thistles out. Feminism suggests that we should do the same with regard to Gen 3:16. We need to do this generation after generation simply because women and men mistake their fallen inclinations for God's intentions in human life.

Thus, plainly, we still need feminist theology. The arguments made by Catherine Fell, by the Grimké sisters, and by more recent feminist theologians, do not persist generation after generation. The default position is deeply embedded in the human psyche. Yet as Christians there is something about the doctrine of fallenness which allows us to say; This is not right. However we interpret the details of fall and original sin, we can at least affirm that sin and brokenness are deeply embedded in human life in a way that is obscure to us, and the gospel calls us to resist evil.

There is something in the way women relate to men which makes possible the ongoing dominance of men, and the appearance that this is a natural human trait. I would argue that it is important to resist this natural dominance and this natural acquiescence. Although there is nothing in Craig's arguments which would encourage general dominance, nor, with due respect, do his arguments help, because they rely upon taking "what is" as "what should be." We are called to resist temptation, and thus, I would argue, to resist these voices, there is still a need for feminist theology today.

THE COMPLEXITIES OF SELF-SACRIFICE

I have looked at why I think historical arguments do not carry weight given a feminist understanding of why women do indeed acquiesce to patriarchal conditions, whether they be mild or oppressive. There are other reasons, though, why women slot into these patterns. In any human relationship or institution it makes sense for people divide labor, at least for a time. Division of labor, once implemented, gives the impression of necessity and permanence. This should not, however, entail complementary gender roles, and certainly not complementary authority. Feminism has long agreed that there may be inherent gender differences, though they are on a continuum and do not apply to any particular case. Moreover, these inherent broad differences should not in any sense determine rigid gender roles. Division of labor, and asymmetrical experiences in child rearing lead to conundrums over roles, inevitably feeding into the human tendencies outlined above.

Humans are characterized by their extraordinary plasticity and adaptability. This plasticity and exocentricity[9] (other-centeredness) is what makes us uniquely human. This trait allows our extraordinary human drive, our intense curiosity, our nobility and our vulnerability in the face of temptation. Humans have the ability to exceed and go beyond the instinctual or the natural, to take on roles for a season, and then to change. In times of extreme hardship however, many roles become again determined by biology. Only in the area of gender do these determinations take on the air of moral necessity. While it may be perfectly healthy for a woman to care for children for five years as the primary nurturer, and even if this is necessary to continue that role, it ceases to be life-giving if the woman or others in her context prescribe certain roles or futures or work paths as a result. If we look to God's creation for guidance we find many different models, female nurturers, male nurturers, mixed models, transsexuality, patriarchal societies, and matriarchal

---

9. J. Wentzel Van Huyssteen uses Pannenberg's term in *Alone in the World? Human Uniqueness in Science and Theology* (Grand Rapids: Eerdmans, 2006) 140.

ones. There is nothing unnatural about women's leadership, and for both women and men to be malleable and adaptable is to be human.

Second, at the heart of our common life together is a puzzle regarding self sacrifice and selfishness. Women are more likely than men to take on nurture of children in early years. Nurturing of children is self sacrificial; women become exemplars of self sacrifice because child rearing demands this. Feminist theology negotiates these waters, but there is much still to be said, and much from our experience to be pondered. There is movement and development in feminist theology, and this relates perhaps to Craig's encounter with a woman who insisted something less than egalitarianism would be enough. In the kingdom of God we obviously do not wish to argue that we should all be standing up for our rights all the time, or even most of the time. The grammars of the kingdom require something more conciliatory. There is give and take in any relationship, in any institution. At the heart of the gospel is the insistence that self sacrifice is the way of life. Women have given up their lives, trying to be good as well as to win the favor and protection and status of men.

Yet self sacrifice is always troubling for women because, as feminism has argued, women are required to sacrifice before they have a self to give away, and because the impetus for sacrifice is often external rather than internal. It was Valerie Saiving who argued first that women have this tendency to give themselves away.[10] Roberta Bondi illustrates vividly and expertly the pathological giving away that is evident in the lives of many women.[11] All of this is, I think, described by Gen 3. Yet we are all told that giving up our lives we will find life, and that love is the primary commandment of God.

Thus the balancing of proper human self respect and self reliance with the religious command to give up the self has always been a difficult one for all of humanity, but all the more so for women, because women have this tendency to give up the self, before they have a self, and the demands of child rearing then reinforce this tendency.

Self sacrifice, however, can be a temptation as well as the highest moral act of a Christian. In the ordinary, every day conflicts of life it is

---

10. Valerie Saiving, "The Human Situation: A Feminine View," *Journal of Religion* 40 (1960) 100–112.

11. Roberta C. Bondi, *Memories of God: Theological Reflections on a Life* (Nashville: Abingdon, 1995).

very hard to balance justice and love, as Reinhold Niebuhr argued so well.[12] Human love should aspire to mutuality. Although agape love is the ideal it can also be idolatrous, when the object of self sacrifice is the male. In all these relationships women, because they have a tendency to self-abnegation, are more likely to find themselves wrapped up in cycles of self giving which are not life giving, and to discover then that they are unable to find a way out of the snare. A slight tendency to self sacrifice, combined with powerful legitimizing religious stories that validate this sacrifice, will make for exactly the sort of difference Craig detects.

The other side of self-sacrifice, however, is vulnerability, and the long-term negotiation by which one person forms, and is formed by, another. Feminist theologian Sarah Coakley has argued that vulnerability is something related to self-sacrifice, which women can share with all Christians. She relates vulnerability to the inner life of prayer which so characterizes the Christian: "What I have elsewhere called the 'paradox of power and vulnerability' is I believe uniquely focused in this act of silent waiting on the divine in prayer. This is because we can only be properly 'empowered' here if we cease to set the agenda, if we 'make space' for God to be God. Prayer which makes this 'space' may take a variety of forms."[13]

Feminist theology, then, has sometimes been characterized as associated only with arguments about equality and justice with men. Coakley exposes the other side, showing that tenderness, vulnerability, mutual formation and longing are a part of the moral apparatus that makes us fully human and spiritual. She finds these are to be affirmed in the interests of feminism, rather than discarded as not being male enough. Thus this is another reason we still need feminist theology, to continue to explore the complexities of intimate relationship, and to affirm the moral virtues that have been associated only with women.

SUMMARY

In summary then I have argued that we still need feminist theology for a wide range of reasons. The biblical and hermeneutical and contextual arguments were all made long ago, but these arguments have never been

12. Reinhold Niebuhr, *Love and Justice*, edited by D. B. Robertson (Louisville: Westminster John Knox, 1957).

13. Sarah Coakley, *Powers and Submissions: Spirituality, Philosophy, and Gender* (Malden, MA: Blackwell, 2002) 34.

finally accepted, and require retelling in each generation. I looked at the way in which the natural tendencies of women to self-abnegation and to accommodation to male authority, noted by Craig, might be connected to the desire for companionship and community. I noted that pathological forms of this acquiescence are predicted in Genesis, and experienced in homes and witnessed in women's shelters around the world. I argue that the hidden faces of oppression and the ambiguities surrounding division of labour and self-sacrifice further exacerbate these tendencies, requiring constant vigilance and ongoing development in feminist theology.

5

The Gender Issue in New Zealand Evangelical History

Peter J. Lineham

OVER THE PAST FIFTY years there has been a huge debate over gender in the evangelical sectors of the church throughout the world. Various solutions have emerged, indicating different views, culture, and theology. evangelicals have lurched between pragmatism and conviction in dealing with the issues. There is much to learn from a retrospective probing of the approaches to the issues.

Over recent years the historiography of these issues has also rapidly expanded. This paper seeks to evaluate this writing, and conceptualise the attitudes to women among conservative Protestants in New Zealand particularly in the late colonial period and the early twentieth century, periods which were critical in the development of this country.

HISTORICAL TRADITIONS IN EVANGELICALISM

It is hardly surprising that Christian visions of the role of women have changed profoundly over the last few centuries, but evangelicalism so prides itself on its fidelity to the Bible's teaching, that the issue was inevitably contested. Yet evangelicalism as a historical phenomenon incorporates a range of groups and identities and faces significant pressures. David Bebbington's identification of the common marks of evangelicalism—conversionism, biblicism, crucicentrism, and activism[1]—has received enough acceptance to provide us with a workable identitikit,

---

1. David Bebbington, *Evangelicalism in Modern Britain: A History from the 1730s to the 1980s* (London: Unwin Hyman, 1989) 282.

although its methodology sidesteps the role of evangelical traditions. Yet the movement, because it lacked formal institutional expression, was shaped by its evolving and diverging heritage. The expressions of evangelicalism have changed significantly over the last 270 years, and so have its views on the role of women.

Interpretations of gender roles did not trouble the first generation of evangelical Christians. They were relatively freethinking about the role of women, although they shared the hierarchical values of the age. The dominance of this patriarchal structure of religion had been challenged by the "prophetism" of the early Protestant sects. Protestantism had curtailed women's religious options by abolishing convents and monasteries, by viewing the family as the only basis for social structures, and by identifying church and state so closely. John Knox was prepared to use the Bible to condemn women rulers in his impolitic *First Blast of the Trumpet against the Monstrous Regimen of Women*.

Some radical reformers had hinted at a different vision of the church. The Anabaptists and several of the English civil war sects encouraged women to exhort as the Spirit moved them. The Camisards, who fled from France when Louis XIV suppressed the practice of Protestantism, included women prophets. Both traditions influenced the eighteenth century evangelicals. Since Methodism was not a church but a religious society, John Wesley cautiously permitted women to exhort "indoors" and to lead women's class meetings.[2] This tradition continued among the Primitive Methodists until about 1850. In the American revivalist scene, where evangelicalism remained less church-bound, women preachers continued. Moreover, evangelicalism in all strands was opportunistic. So Selina, the dowager Countess of Huntingdon, became the sponsor of the Calvinist Methodist denomination in England, despite opposition from some.[3]

Because of their emphasis on individual conversion and salvation, early evangelicals sought to convert women. They used the language of the heart, and since emotions were identified as virtues in women, the

---

2. Deborah M. Valenze, *Prophetic Sons and Daughters: Popular Religion and Social Change in England 1790–1850* (Princeton: Princeton University Press, 1985).

3. For the Countess see the new biographies, by Boyd Stanley Schlenther, *Queen of the Methodists: The Countess of Huntingdon and the Eighteenth Century Crisis of Faith and Society* (Durham: Durham Academic, 1997), and Edwin Welch, *Spiritual Pilgrim: A Reassessment of the Life of the Countess of Huntingdon* (Cardiff: University of Wales Press, 1995).

testimony of assurance gave scope for women's voices. Missionaries took pride in the ministry of liberating women on the mission field. Women were central to a key evangelical strategy of home visitation back in England.[4]

The Bible was read by most Christians of that era as supporting a gender hierarchy. In the Victorian age new gendered behaviour codes developed especially among the middle class. Some historians argued that women were restricted to the private sphere, although evidence suggests that this is rather too broad a generalisation.[5] As evangelicalism became more entrenched in the churches, and as the Victorian code of behaviour became stronger, evangelicals never challenged the male voice in the formal church service. The idea of restricting woman's sphere to the home was an ideal in this period. The more English and the more middle class the environment, the more absolute were these rules.

GENDER FACTORS IN NEW ZEALAND HISTORY

Over the last thirty years historians have reflected extensively on the gendered nature of New Zealand history, and what was distinctive about this, compared to other societies at the same time. Most historians now see the colonial/imperial factor as a key not simply to the colonies but also to the imperial heartland. Victorian notions of gender need to be applied to New Zealand with caution because gender roles were reshaped in the colony.

The disproportion of men to women in New Zealand is usually viewed as a key factor although, as David Thomson has argued, it can be exaggerated.[6] Nevertheless, in the broader context of Australasian culture, single males—tramps and mates and soldiers—influenced the emergence of a very rugged masculinist culture. The image of New Zealand males remained in "cowboy" mode. Fred Dagg and Barry Crump and mud-splattered All Blacks symbolise New Zealand masculinity and this

---

4. See J. N. Ian Dickson, "Evangelical Religion and Victorian Women: the Belfast Female Mission, 1859–1903," *Journal of Ecclesiastical History* 55 (2004) 700–725.

5. See A. Vickery, "Golden Age to Separate Spheres? A Review of the Categories and Chronology of English Women's History," *Historical Journal* 36 (1997) 383–414; A. Clark, *The Struggle for the Breeches: Gender and the Making of the British Working Class* (Los Angeles: University of California Press, 1995).

6. David Thomson, "Marriage and Family on the Colonial Frontier," in *Disputed Histories: Imagining New Zealand's Pasts*, edited by Tony Ballantyne and Brian Moloughney (Dunedin: Otago University Press, 2006) 119–42.

"good keen man" image was rather rough, dirty, violent, and implicitly rather hostile to femininity.[7]

Meanwhile, the colonial pattern of the hardworking wife with few or no servants subtly changed the Victorian ideal of the woman in the home. Women learned to be strong and determined, and challenged the demure image of Victorian women.[8] They gained power from their home base. Women strongly supported the campaign for the prohibition of alcohol and the enfranchisement of women. The WCTU's motto[9] was "for God for home for humanity." Moreover, movements of "scientific motherhood," eugenics and race purity, and above all the Plunket Society, portrayed the ideal woman as domestic in her outlook, giving everything to her children. Probably the early twentieth-century tone placed more restrictions on respectable women.

There were always other dimensions to the story. An influential book by Caroline Daley identifies changing notions of gender and sexuality. In the 1920s and 1930s colonials were exposed to Hollywood's notions of femininity, and women began to conform to changing notions of the stylish body beautiful.[10] This contradiction—women questing for the beautiful and men anxious not to be domesticated—remains a feature of our gender history.

NINETEENTH CENTURY NEW ZEALAND EVANGELICAL WOMEN

One must be careful in using the term "evangelical" in nineteenth century New Zealand. The term was rarely used even in the Anglican setting. It fitted the CMS missionaries, who were shaped by Calvinist Methodism. In their view, propriety was one of the fruits of the gospel, and a very male-dominated order marked their ministry. The missionary home was ruled over by the husband, but with domestic leadership over family and

---

7. See Jock Phillips, *A Man's Country: The Image of the Pakeha Male: A History*, 2nd ed. (Auckland: Penguin, 1996).

8. Raewyn Dalziel, "The Colonial Helpmeet: Women's Role and the Vote in Nineteenth Century New Zealand," *New Zealand Journal of History* 11 (1977) 112–23.

9. Women's Christian Temperance Union.

10. Caroline Daley, *Leisure & Pleasure: Reshaping and Revealing the New Zealand Body 1900-1960* (Auckland: Auckland University Press, 2003). See also *The Gendered Kiwi,* edited by Caroline Daley & Deborah Montgomerie (Auckland: Auckland University Press, 1999).

servants provided by the wife. However they believed that women were as capable as men of salvation and service. As Cathy Ross has shown, missionary women were enterprising, and Marianne and Jane Williams operated large scale domestic economies, ran schools, and ministered to many women. Elizabeth Fairburn, who married and then separated from William Colenso, developed independent missionary work as a translator.[11]

Most of the evangelicals among colonial Anglican clergy were Irish.[12] Methodism retained its evangelical Arminianism but its revivalist tone was in decline. Both class meetings and the language of the heart faded in the colonial environment. Most of the other Protestant denominations had been touched by the evangelical movements, but were gradually trimming their Calvinist theology and spirituality. There seems to have been some freedom from gender stereotypes in the first church services held in homes and open spaces of the new colony, but very quickly small wooden churches were built. These churches depended almost entirely on voluntary effort. Women often demanded that their husbands build churches.[13]

Many women worked to make New Zealand a more respectable place, and connived at their own exclusion from public participation by building church buildings. Sacred space had its own gender codes. Men were involved in the design of the church, women in its furnishing. The church was a place one dressed up to go to; there one behaved properly. Church cleaning, decoration, and sweetening (using flowers), were the tasks and the financial responsibility of women. Women were treated as housekeepers for the real leaders of the church. Because it was a public place, women were systematically excluded from ministry. Woodward Street Congregational Church in Wellington in its founding Articles of Faith and Rules, adopted on June 14, 1842, required that "No female

---

11. C. Ross, *Women with a Mission: Rediscovering Missionary Wives in Early New Zealand* (Auckland: Penguin, 2006); T. Fitzgerald, "'To unite their Strength with ours': Women and Missionary Work in Aotearoa New Zealand 1827–45," *Journal of Pacific History* 39 (2004) 147–61.

12. See A. Galbreath, "The Invisible Irish? Rediscovering the Irish Protestant Tradition in Colonial New Zealand," in *A Distant Shore: Irish Migration & New Zealand Settlement*, edited by L. Fraser (Dunedin: University of Otago Press, 2000) 36–54.

13 See Ruth Fry, *Out of the Silence: Methodist Women of Aotearoa 1822-1985* (Christchurch: Methodist, 1987) 49.

members be allowed to speak in the Church, only to vote according to the command of Scripture."[14]

In institutions, roles were defined for each gender. Men chaired committees, even if women were permitted to play other roles in the organisation. Men were always responsible for finances. All of these rules applied strictly to formal church bodies. Women's place in the church included caring for the needy through very extensive charitable work (although men ran the committees and controlled the funds); they provided informal pastoral care and educated children. Sunday schools were a key function of most churches, and Ruth Fry demonstrates in her study of Methodist women that this was a public role for many.[15]

There was a hierarchy among women. In the church the minister's wife wielded considerable influence. There was however a relatively formal prescription for the role of the wife. She was the classic example of the helpmeet.[16] In her, the strong but domestic role of the Christian woman was modelled for all other women to see.

A major responsibility of women was the church cleaning, catering, picnics, and floral displays. Catering was important and gave women a key role in shaping the framework for sociability. "Ladies a plate please" was uniform in society and church. Some fundraising was also dominated by women, through fairs, sales of work, flower shows, bring and buys, and sewing. Church music offered interesting opportunities for women, for in New Zealand it was shared by men and women (whereas in English Anglicanism cathedral-style choirs of boys became common last century). Women were regarded as competent organists and they dominated choirs. Congregational participation was symbolised by singing, and women's role in this indicated their role as participants but not leaders.[17]

Some women made huge commitments of time, talents, and finances to the church, which often tell us that they were shaped by a profound evangelical vision. Consider the case of Mrs Jane Dickie née

---

14. Cited in J. B. Chambers, *'A Peculiar People': Congregationalism in New Zealand 1840-1984 including the Congregational Union of New Zealand 1884-1984* (Wellington: Congregational Union, 1984) 13.

15. Fry, *Out of the Silence*, 65–74.

16. Ibid., chapter 17 analyses Methodist parsons' wives. Hilda Minnie Ford, *Through Many Doors* (Ilfracombe: Stockwell, 1954) 54, says her husband called her his curate.

17. See Fry, *Out of the Silence*, 178–82.

Smith (died c. 1928), whose involvement in a revival in the Mataura area was evidently significant. Her obituary indicates her great faith and prayer, commenting that "those who were privileged to listen to Mrs Dickie in public prayer felt the definiteness and reality of her petitions," as well as her sense of love and sympathy to the sick, her assistance to her husband, who was for some time a home missionary of the Presbyterian Church, her huge Sunday school class of senior girls and her work for temperance through the Band of Hope.[18] The obituaries of the many such women usually give them the honorific biblical phrase of being "mothers in Israel." Such praise highlights Mrs Dickie not just for her domestic duties but also for her service of the community as a whole.

In the separatist revivalist groups there was greater flexibility in the role of women. Catherine Squires née Dewe (1843–1912), the female preacher in South Otago is a striking example, the more so because her activities seem at odds with her chosen church. Kate was from an English family who emigrated to Milton, where the family were founders of the local Anglican church. After her marriage and move to Tokomairu in 1861, she became involved with the Plymouth Brethren and there Kate was a key force in the Brethren services in Gore. In 1894 a schism took place, and thereafter Kate preached on Sundays to the "Squireites" in a temple attached to her house, while on Monday she visited her neighbours in a buggy to enquire why they had absented themselves. Her diaries suggest some parallels with Jane Dickie, for example her deep concern for others, but they also show her highly organised approach to the spiritual needs of her district in which she took leadership. Retiring to Bluff, she led prayer meetings there and the spiritual authority of "Granny Squires" was recognised although her right to preach disturbed some.[19] Doubtless, there was always opportunity for people of exceptional ability to exercise their gifts, but there was less opportunity for women to play a leadership role once conventional church traditions were established.

---

18. I am relying on a set of clippings on the revival in the Waituna valley in the 1880s.

19. *Dictionary of New Zealand Biography*, vol. 1, edited by W. H. Oliver (Wellington: Allen & Unwin, 1990) 403. Her diaries are in the Otago Early Settlers Museum.

MODIFIED DOMESTIC IDEOLOGY

The Victorian domestic ideal was firmly advocated as a religious and social ideal as New Zealand society became more established. In a debate on women's role in Auckland in 1871, the Bible was repeatedly cited.[20] Yet colonial exponents significantly modified the British middle class vision of feminine delicacy. An article in the *Christian Observer* in 1870 praised the woman of Prov 31, rejecting "dainty" Victorian expectations. The author complained that: "Some seem to be of the opinion that she ought not to be expected to lift anything heavier than pins and needles, and never more than a cotton reel; and that if she faints in a crowd, or sinks down on a sofa with the slightest exertion, she is only giving evidence of her distinctive womanly characteristics."

Yet although the author considered women strong enough to survive the "stern demands of an unsympathising world," the article urged women to marry husbands they could safely submit to and trust.[21] An editorial in a later issue of the same magazine suggested that the colonial woman needed to be Martha—active, working, with a high view of domestic duties—and it therefore reproved too much enthusiasm for clothing as immoral. A woman replied to this editorial, insisting that "I have not learnt that women are vainer than men" but she also denied that she was a champion of women's rights.[22]

Religious authority was constantly used to endorse this ideal. The Rev. James Buller, in a sermon to young women, insisted that the sacred role of women was to be a homemaker and to avoid dancing.[23] When the Anglican Mothers Union was founded in 1886, its listed "objects" focused on children and the sacredness of marriage.[24] The WCTU superintendents' watchword was "For God, for Home, and Humanity."[25]

---

20. J. E. Malone, "What's wrong with Emma: The Feminist Debate in Colonial Auckland," in *Women in History: Essays on European Women in New Zealand*, edited by B. Brookes, C. Macdonald, and M. Tennant (Wellington, Allen & Unwin, 1986) 81.

21. *Christian Observer* 1.1 (1870) 3–4.

22. *Christian Observer* 1.8 (1870); *Christian Observer* 1.9 (1870) 138.

23. *New Zealand Wesleyan* 2.20 (1872) 115–17.

24. Nancy Robertshawe, Thora Holland, and Barbara Archer, *A History of the Mothers' Union and the Association of Anglican Women in New Zealand* (Association of Anglican Women, 1980) part 1, 2.

25. *Leader* (20 July 1888) 101.

The domestic ideal was under some attack in the 1890s, but it revived in the early twentieth century.

There was warm support for women's education among church people, to judge by the applause when Major Richardson spoke on the subject in Knox Church, Dunedin, in 1870,[26] but this education was expected to be very practical. The churches sponsored girls' schools, and had clear views about their curriculum.[27] There was no advocacy of equality, and the demands on daughters were strict.

Some changes in opportunities for women developed by the late nineteenth century, in particular the formation of separate women's organisations. Mother's Unions (with the vicar's wife presiding at the parish branch and the bishop's wife at diocesan level) became common in the Anglican parishes from 1886, and the wife of the Governor Lord Glasgow helped these bodies to develop rapidly in the 1890s.[28] In the Nonconformist world, Women's Missionary Unions flourished in the same period. The significance of such organisations was partly financial. The Ladies Guild raised one quarter of Upper Riccarton Methodist Church's income in the inter-war years.[29] So a greater degree of female autonomy slowly emerged, in which these organisations were instrumental.

The first national women's bodies were not denominational. The undenominational WCTU was founded in 1885, the National Council of Women in 1896. The national denominational bodies came later: the Methodist Women's Missionary Auxiliary was founded in 1902; the Baptist Women's Missionary Union in 1903 and the national Presbyterian Women's Missionary Union in 1905. The Mothers' Union Dominion Council was not formed until 1926. It was not until the 1920s that more

---

26. *Evangelist* 2.11 (1870) 345.

27. V. Johnson and H. Jensen, *A History of Diocesan High School for Girls, Auckland, 1903-1953* (Auckland: Whitcombe & Tombs, 1956); K. Carpenter, *Marsden Women and their Worlds: A History of Marsden School 1878-2003* (Wellington: Samuel Marsden Collegiate School, 2003).

28. A *History of the Mothers' Union and the Association of Anglican Women in New Zealand*, part 1, 1-5.

29. J. E. Cookson, *Upper Riccarton Methodist Church: A Centennial Retrospect 1886-1986* (Christchurch: Upper Riccarton Methodist Church, 1986) 24. See H. D. Morrison, "'It Is Our Bounden Duty': The Emergence of the New Zealand Protestant Missionary Movement 1868-1926." Massey University PhD thesis in History, 2004.

broadly based women's guilds were approved by denominations.[30] For example Mrs Gray of the BWMU spoke at the annual conference held parallel with the Baptist Union's annual conference, on "the position women occupy in the scheme of the Christian faith and its propagation," but her talk focused on their equality in salvation and evangelism, not in church government.[31] Yet such bodies had virtually no presence in the denominational courts. Women were sometimes allowed to comment on missionary matters since most of the missionaries were women. Baptists allowed women to be elected onto the BMS executive from 1907 but not as office holders. They allowed women to speak to a report at conference in 1912.[32]

WOMEN MISSIONARIES AND PREACHERS

Perhaps the most significant change was the move to permit single women to go as missionaries to the heathen, initially to the separate world of the "Zenana" women of India. Rosalie MacGeorge may have been the first single missionary from New Zealand, going out as the first worker with the Baptist Missionary Society (a body established at the urging of a visiting woman missionary, Ellen Arnold) in 1886.[33] It was this move which stimulated other changes including missionary organisations to support them and opportunities for them to write and speak about their work. Local missionaries also won respect, including Susie Mactier née Seaman, an evangelist with the Auckland YWCA, who organised a "flower mission" motivated by "a passionate desire to win girls to Christ."[34]

30. Fry, *Out of the Silence*, 114–25; Alice Henderson, *Women's Work for Missions: The Story of the Beginnings and Growth of the Presbyterian Women's Missionary Union of New Zealand* (Christchurch: Presbyterian Bookroom, 1939); Vera L. McLennan, *These Seventy-Five Years: A Short History of the Baptist Women's Missionary Union* (Palmerston North: BWMU, 1978). I have explained the development of national religious organisations in Peter J. Lineham, "Finding a Space for Evangelicalism: Evangelical Youth Movements in New Zealand," in *Voluntary Religion*, edited by W. J. Sheils and Diana Wood, Studies in Church History 29 (Oxford: Blackwell, 1986) 477–94.

31. *New Zealand Baptist* 28.347 (November 1912) 25–26, cited by S. Hewlett, "'Adam's Helper': Women's Roles in Evangelical Churches in New Zealand from Colonial Times to the End of the 20th Century," Massey University MA thesis in History, 20.

32. Hewlett, "Adam's Helper," 24.

33. See *Baptists in Colonial New Zealand: Documents illustrating Baptist Life and Development*. Edited by M. Sutherland (Auckland: N.Z. Baptist Research and Historical Society, 2002) 109–19.

34. Sandra Corney in *The Book of New Zealand Women.*, edited by Charlotte

These missionaries reflected a wave of women speakers within the Protestant community. Visiting women evangelists included Mrs Baeyertz, who visited in 1890, Eliza White, who visited to found the YWCA and Mrs Leavitt who founded the WCTU. An even more striking and earlier example is Mrs Margaret Hampson, an evangelist on interdenominational lines, who had come from Liverpool after the death of her husband, it would seem, and preached extensively in New Zealand from 1880 to 1882 in most of the leading non-Anglican Protestant churches.[35] In Auckland she spoke at the central Baptist and Methodist churches, and went on to Thames, a town famous for its active churches. She went to Dunedin in April 1881, then visited Waimate, and by 1882 was in Wellington, then Nelson, then Christchurch, then New Plymouth, and was last reported in Wanganui in October 1882.[36] She was active in Australia in 1884.[37] Further research on Mrs Hampson is currently being undertaken by Janet Crawford.

Mrs Hampson was a brilliant speaker, much noted for her ability to grip the emotions as she modulated her voice from shout to whisper, using charm and threat alternately. Dunedin observers noted that she was a master of the anecdote; she would, for instance, describe the distress and agony of the mother hearing of her shipwrecked son. Vicesimus Lush's jaundiced account of the Thames campaign reported "screaming—screechings—groaning and shouts 'I have found Him,' 'I am saved' takes place in the body of the hall."[38] Others insisted that her ladylike tone attracted when other women speakers offended. She worked for the cause of gospel temperance, handing out the blue ribbon to those signing the pledge.[39]

Macdonald, Merimeri Penfold, and Bridget Williams (Wellington: Williams, 1991) 396–98.

35. David Hilliard, *Popular Revivalism in South Australia from the 1870s to the 1920s* (Adelaide: Uniting Church Historical Society, South Australia, 1982) 14–17.

36. *New Zealand Herald* (24 January 1881) 4; *New Zealand Herald* (14 March 188) 4; *New Zealand Herald* (5 February 1881) 4; *New Zealand Herald* (19 February 1881) 4; *The Thames Journals of Vicesimus Lush 1868–1882*, edited by Alison Drummond (Christchurch: Caxton, 1975) 236–37; Alexander Turnbull Library: Terrace Congregational Church Minutes, 11 January 1882; *Echo* (7 May 1881) 2, 3; *Echo* (22 April 1882) 2; *Taranaki Herald* (23 September 1882) 2.

37. *New Zealand Methodist* 1.13 (Sept 1884) 5.

38. Lush, *The Thames Journals*, 236; *Echo* (30 April 1881) 2, 3.

39. *New Zealand Wesleyan* 11.9 (Sept 1881) 205.

There were some local speakers in the same vein. Mrs Joan Scott née Boag (c. 1828–1912), the husband of Andrew Scott of Christchurch, was a Methodist woman who for forty-nine years held occasional services in country Methodist churches. She was buried with virtual ministerial honours.[40] Again success made her ministry acceptable; prejudice against her preaching declined after a series of striking conversions.[41]

These women were welcomed because they were successful evangelists. The evangelist was not a pastor; she had an irregular ministry and therefore posed few challenges to customs. But when such women attracted male audiences, some questions were asked. Samuel Deck had to defend Mrs Hampson from criticism: "How shall we receive such Christlike devotion? Thwart, insult, hound her down, simply because she is a woman? Perish such cold, unmanly, heartless Christianity."[42] Broadley sets the support for her within an evangelical culture of subversive female oratory.[43] This evangelicalism was a liberal movement challenging denominational controls, not the conservative evangelicalism which flourished in the early twentieth century.

THE WCTU AND ITS VALUES

The Women's Christian Temperance Union arrived in the colony at the high point of this wave of women's activism. The American "Women's Crusade" against the liquor industry, which was the origin of the WCTU, grew out of the 1859 revival. The visit of Mrs Leavitt in 1885 was successful because enough women had caught the vision of a role they should play in society. The temperance issue was the starting point for reform.

In essence it was Christian duty which inspired the women of the WCTU. Mrs Schnackenberg in her 1888 address cited Miss Willard, the American founder of the organisation, that there was no more important work: "than in re-constructing the ideal of womanhood. In this age woman has strength and individuality, a gentle seriousness, and is be-

---

40. See Fry, *Out of the Silence*, 209. See *New Zealand Wesleyan* 11.9 (Sept 1881) 214.

41. *New Zealand Methodist Times* (15 June 1912). See T. G. Carr, "My Life's Story" (Alexander Turnbull Library MS papers 316, c. 1926) 33.

42. *New Zealand Christian Record* (20 May 1881) 11, and *New Zealand Christian Record* (24 June 1881) 7, cited in S. Broadley, "Spirited Visions: A Study of Spiritualism in New Zealand Settler Society," University of Otago PhD thesis in History, 2000, 167.

43. Broadley, "Spirited Visions," 164.

coming what God meant her to be—the companion and counsellor, not the toil and encumbrance, of man."[44]

The women's campaigners made a great impact in the Protestant dissenting world. When W. M. Grant heard Mrs Mary Cleaver Leavitt, he was impressed that she was "one of the most telling Temperance Advocates I have yet heard." Mrs Leavitt was allowed to speak in churches normally closed to female speakers.[45] Most of the key supporters of the Union were middle class Christian women. The wives of non-Anglican clergy and lay leaders were particularly important. The wives of the Dunedin clergy were made vice-presidents of the Union in its early days.[46] Mrs Annie Schnackenberg, who was the widow of a Methodist missionary, in her 1888 address as President to the Annual meeting of the Auckland branch of the WCTU appealed for "the sympathy and help of all ministers and their wives, who can do so much in their various congregations, also the help of all Christian workers and reformers."[47]

The Christian respectability of the leaders gave the movement its opportunity. Earlier attempts to mount a campaign on a secular basis had been abortive.[48] The electoral goals of the WCTU gained the general support of leading middle class Christian women because the vote was described by the WCTU as a "sacred possession, for the protection and welfare of your sex, your homes and the moral benefit of the community at large."[49] The WCTU was primarily a movement for temperance and moral purity. The temperance reformers were sure that Christians were called to change the world. Gaining the franchise extended their opportunity to do good. Miss Morison commented "We want that franchise, not because of any special thing, but because we are women and consider we have a right to vote on all social and political questions affecting the

44. Cited in the *Leader* 4.147 (20 July 1888) 101.

45. See *Freethought Review* 2.22 (July 1885) 8.

46. See Bunkle, "The Origins of the Women's Movement in New Zealand: The Women's Christian Temperance Union, 1885–1895," in *Women in New Zealand Society*, edited by P. Bunkle and B. Hughes (Auckland: Allen & Unwin, 1980) 57.

47. *Leader* 4.147 (20 July 1888) 101.

48. Robert Stout's newspaper, the *Echo* mounted an earlier campaign See *Echo* (27 August 1870) 2; *Echo* (5 November 1870); *Echo* (17 July 1880) 3. For evidence of the religious background of Auckland women leaders of the Y.W.C.A. see Sandra Coney, *Every Girl: A Social History of Women and the YWCA in Auckland 1885–1985* (Auckland: Y.W.C.A., 1986) 18.

49. *Prohibitionist* 89 (21 October 1893) cited by Bunkle, 67.

community."[50] Men were nervous about such arguments. Some thought political involvement would rather worsen women's status. "Instead of the female mind purifying our politics, there would, we suspect, be some danger of our politics contaminating the female mind."[51]

In a very significant article Phillida Bunkle has shown that "purity" is the unifying concept of the temperance world view. Purification of politics had deep symbolical significance, for it meant not just female votes, but also women's moral power. Bunkle relates the essence of the WCTU's work to the campaign for social purity, and thus relates it to the campaign for the repeal of the Contagious Diseases Act.[52] This act for the registration and inspection of prostitutes but not their male clients had been repealed in Britain in 1885 on account of pressure from women and Nonconformist church leaders, but survived in New Zealand until 1910.

The purity motif made sexual values the central character of the female political mission. There was a strong emphasis on the evils of sexual impurity among the WCTU.[53] Hence marriage was a way to purify man's sexual lusts, "Social purity protects the home in its innermost sanctuary—*marriage*."[54] Thus the movement endorsed the domestic character of women's power. So perhaps we should not be surprised that the domestic ideal grew in force after the triumph of first wave feminism.

Although the founders of the WCTU were involved in the churches, they were frustrated by them. Mrs Amey Daldy commented: "The churches—oh the churches—can they not see that good may be done for the people outside their walls? They will learn their lesson some day after paying dearly for it. With all our vaunted progress, we are still very narrow and can have no dealings with the Samaritans."[55]

Some leaders of the WCTU were anything but conservative in faith or politics. Kate Sheppard, and the Edger daughters were highly unortho-

---

50. Cited by P. Grimshaw, *Women's Suffrage in New Zealand* (Auckland: Auckland University Press, 1972) 50.

51. *N.Z. Presbyterian* (1 October 1892) 71.

52. Phillida Bunkle, "The Origins of the Women's Movement in New Zealand," 62–63, 67. See also Coney, *Every Girl*, 52–55.

53. Bunkle, "The Origins of the Women's Movement in New Zealand," 70–71.

54. Ibid., 73, citing Minutes, 3rd A.G.M., Dunedin, February 1888, 26.

55. Cited by Grimshaw, *Women's Suffrage in New Zealand*, 57.

dox in their faith. However as a whole the WCTU was evangelistic; it had an active evangelistic department and a strong emphasis on outreach to the young. Most of the members of the WCTU were broadly evangelical and others were distinctly pietist and wanted to make conversion a condition for joining the WCTU. However, they were outvoted, and the New Zealand body was from the beginning open to a reasonably wide group, reflecting a growing pattern also evident in the YWCA and the Student Christian Movement.[56] So while some conservative evangelical women would have nothing to do with such a worldly organisation, after 1910 the WCTU leaders became increasingly conservative. It was a reflection of decline of radical first wave feminism. At much the same time, in the Salvation Army women officers lost status and achieved significance almost entirely through their husbands.

DEACONESSES

The title of deaconess was introduced in the late nineteenth century church as a way of giving formal status to women's ministry. Protestant churches at the time of the Reformation abolished convents and thus excluded women from formal roles. The informal roles that grew in the late nineteenth century seemed to allow a significant degree of independence from the denominational bodies. Perhaps this is why regulation followed so quickly. The churches that accepted this role were prepared to formalise the role of women, doubtless aware of competition in ministry from other religious bodies. The Salvation Army, a split from the Wesleyan Reformers, came to New Zealand in 1884 and was very active in many town communities. From the very beginning they employed women officers in their own right.[57] The revival of the Catholic wing in the Church of England seems to have provided a competitive factor to other denominations. In 1892 the Christchurch diocese admitted women as deaconesses, and Auckland followed. These deaconesses were supported by the Catholic part of the denomination and were soon organised into religious orders.[58] This seems to be the background for the use of the

56. Bunkle, "The Origins of the Women's Movement in New Zealand," 59.

57. B. Sampson, *Women of Spirit: Life-stories of New Zealand Salvation Army Women for the Last 100 Years* (Wellington: Salvation Army, 1993).

58. See *The Journey and the Vision: A Report on Ordained Anglican Women in the Church of the Province of New Zealand*, edited by Rosemary Neave (Auckland, Women's Resource Centre, 1990) 1/1–2, 2/1–2.

title in the Protestant churches. Sister Christabel was appointed to work in Rutherford Waddell's Presbyterian congregation in Dunedin in 1901. The General Assembly of the Presbyterian Church created its deaconess order in 1903. The Methodist Order was established in 1907. In both cases a training institution was established at an early stage.[59] Some Baptist churches appointed deaconesses, but their denomination did not do so at this time. Curiously the Presbyterian Church took opportunity to authorise the existing ministry of its women missionaries and "all women now acting as Church visitors or Bible [women] with or without salary" as deaconesses.[60] Thus women's ministry was regularised.

THE LIBERALISING OF PROTESTANTISM

Most of the churches took sides in the franchise debate, but this immediately raised the issue of what women were permitted to do in the denominational setting. There were ardent advocates of change like Harry Driver, the Baptist leader.[61] When the franchise debate was at its height, the Congregational Union (doubtless pressured by Kate Sheppard, who was a Congregationalist) resolved "that this council expresses its sympathy with the efforts of women to obtain the right to exercise a general franchise in this colony" and also resolved "that female representation on the council of the Union is desirable." They noted the "commendable audacity" of the English Union in admitting women as delegates.[62] In 1892 the Union "expresse[d] its cordial sympathy with the admission of women to the Parliamentary franchise and appeals to the members of

---

59. See J. D. Salmond, *By Love Serve: The Story of the Order of Deaconesses of the Presbyterian Church of New Zealand* (Christchurch: Presbyterian, 1962); Nancy J. Burgess, *Except a Grain of Wheat: The Ensuing History of the Order of Deaconesses in the Presbyterian Church of New Zealand 1961–1975* (Wellington: Presbyterian Church of New Zealand Ministry Committee, 1979); Wesley A. Chambers, *Not Self—But Others: The Story of the New Zealand Methodist Deaconess Order*, Wesley Historical Society (N.Z.) Proceedings, no. 48, 1987. See also E. Bolitho, "Women in New Zealand Churches," *Stimulus* 1.3 (1993) 25–32 and 1.4 (1993) 28–37.

60. Presbyterian Church of New Zealand *Proceedings of General Assembly*, 1902, 193.

61. Cited by Hewlett, "Adam's Helper," 25.

62. Congregational Union Yearbook 1891, 11, 34.

our churches for their hearty support of this beneficent and just reform."[63] Unfortunately not all churches followed the lead of the Union.[64]

The New Zealand branch of the Wesleyan Methodist church supported the same cause in its meeting in late 1890 and in 1893 it complained that "a measure essentially just and liberal" was being placed low on the agenda by the Premier, Dick Seddon.[65] Still it was only after Methodist Union in 1915 that the conference declared that all lay positions were open to women and not until 1933 was a woman sent as an official delegate to the Wesleyan Conference, although some of the smaller Methodist bodies had allowed this in the 1890s. The Baptist Union, although its churches had supported the franchise movement of the 1890s, did not admit women to its union as delegates until 1908, and they took part from 1909.[66] Anglican and Presbyterian Churches were more regulated and more cautious. Presbyterian regulations forbad women elders until 1953. The occasional woman was elected onto an Anglican vestry despite the rules,[67] but in most dioceses and in the General Synod clergy and episcopal hostility until 1919 vetoed legislation to permit women to vote in parish meetings. There were liberal voices, including the evangelical bishop Stuart of Waiapu, but the more evangelical diocese of Nelson was conservative on the issue.[68]

Significant changes in the role of women in denominations came through their youth organisations. Young Women's Bible Class Unions began to emerge alongside boys' Bible classes, beginning in the Presbyterian Church in 1904. These Bible classes were often relatively liberal in outlook, often espousing "a moderately modern view of religion and life."[69] The Student Christian Movement campaigned for more

---

63. Congregational Union Year Book 1892, 11.

64. Congregational Union Yearbook, 1896, 49.

65. Wesleyan Methodist Church *Minutes of Annual Conference*, 17th Conference, 1890, 80; ibid., 20th conference, 1893, 108.

66. Fry, *Out of the Silence*, 201–4; J. Ayson Clifford, *A Handful of Grain. Vol. 2, 1882–1914* (Wellington: Baptist Historical Society, 1982) 92–93; Hewlett, "Adam's Helper," 31.

67. *Press* (15 Feb 1894): 4.

68. H. F. Ault, The *Nelson Narrative: The Story of the Church of England in the Diocese of Nelson New Zealand 1858–1958* (Nelson: Diocesan Standing Committee, 1958) 134, 192–93; W. P. Morrell, *The Anglican Church in New Zealand* (Dunedin: Church of the Province of New Zealand, 1973) 131.

69. Quotation from New Zealand Young Women's Presbyterian Bible Class Union *Souvenir Booklet 1904–1925* (Dunedin: Otago Daily Times for the Union, 1925) 7; see Ann Allan, *Life upon Life: A History of the Presbyterian Young Women's Bible Class Union*

change, and gradually the denominations overrode theological sensitivities. But regulation does not necessarily mean real change at congregational level. Although the Presbyterian Church permitted women elders in 1953, until about 1987 individual churches were permitted to prevent women elders, and only 1211 out of 6818 members of session were women in 1975.[70]

By the 1950s, while there were some pressures for the ordination of women, the domestic ideology reigned supreme, and churches of whatever hue reinforced this role. In the Wells Organisation's fundraising carried out by the Anglican Church in the 1950s, arrangements committees and hostess committees were organised by women, under the firm control of the vicar's wife. Young women were questing after better education and vocational opportunities, but the churches had little to offer beyond the Bible classes. The conservatism of the evangelical churches has to be seen in this light.

CONSERVATIVE EVANGELICALS

In the early twentieth century while many Protestants broadened in their outlook, others became more conservative or Fundamentalist, and these groups wanted nothing to do with changing the role of women. A rift over theology changed the situation for women. The rise in status of "restorationist churches," which aimed to return to biblical patterns, helped this. Brethren assemblies became a very significant group in the bush farming districts of the colonies from the 1880s, and grew rapidly in the early twentieth century. For Brethren, the veiling and silence of women was virtually a constitutional matter, but their only constitution was the Bible, so change involved biblical interpretation. Since most of the conservative groups held their services in hired buildings or erected very plain halls for their meetings, the role of the woman as furnisher was restricted. Among the Brethren the notion that physical things could facilitate worship was disdained, and women were rarely allowed to adorn their halls with flowers.

(Christchurch: Presbyterian, 1954); Olive Mary Cook, *History of the Young Women's Methodist Bible Class Movement, 1906-1926* (Christchurch: Whitcombe & Tombs, 1927).

70. See *Enquiry into the Status of Women in the Church*. Edited by Jan Cormack (Christchurch: National Council of Churches, 1976) 12.

Such churches strongly criticised the forward position of women in other churches. Because interpretation of the Bible was the responsibility of all, there was little respect for cultural factors interpreting the Bible. Inevitably questions of application remained. The question of whether women should be allowed to pray in prayer meetings was debated by some; and the issue of the role of women in cottage meetings was raised at an early stage, although most Brethren took a hard line on this. A further issue was the insistence on the head covering as the symbol of submission. Should non-believers be expected to wear it to the gospel meeting? Should they be worn to young people's meetings?[71] Yet as the Brethren assemblies grew rapidly in the 1940s and 1950s, evangelistic opportunities led to new initiatives and encouraged "exceptions." Women's testimonies, women singing solos, women's missionary support meetings, and women's Christian work and secular work and dress beyond the assembly began to be advocated by some. By the 1950s such issues were the subject of widespread discussion.[72] Women dominated numerically the very large Brethren missionary force, yet they could not report back to their assemblies about their work. A story is told that on one occasion when a notable woman missionary came to speak to the women in an assembly, males listened to her from behind a curtain hung half-way down the hall. One of the few Brethren theological writers, Kate Dawson of Auckland, never used her Christian name in her publications so that people would be willing to read what she said. Some doubted that the Brethren magazine should carry contributions from women missionaries on their work, but the editors, otherwise stout conservatives, always allowed this.[73]

The Christadelphians took submission to an extreme. Their Sister Walker had been involved in politics (perhaps meaning the WCTU) as a school mistress in Mercer before joining the sect, but thereafter would not even speak in Bible discussion groups. Some women otherwise attracted to the Christadelphians were held back by such rules. A leading Christadelphian acknowledged in 1896 that women needed to be

---

71. *Treasury* 4 190; *Treasury* 27 (1925) 68–69, 175; *Treasury* 34 (1932) 29; *Treasury* 47 (1945) 77; *Treasury* 50 (1948) 173.

72. *Treasury* 53 (1951) 73; *Treasury* 56 (1954) 89, 135; *Treasury* 63 (1961) 339.

73. *Treasury* 5 (1903) 26.

respected and permitted them in the absence of men to conduct the breaking of bread and read sermons.[74]

In the Reformed churches Scripture was viewed as normative law, and consequently what Scripture forbade could not be contemplated. The revival of Calvinist traditions among conservative Presbyterians was a response to the growing liberalism, and the role of women seems to have been one aspect of the conservatism among the Calvinist minority led by P. B. Fraser and later by the Rev. Thomas Miller. Women elders were rarely accepted in evangelical congregations. The Reformed Church, founded by conservative Dutch migrants, differentiated itself from the Presbyterians partly over its view of the role of women in the church.[75]

The issue of women's role in the church often awoke sharp controversy. For example a Methodist home missionary in Dannevirke was inspired by Catherine Booth's pamphlet on women preaching to challenge the views of local Brethren.[76] Some twentieth century evangelicals took divergent approaches towards women's ministry. The Richmond Mission was founded in Christchurch about 1910, by David Thomas Smith and his wife, Florence Caroline Smith (née Pashby). It became a well-known independent evangelical centre. From 1919 until their deaths in 1962 and 1963 Mrs Smith was the principal preacher because of her outstanding evangelistic gift, and her husband's role in the mission complemented hers.[77]

The Pentecostal tradition read the Bible in a different way than other conservatives. While the Pentecostals were proudly Fundamentalist, they discovered that the power of the Holy Spirit was often manifest in women. Aimee Semple McPherson, the Canadian Pentecostal, visited New Zealand in 1922, and drew large crowds.[78] Strong women participated in leadership of the New Zealand evangelical Mission, the first Pentecostal body, comprising five of the twenty-six delegates to the

---

74. R. Roberts, *Diary of a Voyage* (1896) 111, 113–14, 142.

75. See R. P. Flinn, "Convention: What Is Involved?," *Challenge Weekly* (24 February 1984) 12.

76. George Cook, in Alexander Turnbull Library MS Papers 2205, 32.

77. I am grateful to Mary J. Petersen for this information, and to the Rev. Graham Reddell, the first minister of North Avon Baptist church, the successor to the mission.

78. J. E. Worsfold, *A History of the Charismatic Movements in New Zealand* (Bradford: Julian Literature Trust, 1974) 136–37.

November 1924 conference and twenty-six of the sixty-one delegates in December 1924. Women were among those set aside for ministry in the 1926 conference. The Assemblies of God in 1927 adopted articles of faith which emphasised equality for all in salvation and power to prophesy. Although women were not to take authority over men, they resolved to "recognise their God-given right to be ordained, not as Elders, but as Evangelists . . . and that they serve as assistant Pastors, Missionaries, or as Evangelists."[79] This approach attracted some evangelical women into the movement. Three Brethren women missionaries to the Maori in the Te Puke area, Elsie Phillips, Katie Rout, and Sylvia Martin affiliated for a time to the Apostolic Church because they wanted greater freedom to minister.[80]

All evangelicals permitted women to minister to children and young people, although some were uncertain about their appropriateness for young boys. Bible classes were divided by gender, for it was believed that men ought to provide spiritual guidance to young men as they matured. Sunday school superintendents were typically male, although Hewlett cites an example of a woman superintendent in 1912.[81]

INTERDENOMINATIONAL ORGANISATIONS AND WOMEN

The Brethren had a huge influence on the leadership and the teachers of much of the evangelical world in New Zealand, including many who became women leaders in other settings in the inter-denominational organisations or in other churches. Thus the Brethren view frequently inspired debates in the evangelical world. For example, it seems likely that Brethren members of the Canterbury University Evangelical Union were responsible for the queries in 1955 over women students praying aloud.[82]

Another factor was the growing influence of American and British Fundamentalism, often associated with the arrival of Joseph Kemp in 1919, to serve as pastor of the large Auckland Baptist Tabernacle. Baptist

79. Worsfold, *History of Charismatic Movements*, 162–64, 175, 202.
80. Ibid., 258; Sylvia Martin, *God's Hand in Maoriland* (Tauranga: the author, 1975); P. J. Lineham, "Tongues must cease: the Brethren and the Charismatic Movement in New Zealand," *C.B.R.F. Journal* 96 (Dec 1982) 8.
81. Hewlett, "Adam's Helper," 28.
82. Minutes Canterbury University College Evangelical Union (held in Tertiary Students Christian Fellowship Archives, Wellington) May 28, 1955.

observers contrasted the Tabernacle with the more tolerant traditions in other Baptist churches further south. However, Kemp was not particularly conservative on the role of women, and from the first wanted to use their energies. The Bible Training Institute, which he founded in Auckland in 1922, began with five men and five women students and attracted significant enrolments from women, who had few other opportunities for theological training, especially if they came from the Brethren. A women's hostel was commenced and a series of redoubtable matrons played a significant role in the BTI, including Annie Grantham (1924-1946) and Jean A. Jaggers (1947-1970), enforcing a strict protocol of appropriate behaviour. No women served as teaching staff or members of the Board of Directors, although there was an active Ladies' Committee, the so-called "prayer ladies."[83]

When the Crusader Movement was established in the state schools in 1930, problems arose through Howard Guinness's visits to girls' schools, and the first Secretary, John Laird, recognised that headmistresses of girls' schools would exclude the movement, unless it could find outstanding women leaders. Consequently Margaret McGregor, a Brethren woman trained at the BTI, was appointed as a staff member, and served in this role from 1931 until 1950. McGregor had a cautious but dignified and firm approach as woman's travelling secretary. Her successors in the 1950s and 1960s including Madge Logan, Jane Morrison, and Margaret Lamb exuded a tough extroverted activism, which was anything but the domestic ideal. Some of these women seemed to express or sublimate their sexuality in their role. Women also served on the Crusader committee, but they were not expected to be too outspoken.[84] Margaret Malcolm, who was a member of the Council from 1964 to 1977, later commented that she felt like a tea lady at times.

There were continual attempts to distinguish gender roles in the BTI and at the CSSM, but the leaders often felt as though they were battling against wider social trends. Separate boys and girls Crusader camps were continued until enrolments began to decline. In 1965 the Executive approved the appointment of Averil McIntosh as overall leader of a CSSM

---

83. J. Oswald Sanders, *Expanding Horizons: The Story of the New Zealand Bible Training Institute* (Auckland: Bible Trianing Institute, 1971) 13–15, 126–30.

84. Peter J. Lineham, *No Ordinary Union: The Story of the Scripture Union Children's Special Service Mission and Crusader Movement of New Zealand 1880-1980* (Wellington: Scripture Union, 1980) 55, 58–60, 123, 148.

beach mission.⁸⁵ By then few were prepared to defend the "parallel but equal" approach. The Inter-Varsity Fellowship (now Tertiary Students Christian Fellowship) from the first attracted women and men alongside each other. Relationships within the groups were curious. The role of women's vice president was an important one on evangelical Union committees, and women often held other positions as well, but the EUs were often seen as strong because (unlike the SCM groups) they were not dominated by women.⁸⁶ The founders and sponsors of the movement were all male, and yet in fact women played an important role in the origins of several groups. For example, the Canterbury University College EU was virtually founded by Elizabeth M. Herriott, a demonstrator and the lecturer in the Biology Department from 1916 until her death in 1934, and a member of the Worcester Street Brethren assembly. She gathered the members of the future EU in her office for prayer meetings.⁸⁷

So while the evangelical movement was socially conservative, in emphasising separate roles of men and women, within the voluntary societies there was considerable scope for women. One should recall that until the 1960s it was widely held that girls would flourish better in separate schools and so the evangelical organisations among youth were effectively following current trends.

THE EVANGELICAL CHURCHES

The evangelical denominations slowly followed the lead of the interdenominational organisations, but were much more cautious to adopt this pattern. The Brethren only established the Assemblies Bible School in the 1950s and for its first twenty years the women's courses were always held at a separate semester from those of the men students. The Baptist Union commenced a deaconess course at its College in 1956. In 1972 the first deaconess, Pat Preest, retrained as the first full minister,⁸⁸ but the

---

85. Scripture Union Executive minutes (held in Scripture Union Archives, Wellington), 18 Nov 1965.

86. Peter J. Lineham, "Evangelical Witness in Canterbury University" (unpublished MS, 1973, held in archives of Tertiary Students Christian Fellowship, Wellington) 13.

87. Ibid.; W. J. Gardner, E. T. Beardsley & T. E. Carter, *A History of the University of Canterbury 1873–1973* (Christchurch: University of Canterbury, 1973) 462.

88. S. L. Edgar, *A Handful of Grain: The Centenary History of the Baptist Union of New Zealand*, vol. 4 1945–1982 (Wellington,: Baptist Historical Society 1982) 69–73.

move towards permitting women into the ordinary orders of ministry common in other churches—Congregationalists in 1951, Methodists in 1959, Presbyterians in 1965, and Anglicans in 1976—took longer to take hold in the evangelical world. Effectively the "separate but equal" philosophy remained dominant among evangelicals.

Such a philosophy represented a distinctive culture that worked well in the period from 1945 to 1965. Patterns of sisterhood were deeply felt within the evangelical world. In the Brethren, women's meetings were initially disapproved, but eventually women's missionary conferences provided the major opportunity for "the sisters" to hear women speakers. Organisations like Council of Christian Women in Auckland, founded by the wife of the Baptist Pastor of the Auckland Baptist Tabernacle, Mrs Hodge, gave further opportunities for women.[89] Sisterhood meant a distinctive female perspective on issues, an identity with one's gender. Some Brethren women were adept at demure submission in public contexts while privately using their skills to persuade their husbands into action. Such women became formidable opponents of the feminist movement.

The informality of evangelical churches meant that formal changes were difficult to implement. Moreover conservative voices were not easily checked. Institutions with written rules and constitutional procedures are much easier to reform than informal bodies, because there are procedures for change. Each denomination had to grapple with caution and tradition. The 1972 report of the Provincial Commission of the Church of the Province of New Zealand on the ordination of women studied and set aside the biblical and theological problems.[90] But how were evangelical attitudes to be changed in the absence of a recognised forum?

Conservative evangelicalism in New Zealand had a strong Brethren element in it, along with a Reformed Presbyterian faction, and as a result its pragmatic element has been restrained. In recent years these voices have weakened, with the rise of the Charismatic/Pentecostal movement. While Pentecostals have urged "biblicist" stances on the role of women and on sexuality, they have been relatively pragmatic on the role of women in ministry, following a wider tradition within the Arminian tradition of evangelicalism and Pentecostalism.

---

89. *Reaper* 17 (July 1939) 132.
90. Anglican Church, Proceedings of General Synod, 1972, iv–v.

CHARISMATIC PATTERNS

The development of the embodied masculinist and feminist cultures in the twentieth century was evident in religious changes from the middle of the twentieth century. The appeal of the Charismatic Movement undoubtedly had a gendered element. The exclusion of the Te Papapa assembly from the Brethren Movement was justified not because they permitted the exercise of charismatic gifts, but because they permitted *women* to use these gifts and minister audibly.[91] Perhaps the most notable woman associated with the New Zealand charismatic movement, Joy Dawson née Manins who was the daughter of a very well-known Brethren leader, established with the help of her husband Jim a charismatic prayer group in the Waikowhai Brethren assembly in the early stages of the renewal, then joined Hillsborough Baptist Church and pioneered the work of Teen Challenge, and eventually became a leader of Youth with a Mission.[92] Dale Garrett née Sweet is another such example. Freedom to minister was thus a factor in attracting some strong evangelical women into the charismatic movement. They were not directly rejecting the Brethren ideology but reinterpreting its interpretation in the public space. The "spirit endued woman" became a significant figure in the charismatic landscape, because her special endowments enabled her to rise above restrictions without rejecting them. Nancy Campbell and her *Above Rubies* magazine published from 1977 had an extensive influence, promoted the domestic ideology. Cecilie Graham's charismatic ministry began alongside her husband where she exercised the extraordinary gift of the word of knowledge. As this developed into a world-wide speaking and healing ministry, the role of her husband diminished and her speaking and healing ministry became more like that of any other international charismatic superstar.[93]

Such women were exceptional. *Above Rubies* was filled with stories of women who returned to a traditional role as wife and mother. Women leaders in the Pentecostal Movement were increasingly portrayed as submissive and happy wives beside their virile pastor husbands. Brian and Hannah Tamaki took this style to an extreme. So while the charismatic movement began as a movement for spiritual freedom, it increasingly

---

91. Lineham, "Tongues Must Cease," 30, citing *Treasury* 67 (April 1965) 19.

92. *Massey Conference Report*, 1964, 39; Lineham, "Tongues Must Cease," 29.

93. Cecilie Graham, *Fresh Beginnings* (Auckland: Fresh Beginnings Outreach Ministries, 1989) 34, 41, 58, 62.

emphasised spiritual leadership and the "covering" of a spiritual leader. This was accentuated by teaching on submission in some charismatic networks. Perhaps it was logical that submission to the pastor became linked to a renewed emphasis on submission to the husband. So deeply is this felt that charismatics were prepared to ally with conservative Catholics in the cause of defending the family.[94]

The reassertion of the domestic ideal represented an attempt to preserve the family at a time when the rising divorce rate suggested that it was under threat. Pastors' wives were significant role models and they defended the traditional women's role in the family. Maribel Morgan's book *The Total Woman* with its emphasis on the deployment of feminine charm was the textbook for this ethic. There was also extensive segregation of the sexes in charismatic circles; for example the Aglow fellowships are for women, while the Full Gospel Businessmen's Fellowships are for men. Charismatic female leaders were as capable of strong and effective action as any feminist. Ian Breward notes that "the growth of the charismatic movement may strengthen traditional attitudes, because of the literalness with which Biblical teaching on women's roles is taken."[95] Yet in fact the charismatic movement had modified the traditional approach.

Nevertheless, the charismatic movement is certainly in the fundamentalist tradition. Its understanding of Scripture is literalist. Moreover many of its early (male) leaders were drawn from the Pentecostal tradition, the Brethren and other fundamentalists. Although they made significant changes to the interpretation of Scripture it was in a more literal, not a freer direction. Thus at a time when evangelicalism as a whole was becoming more culturally sensitive in its interpretation of the Bible, they reasserted older traditions, and became increasingly resistant to the ordination of women. The AOG movement, for example, took until 1986 to allow women's ordination and then only in exceptional circumstances.[96]

The advent of youth culture and youth work also created a strange combination of highly gendered models for youth work. The advent

---

94. See the comment by Janet Crawford, "Challenging the Churches: Women are Questioning Male Attitudes," *Accent* (July 1986) 8–12.

95. I. Breward, "The Protestant contribution," in *Religion in New Zealand Society*, edited by Brian Colless and Peter Donovan (Palmerston North: Dunmore, 1980) 138–48; 76.

96. I. G. Clark, *Pentecost at the Ends of the Earth: The History of the Assemblies of God in New Zealand (1927–2003)* (Blenheim: Christian Road Ministries) 173–74, 197. Also Hewlett, "Adam's Helper."

of divorce and its incidence in the Christian community are awaiting a solid study but marriage registers (which have to be marked after a divorce) do suggest a considerable incidence of marriage breakdown is becoming quite common in these contexts.

FAMILY RELIGION

The gender debate in the 1960s was part of a broader theological and social debate as well. It is little wonder that evangelicals and Pentecostals took the conservative side on gender. In the opposition to the ratification of the United Nations Convention on women, one leaflet expressed as its key concern: "Did you know that the feminist aim is to destroy the family," citing as its evidence the Socialist Action League's submission to Parliament in 1974.[97] Family and home were seen as the abiding centres of evangelical life and faith, for evangelicalism is a lay movement, in which church is often peripheral. The family was the centre of evangelical religion, and its stable core. The care of children and provision for them was viewed as the particular responsibility of women. Therefore any attempt to change the family was very serious. There was alarm in the 1984 pamphlet because they believed that the aim was "to get mothers out of the home" and make maternity a "social function."

Evangelicals were initially as alarmed about contraception as Catholics. Sexual activity was a duty owed by the wife, and sexual feelings in themselves were supposed to be suppressed. The good wife was therefore the one who took responsibility and covered for her husband. Janet Crawford comments that such a view is based on a narrow conception of a "white, middle class nuclear family, with breadwinning father and homemaking mother"[98] but the advocates defended this narrowness, because only if this style of family was the norm could society be stable. Yet at the same time the divorce rate began to have its impact among the churches, straining the old domestic ideology even further,

---

97. This is a photocopied sheet headed "Why oppose the U.N. Convention on Women?" (no place, no date). See R. E. Low, "The United Nations Convention on the Elimination of all Forms of Discrimination against Women (UNCEDAW) Debate: a Clash of Ideologies." Massey University M.A. Honours dissertation, 1994. Also R. E. Low, "The Debate on the United Nations Convention for the Elimination of all Forms of Discrimination against Women: Motivated by Fear or a Clash of Ideologies." *Stimulus* 13 (2005) 23–30.

98. Janet Crawford, "Challenging the Churches: Women are Questioning Male Attitudes." *Accent* (July 1986) 10.

and the new style of Pentecostal pastor seemed to have a very high level of risk to his marriage on account of the three temptations of gold, glory, and girls.[99] Yet Pentecostal churches were very reluctant to approve the remarriage of divorcees or their return to ministry, and many pastors with broken marriages created independent churches when they lost their denominational credentials.

In more recent years gender issues have been subordinated to defence of the family, as the evangelical agenda has been politicised. The rise in the level of abortions, the tightening up of adoptions, the decline in marriage, the issue of adoption into non-conventional families, and the issue of what is a family have clearly stirred evangelicals to identify this as the cause of the "moral majority." In fact community tolerance has left evangelicals more isolated on these issues than anticipated.

Catherine Benland has argued that evangelicalism is male dominated by definition. Commenting on the conservative Christian women who invaded the women's forums in 1984, she remarks: "One's sense of identity is possibly one's most precious possession, and if this is inextricably bound up with one's roles as mother, wife and daughter as ordained by God, then resisting change becomes a matter of life and death. When the surgeon is a parvenue female politician, she is no match for the local male pastor or priest whose authority comes from a heavenly father."[100]

Doubtless there is some truth in this argument, but the beaten and abject women whom she pities for taking refuge in male symbols might just as well be seen as finding security and hope in a recognition of their own ability to know the divine.

In practice the evangelical position is not as absolute as it was. A sharp debate erupted in St Paul's Symonds Street over the role of women in the late 1980s when Lorna Balfour sought recognition of her gifts for ministry.[101] Advocates of a different role for women campaigned in the Annual Meetings of the Baptist Union, and very capable women like Bev

---

99. Clark, *Pentecost at the Ends of the Earth*, 229. The debate over divorce in the Assemblies of God was a bitter one over many years. See Clark, 141–42, 179–80, 208–9, 224, 226–27.

100. "Womb Makers and Womb Breakers," in *Public and Private Worlds: Women in Contemporary New Zealand*, edited by Shelagh Cox (Wellington: Allen & Unwin, 1987) 169.

101. L. Balfour, "It's Different when it's your Wife," in *Opening the Cage: Stories of the Church and Gender*, edited by M. A. Franklin and R. S. Jones (Sydney: Allen & Unwin, 1987) 1–21.

Holt within the structure were able to press for change. By then a number of Brethren assemblies were cautiously changing the rules for women's participation.[102] Eventually the Brethren magazine, the *Treasury*, admitted that there was an issue to debate.

The pressure for change was evident particularly in the organisations with more of a public face. TSCF established the Women Men and God Movement in the early 1980s, based on an English model, and for a period this probed questions for a range of women throughout the country. The Bible College of New Zealand established formal rules to establish the equality of women in its ministry, and required students to present their work in gender-inclusive language.

At the grass roots such steps were criticised. Women were ordained to the Baptist ministry, although it took a very long time for them to be appointed as sole pastor of a local church. Modern evangelical churches are developing a new hierarchy of leadership and no women have ever been appointed "senior pastor," although it is now common to find women lower down in the hierarchy. Masculinist images abound in the evangelical and Charismatic church worlds. TSCF and BCNZ were both tarred with a liberal epithet in the eyes of some over precisely these issues. The wider evangelical movement sharply divided over the gender issue, and over the issue of how to interpret the Bible on the subject. Moreover the broader struggles of Christianity in a secular world had the effect of consolidating the conservatism of those who remained, and there seems to be a new flurry of conservatism among the younger members of these churches.

There is a contrast in this story between the patterns of Australian and New Zealand evangelicals. More New Zealanders accepted gender equality than Australians. Secular and church bodies moved to recognise women in leadership. The use of Scripture changed to reflect the different practice. By and large, Pauline instructions on the household are now "put in context" in many evangelical circles, if they are ever mentioned. Even where they are stoutly defended, the traditional exclusion of women from public ministry and the demand for demure dress seem to have been quietly dropped.

---

102. Hewlett, "Adam's Helper." Chapters deal with all three groups.

CONCLUSION

The early twenty-first century has seen a sharp reduction in the debate over gender issues. Current practices are defended cautiously. The modest toning down of biblical material is seen as a proper contextualisation within our own society, while maintaining the authority of scripture. Historical study does lead one to be cautious about such statements. Evangelical interpretation of Scripture seems to change in order to defend current practice. There is an applied character to much evangelical biblical interpretation, although this has not always been the case. So it ill becomes ardent advocates of the current position to attack others as "unscriptural" unless it is clear that there is a consistency in their own position with that of Scripture. The biblicism of evangelicalism was always only one factor alongside the tradition of activism which Bebbington also identified. One cannot explain either independently.

6

Is Christianity Good for Women?

A Response to Peter Lineham

CATHY ROSS

INTRODUCTION

IN 1927 WOMEN CONNECTED with the International Missionary Council (IMC) published the first report ever on the condition of women in the world church. The report affirmed the superiority of Christianity for women because "women find in it a religion that compliments them by ignoring them as women. Christ laid down no rules for women as separate from men."[1] Presumably this statement is alluding to the fact that there is no gender bias against women in Christianity. It is an intriguing and ambiguous statement because while most women would applaud that sentiment, they may also wish to be acknowledged as women and not ignored.

Nearly eighty years later, in 2006 Dana Robert asserted that world Christianity is in fact a women's movement, "based on the fact that even though men are typically the formal, ordained religious leaders and theologians, women constitute the majority of active participants."[2] She goes on to deplore that fact. As in other areas of research, "the same path is being trod ... namely to bury women's participation in a larger narra-

---

1. IMC, 1927, 37, quoted in D. Robert, *Gospel Bearers, Gender Barriers, Missionary Women in the Twentieth Century* (Maryknoll, NY: Orbis, 2002) 11.

2. D. Robert, "World Christianity as a Women's Movement," *IBMR* 30.4 (2006) 180.

tive, in this case one called 'world Christianity.'"³ So is Christianity good for women? If women do form the majority in our churches, why is this? Can we simply assume that it is good for women because the women remain there? This response can only begin to ask the questions and explore some of the issues.

Peter concludes his chapter by asserting that the "early twenty-first century has seen a sharp reduction in the debate over gender issues." This may be the case, although I am not convinced, but it does not mean that the issues are no longer there. As Robert pertinently asks, "What would the study of Christianity in Africa, Asia, and Latin America look like if scholars put women into the centre of their research?"⁴ Or put even more trenchantly by a South African scholar, Puleng LenkaBula: "Many scholars who portray a triumphal tone in the shift of gravity to Africa, have a tendency to omit or exclude questions such as: Where and how are power, administration, management or leadership of the neo-Pentecostal, charismatic and AICs [African Instituted Churches] located, lived out and what are their impacts on women and the general church and society? This is often overlooked, downplayed or even ignored by scholars who emphasise these developments."⁵ The cry seems to be that once again, women are marginalised or ignored. She also points to the structural and leadership issues that can so easily marginalise, exclude and disempower women.

WOMEN'S INVISIBILITY

Peter reminds us of the new gender codes that developed during the Victorian era and of the ideal of women's sphere being in the home. He describes the "rugged masculinist culture" that developed in both New Zealand and Australia where women featured only on the margins, if at all. New Zealand historian, Labrum explains why women were invisible: "As the story of the European settlement of Aotearoa has been told, gold-diggers, missionaries, pastoralists, soldiers, adventurers and agricultural labourers have been brought into view. It is the men who settle the country and break in the land. Women are viewed only in terms of

---

3. Ibid.
4. Ibid.
5. Puleng LenkaBula, "The Shift of Gravity of the Church to Sub-Saharan Africa: Theologies and Ecclesiological Implications for Women," *International Journal for the Study of the Christian Church* 8.4 (2008) 303.

their relationship to men: 'The pioneers and their wives.' They are mute appendages, unnamed and therefore unidentified."[6]

Women's invisibility in church history is well documented and readily acknowledged. It is as though women have trained a camera lens through the ages of the church and have found the women missing. As Patricia Hill commented, "The women have simply disappeared."[7] However, it is not that women were absent from church history. Women have always been there; but history has been written from a standpoint from which women were often excluded. Peter's chapter is a good example of trying to make women visible within the church, finding them sometimes in unexpected places and bringing to light and affirming work that has not often been affirmed or acknowledged. Church cleaning, catering, and floral arrangements are affirmed as providing a "key role in shaping the framework for sociability." However, when they cross over to the more public roles, it seems that tensions begin to occur. Observations such as "Women were sometimes allowed to comment on missionary matters since most of the missionaries were women," and "but when such women [evangelists] attracted male audiences, some questions were asked," indicate that women had their place but that there were indeed "rules for women as separate from men."

Women's invisibility is still an issue today. Young Lee Hertig tells a story of Korean Bible women in both the nineteenth and twentieth centuries. In a moving article, entitled "Without a Face" she catalogues the work of nineteenth century Korean Bible women who were effective evangelists and informal leaders. However, she claims that once the church began to become institutionalised, "masculinization of the Korean church took place, and the hard labour of the Bible women remained invisible and faceless. Patriarchal leadership took over and continued to harvest the Bible women's work with women's labour credited to male leadership."[8]

The situation had not improved for Korean Bible women by the twentieth century. She cites a distressing example from 1922 where 300

---

6. Bronwyn Labrum, *Women's History: A Short Guide to Researching and Writing Women's History in New Zealand* (Wellington: Williams, 1993) 9–10.

7. Quoted in Janet Crawford, "Church History," in *An A to Z of Feminist Theology*, edited by Lisa Isherwood and Dorothea McEwan (Sheffield: Sheffield University Press, 1996) 27–30.

8. Young Lee Hertig, "Without a Face," in *Gospel Bearers, Gender Barriers*, edited by D. Robert (Maryknoll, NY: Orbis, 2002) 186.

Southern Methodist women *jeondosa* (evangelists) protested about salary inequalities compared with male colleagues, a male-only ordination policy, and their low social rank—being referred to as a "rag." Being either single or widowed, these Bible women had a low status in a patriarchal society. According to Hertig, Korean women *jeondosa* today still struggle with discrimination. A similar situation exists in India, where at the Church of South India's Golden Jubilee in 1997 the total number of women in fulltime pastoral or evangelistic work had declined dramatically over the previous fifty years. Ironically, "Under devolution, Indian women exchanged leadership and support by foreign (American) women for control and maintenance of traditional cultural assumptions by Indian men."[9]

Invisibility is not the only issue that may prevent women from flourishing in church. Others may be lack of respect for women, power and patriarchy, the fact that women's opinions not taken seriously, and that churches follow cultural rather than Christian values. Women may internalise certain cultural values, believing themselves to be of less significance, and this can take on a Christian meaning. This is especially dangerous when women exaggerate Christian attitudes of service and self-sacrifice, resulting in unhealthy oppression of women.

Culture can certainly be a source of oppression and this was readily acknowledged by early missionaries; foot binding of women in China and *sati* in India are obvious examples. More subtle examples such as tribalism can deeply embed male power. These issues are too sensitive to address openly in the Majority World and are hardly acknowledged in the West, although the "old boys clubs" are clearly operational in both church and society in UK.

This form of oppression maintains the invisibility of women in the church and can exclude women from church structures, worship leading, and leadership teams. A quick look at the term card of a local church here in Oxford shows fifty-nine sermons will be preached over a three month period, two by women. There seems a very basic imbalance and injustice to this, especially if the majority of the church members are women.

We become blinded by this the prevailing culture and fail to see and name this oppression as sin. As feminist theologian Serene Jones

---

9. Deborah Gaitskell and Wendy Urban-Mead, "Transnational Biblewomen: Asian and African Women in Christian Mission," *Women's History Review* 17.4 (2008) 490.

writes, "we must strain hard to see, given the powerfully destructive ways in which oppression structures our thinking and makes even the most profound forms of brokenness seem normal."[10] Because oppression works like a blinder preventing us from seeing that we are caught in sin, domination abounds and women become disempowered and invisible. A Roman Catholic sister from India told me that "women are like curry leaves. Curry leaves are used in cooking to give a nice flavour and taste. When people eat food they throw the curry leaves away. Like this, women are used and thrown out." She grieved over the plight of women in her church. After women give flavour they are discarded as they have served their purpose. Sometimes it is difficult not to become overwhelmed by attitudes and structures that prevent women flourishing.

If this were the whole story, we would know that Christianity is not good for women.

WOMEN'S INVOLVEMENT

And yet it is often women who pave the way for Christianity. Consider this example from the Solomon Islands: "I recall my mother, telling us as children how the gospel came to her area through one of our pioneering men, Peter Ambuofa. The women and children were his first converts. This was a cultural intention so that if Peter Ambuofa's God killed the women and children, the men would survive. It was when their superstitious beliefs were proved wrong, that they too became followers."[11] In this short episode we see many of the themes that recur again and again when we think about women's involvement in the church and in mission. It was the mother who kept the gospel heritage alive by telling it to her children. So often it is the mothers and grandmothers who keep the faith alive, who tell it and model it to their children, who keep the memories vivid by recounting the old stories to their families. It is the women who are the hub of the family and community, passing on vital information, keeping the valued traditions alive.

The women and children became the first Christians. Did they know the tremendous risk they were taking on behalf of their men? Did they realize that they were endangering their lives, and the lives of their

---

10. Serene Jones, *Feminist Theory and Christian Theology: Cartographies of Grace* (Minneapolis: Fortress, 2000) 109.

11. Interview with Lois Kusulifu. Unpublished interview, conducted at Laidlaw College (formerly Bible College of NZ) June 2002.

children, in converting? Whether they knew or not, they accepted this previously unknown faith and courageously committed themselves to this new God for the sake of their communities. Women bravely shouldered this responsibility, and women and children who brought their men to Christ.

A similar story occurs in other parts of the world. Robert cites the first missionaries to Hawaii, greeted by messengers from a female chief. She became an early convert and sponsor of the new faith. In Africa the first converts were often women also. Adrian Hastings has analysed this and concluded that these first women converts saw the "relative equality in Christianity as providing an escape from patriarchal customs that oppressed women,"[12] even though over time the church followed the societal pattern of male domination and women lost that initial freedom. Elizabeth Isichei from Nigeria reminds us that generally, in Africa, women experienced Christianity as empowering. "It gave them a place on which to stand, from which they could bypass or challenge male-dominated sacred worlds. Truth is always complex, however, and sometimes Christianity paved the way for new forms of marginalization."[13]

In a fascinating study on two women-led African Instituted Churches (AICs) in Kenya, Philomena Mwaura notes the preponderance of women in these churches, not just as participants but also as pastors. She notes that this is in sharp contrast to the Western mission-founded churches where women were only participants. She explains that leadership remains male in the mainline churches while classical AICs draw from traditional African religious structures. Consequently, women are attracted to AICs as founders, healers, prophetesses, prayer-leaders and evangelists.[14]

Many scholars acknowledge that women have a more holistic approach to life and work and that when women come into a church community they bring their families. Women tend to join churches because they hope to find female solidarity and support for their families. Robert

---

12. Quoted in Robert, "World Christianity," 184.

13. Quoted in M. Adeney, "Do Missions Raise or Lower the Status of Women?" in *Gospel Bearers, Gender Barriers, Missionary Women in the Twentieth Century*, edited by D. Robert (Maryknoll, NY: Orbis, 2002) 220.

14. P. Mwaura, "Gendered Appropriation of Mass Media in Kenyan Christianities: A Comparison of Two Women-led African Instituted Churches in Kenya," in *Interpreting Contemporary Christianity, Global Processes and Local Identities*, edited by O. Kalu and A. Low (Grand Rapids: Eerdmans, 2008) 274–95.

claims that "women are attracted to new Christian movements because they hold out hope for healing, improved well-being, and reconciliation with others in their communities."[15] Korean missiologist, Chun Chae Ok, claims that women are vehicles for evangelism for their families and neighbours more than men. However, the work often performed by women, hospitality, visiting, counselling, ministries of compassion and children's work, is sometimes seen as secondary to the primary tasks performed by men. She notes that Christian women's roles in church and mission have not been recorded nor sufficiently recognised: "Women evangelists, women deacons, mothers and daughters are the ones who most of the time, give their total service for the faith community and its neighbours in visiting, in prayers, in counselling and in a variety of aids . . . Women's witness with the gospel to the world is carried out in weakness and selflessness."[16]

She goes on to talk about women exercising a missiology of emptiness, a missiology of comforting and a missiology of healing, both for humanity as well as for nature. Philomena Mwaura claims that women's healing roles and holistic approach are an extension of their gendered roles on society.[17] These may well be qualities that women are uniquely placed to offer the church.

WOMEN'S SEPARATE SPACE

New Zealand scholar, Eleanor Sanderson writes of her experience with a Mothers Union (MU) group in Tanzania. The MU was founded in England in 1876 by Mary Sumner and now exists in seventy-seven countries with 3.6 million members. It works to support family life and empower women in their communities through supporting the needs of families, tackling the causes of injustice and providing a network to strengthen members in their Christian faith. The MU groups provide a separate space where women can meet together to discuss, express and minister in their faith. "Heart and home of change" is the metaphor they use to speak of hospitality offered, care for widows and children, craft

15. Robert, "World Christianity," 185.

16. Chun Chae Ok, "Integrity of Mission in the Light of the Gospel: Bearing the Witness of the Spirit: An Asian Perspective." Unpublished paper, 11th Conference of the International Association for Mission Studies, Port Dickson, Malaysia, August, 2004.

17. Mwaura, "Gendered Appropriation of Mass Media in Kenyan Christianities," 294.

work, prayers offered, joys and sorrows shared, community development embodied. This group of women provide powerful, practical support and sustenance for their community, "the affirmed fellowship of love, the women who support you to leave an abusive husband and work to provide you with a house of your own, the receipt of needed food, the new family after losing your own."[18] Here is a group of women finding huge empowerment and support through their life together.

A similar story is told in the Roman Catholic church among the Maasai in Tanzania. In the last decades of the twentieth century, women poured into the church. In the church they found a sacred space, healing and female solidarity, "an alternative female community beyond the control of Maasai men."[19] Reality is indeed complex. Church structures can oppress women, alienate, marginalise, and disempower them. Their responses vary. Some leave, hurt and alienated by the church. Others choose to remain in the church and try to subvert the structures through female solidarity. Some women join the church because it is better than the prevailing mores in their societies.

Robert suggests three reasons why women participate in church. First, women find female solidarity and support for their roles in the family and community. This is vital for women negotiating a patriarchal society. For many this community with other women in church may be more important than challenging unjust patriarchal structures in their churches.

Second, the church offers hope for healing, improved well-being and the possibility of reconciliation in broken lives and communities. Where women experience brokenness, whether through increasing family breakdown in the West, rape as an instrument of war to terrorise and humiliate women and whole communities,[20] or the daily grind of gender discrimination or racist structures in the workplace, churches can offer healing and grace to broken and scarred women.[21]

---

18. E. Sanderson, "Women changing: Relating Spirituality and Development through the Wisdom of Mothers' Union Members in Tanzania," *Women's Studies Journal* 20.2 (2006) 83–100, 95.

19. Robert, "World Christianity," 185.

20. For example, see http://www.amnesty.org.uk/actions_details.asp?ActionID=534 which relates the story of Justine Bihamba working to protect women from rape in the Congo.

21. See Jones, "Sin: Grace Denied," in Jones, *Feminist Theory,* 94–125.

Serene Jones describes the experience of her Tuesday night women's group undertaking a study of sin in Lent. She outlines the various forms of sin that these women were experiencing both within church and society and how they found understanding, solidarity and a certain amount of healing in sharing these together in their women's Bible study group.

Third, church women's groups provide contexts for women to exercise their gifts in ways that may not be possible in society, as we saw with the example from the MU. "The MU groups are an autonomous space for Christian women to discern, express, teach and minister in their faith. This is particularly significant given that in their immediate church context there have not been, nor are there currently female ordained ministers."[22] So this may mean discipleship training or opportunities for leadership. And although this can take generations, Robert reminds us that in "the twentieth century, Christian women became the first medical doctors, college presidents, social workers, community organisers, and politicians in many countries of the non-Western world."[23]

CONCLUSION

Is Christianity good for women? Recently I attended a meeting of about forty Anglican women theological educators from all around the world. Every one of them said they felt excluded in some way from their church context. This has to be taken seriously. Churches can offer safe spaces, places of healing and reconciliation, places of female solidarity. However, as Isichei reminded us, "sometimes Christianity paved the way for new forms of marginalization" so that women can feel excluded and invisible. At the turn of the millennium, Robert wrote, "As I have gone around interviewing women mission activists in conservative churches, I have heard the same sad refrain: there is less room for women's mission today than there was twenty or thirty years ago."[24] She continues that stories of gender bias and dismissal of women's gifts would "break your heart."

Sometimes women collude in this. We do not speak out about injustice or say that we are marginalised or silenced in various ways, that we are slow to offer our gifts and insights for fear of rejection.

---

22. Sanderson, "Women Changing," 84.
23. Robert, "World Christianity," 185.
24. Dana Robert, "Women and Missions: Historical Themes and Current Realities." In *Twentieth Century Missions and Gender Conference* (Boston University: Unpublished, March, 2000) 12.

Strangely we collude in our oppression. A feminist analysis of sin tells us that women need to be challenged to hear different things from men. Traditional models of sin assume an audience of men who are socialised into autonomy and power. Women's sin may be better described as the "sin of hiding." Hess suggests that, "by encouraging woman to confess the wrong sin, and by failing to judge her in her actual sin, Christianity has both added to woman's guilt and failed to call her into her full humanity."[25] This is not to say that women are not guilty of pride and self-assertion common to all humanity but rather our strong ethic of care-giving and nurture can lead us to keep the peace at any price. In this way Christianity has not helped women to flourish but has rather added to our burden of struggling with our role and place in church.

And yet many women around the world (not all) remain in church.[26] We know that Jesus is good for us. Dorothy Sayers wrote in her essay, "The Human-Not-Quite-Human" that "it is no wonder that the women were first at the Cradle and last at the Cross. They had never known a man like this Man—there never has been such another."[27] Jesus took women seriously and always treated women with dignity and respect in the Gospels. He discussed theology with women (the Samaritan woman at the well), he liberated women from bondage (the women with the issue of blood), he challenged gender bias (the woman caught in adultery), the first people he entrusted himself to after the resurrection were women, he had women among his disciples and was financially supported by them, he selected images and parables to communicate on a deep level with women as much as men.[28]

To go back to the ambiguous comment from the 1927 IMC report. Women do not want to be ignored as women, but rather affirmed as women and for what women have to offer. Women long to be in a church where there are indeed "no rules for women as separate from men." However, perhaps we will all be able to answer this question more accurately and comprehensively if we decide to pay more attention to

25. C. L. Hess, "Education as an Art of Getting Dirty with Dignity," in C. C. Neuger, ed., *The Arts of Ministry: Feminist-Womanist Approaches* (Louisville: Westminster John Knox, 1996) 60–88, 69.

26. For example, see http://www.spiritedexchanges.org.uk/index.php?id=87, Christine's story.

27. Dorothy Sayers, *Are Women Human?* (Grand Rapids: Eerdmans, 1971) 68.

28. See Kenneth E. Bailey, *Jesus through Middle Eastern Eyes: Cultural Studies in the Gospel* (London: SPCK, 2008) 194–95.

Dana Robert's plea, "What would the study of Christianity in Africa, Asia and Latin America look like if scholars put women into the centre of their research?"

7

God and Gender

The Relational Center

IRENE ALEXANDER

A PROFOUND MISUNDERSTANDING

THE ENGLISH LANGUAGE SETS us up for one of the most profound errors about relationship with God, and because we think in terms of language we do not see the error. We are concerned that we believe the right things as if at the gates of heaven there is a checklist, ensuring we answer correctly before we are allowed in—like a catechism class. But no, instead the father comes running to welcome us—"At last you've come!" He flings his arms around us, saying "Come and see what you've never dreamed possible!"

We may ask: doesn't the Bible show that God might say, "Depart from me, I never knew you"? (Matt 7:23). Here indeed is the key. Does God know me? In English, unlike many other languages, the word "know" has a number of meanings—to *know* a fact, to *know* a person, Adam *knew* his wife Eve. Recently someone asked me if I knew a certain writer—meaning, did I know his books. "Yes," I said. "Actually I know him." It's possible that the man questioning me knew this person's writing better than I did, could say, as we might of other writers, "Oh yes, I know C. S. Lewis." But have I ever met him? Do I know him as a friend? Does he know me? This is the point. When I run to the gates of heaven will God say—"Ah, here is my friend"?

It has been said, "The Word became flesh, but we evangelicals have made him the Word again." God became a man not so we could read and write books about him, but so we could run into his arms, saying, "I'm home!" Jesus came to show us the Father (John 14:7), to model that relationship. He demonstrated how to relate to God as Abba-Father, so we could relate to God like that too.

Around the topic of gender, relational rather than academic knowing is all-important. If we discuss God and gender as though we are talking about facts and ideas only, we miss the whole point. "God and gender" is about me—who I am, my gender, my sexuality and what those mean to me—and about God, who God is, the quality of God's relationships including gender and sexuality. And—most importantly—how God and I relate, given that I am female, heterosexual, and this is part of my core sense of who I am.

The following explores some images of God and some experiences relating to these. But first, some groundwork in terms of "masculine and feminine ways of knowing," epistemic maturity, and some psychological understanding of the development of our images of God—and therefore relationship with God.

WAYS OF KNOWING

I suggest that the issue of "gender and relationship with God" requires that we reflect carefully on ways of knowing, and our sense of self as gendered beings. For many of us our core awareness of self seems to relate to our gender. Our experience of God is often profoundly affected by our gender, our experience of the meaning of our gender, and our sexuality. While we may be able to discuss these ideas intellectually, it is not until we reflect personally on our experience and self-image, that we will engage honestly.

One of the purposes of our education system is to teach students how to think and this, in turn, depends on an understanding of epistemology, or epistemics, to use a more psychological, interdisciplinary term. Rational thought, scientific method, objective analysis, rules of evidence, presuppositions are all part of a system of knowledge. But so is intuition, revelation, experience, and empathy. While the academic world has chosen to privilege rational thought and scientific method, the church has also kept alive the value of revelationary knowing. A postmodern shift has allowed the revaluing of intuition, experience, and personal interpretation. In the space of a lifetime, acceptable academic epistemology has changed and ways of knowing can now, respectably, include personal experience, as long as it is carefully contextualised and owned.

Not only has there been a philosophical shift over the last fifty years, there has been unfolding understanding of the developmental process of ways of knowing across the lifespan. A 1960–1970s Harvard study, reported by William Perry, described a pathway of epistemic positions based on the changes university students make as they are taught the disciplines of academic thought.[1] It is worth understanding these positions to lay a foundation for recognising possible ways of knowing as relational or intellectual, as developmental, or dependent on worldview. A Christian worldview necessarily changes one's perspective on ways of knowing, thus allowing different perceptions of the possibilities and positions described.

Perry described a number of positions summarised here to four. The first position, that of older children—and many less mature Christians—is termed Dualism, because of the basic duality perceived as we-right/good versus other-wrong/bad. The next major position, Multiplicity, expresses an "egocentric personalism." This is the stance of many non-religious people, a position in which, if there is uncertainty, one person's opinion is just as right as anyone else's. Many people remain in either of these two positions for all of their lives. However secondary schools, and universities in particular, teach students to reassess their understanding and evaluation of knowledge and authority, to examine their own thinking, to compare knowledge claims through rules of evidence, and to recognise theories as models rather than "truth." This leads to a position of Contextual Relativism, in which the students come to perceive all knowledge and values as contextual and relativistic. The final position in this scheme is one of ongoing, unfolding action in which the knower is both committed and tentative, in a continuing dialectical process, having moved from a received belief to a creative faith. Perry uses the term "faith" here, not in a religious sense, but in the recognition that we do not "know" with certainty.

---

1. W. G. Perry, "Cognitive and Ethical Growth: The Making of Meaning," in *The Modern American College*, edited by A. W. Chickering (San Francisco: Jossey Bass, 1981).

WOMEN'S WAYS OF KNOWING

In the 1980s a further study was published, from which a major finding has relevance for Christians, and for the present topic. The researchers called their book, *Women's Ways of Knowing*[2] as the interviewees were women. They found similar positions as Perry's (1981) Harvard study, but there were important differences. They reported on the learning that is necessary for students to shift from Multiplicity (everyone's opinion is as good as everyone else's) to Contextual Relativism. The Harvard study had mentioned the academic disciplines of argument, evidence, and scientific method. The women's study introduced a new perspective.

The authors called the shift into academic knowing reported by Perry as Procedural, (because students learn a rigorous procedure) and Separate Knowing (because the process involves separating "knowing" from my "self," learning to be objective, rational, assessing evidence). This they termed a more masculine way of knowing because these researchers discovered that women use a different procedure. As a woman, a Christian, and a counsellor, I found their "feminine" Procedural Knowing rather fascinating. They call it Connected Knowing. It is much more like relational knowing—knowing "from the inside" rather than "from the outside."

Many women experience Separate Knowing arguments as attack, because their knowledge and their "self" are connected, not able to be separated. Sometimes this is interpreted to mean that a woman has not learned the skills of the Procedural Separate Knowing game. Frequently women prefer Connected Knowing which is just as procedural, just as rigorous—but relational. Connected Knowing is taught in counselling training—to both men and women—as a way to listen and to know: the "Believing game."[3]

When I listen to a counsellee, I need to be able to suspend my judgement, my perceptions, my advice, even my disbelief. I need to learn how to hear the person "from the inside," understand their experience from inside them. I have to be able to listen to my own intuition and reactions but know they are my subjective reactions. I am listening to the other person with empathy, and listening to myself, and knowing

---

2. M. F. Belenky, B. M. Clinchy, N. R. Goldberger, and J. M. Tarule, *Women's Ways of Knowing: The Development of Self, Voice, and Mind* (New York: Basic, 1986).

3. Elbow uses this term to teach critique of literature. P. Elbow, *Writing Without Teachers* (Oxford: Oxford University Press, 1975).

which is which. Carl Rogers, the influential humanist therapist describes the process like this: "To sense the client's private world as if it were your own, but without ever losing the 'as if' quality—that is empathy, and this seems essential to therapy. To sense the clients, anger, fear, or confusion, as if it were your own fear, anger or confusion but without getting bound up in it."[4]

I am explaining this in some detail because I am wanting to point out that this more commonly "feminine" way of knowing is a relational knowing but is also rigorous and challenging, no less "academic" than Separate Knowing. No less "academic" in rigour, only less academic in being more to do with an awareness of feeling than a head process. This way of knowing has thus become more acceptable, more validated in the academic world. Christians hopefully, with our greater understanding of relational knowing and spiritual perception, have been able to recognise it as a valid epistemic process.

KNOWING AND GENDER

As is common in psychological studies which explore "masculine" and "feminine," the disclaimer is that not all men use "masculine" ways of knowing, and women "feminine" ways of knowing. Most people use both. But it can help us make sense of experience to find the broad stroke differences; as well as to recognise the different ways of knowing in our own repertoire, and our attitudes towards them. In fact, the most mature position epistemically, is the position of being able to use numbers of different ways of knowing, and being able to evaluate which is most appropriate for the task at hand.

Perry considered the most mature position to be one of "faith" and "commitment"—not Christian terms in his context. Rather they are a recognition that all our knowing has elements of faith—there is uncertainty, theorising, and subjective contextualisation in everything, but to live in this world we need to make choices, this is our commitment to a worldview, to a way of understanding.

The proposition of this paper is that appropriate knowing concerning God and gender, must include Connected Knowing, experiential reflection, a willingness to be self-aware, and to explore our childhood and

---

4. Rogers (1957) cited in J. Rowan, and M. Jacobs, *The Therapist's Use of Self* (Oxford: Oxford University Press, 2002) 12.

adult experiences. This involves self-awareness around our own gender experiences as well as our evolving images of God, as well as the dimensions of our relationship.

IMAGES OF GOD

In *The Birth of the Living God*[5] Ana-Marie Rizzuto explores people's understanding of God—their images of God. She claims that our images of God have a primary experiential base. Church attendees may be able to describe what they have been taught God is like—a "God concept"—as in Dualistic or Multiplistic Knowing or, if they have been educated in this way—in Procedural knowing terms. However their relational knowing, their experiential grasp, their image of God, is very likely to be different. By interviewing adults about their images of God through their lives, Rizzuto confirmed the theory that our image of God is initially based and deeply rooted in our childhood experiences of those around us, especially our parents. Over time however, these representations of God may change, especially during times of crisis.

Rizzuto's exploration of our changing images of God reminds me of the spiritual director's ever-present question: Who is God for you now? As I have engaged in spiritual direction over a number of years my director's gentle probing has helped me see where my relationship with God and my image of God is changing—or needs to change. Rizzuto says: "The process of continuous reshaping of the God representation is delicate." Indeed this is my experience: that only in a context of great respect for my experience and my relationship with God, am I able to be open, and willing to change.

An exploration of God and gender is in the territory of Connected Knowing and of faith rather than in the theology of Separate Knowing. To use Cantwell Smith's definition:[6] "Faith is the internal attitude of trust with which each person or community responds to the demands of life." "Faith is one's existential engagement with what one knows to be true or good." "Since it is an engagement, to know faith authentically is to become oneself involved . . . This is *fides quaerens intellectum*, faith in

---

5. A. Rizzuto, *The Birth of the Living God: A Psychoanalytic Study* (Chicago: University of Chicago Press, 1981) 210.

6. W. Cantwell Smith, *The Meaning and End of Religion* (San Francisco: Harper, 1978).

pursuit of self-understanding."[7] Exploring God with awareness of our gender is necessarily a Connected Knowing process, beginning with our relationship with God, our experience of God—and working out from there. How then are we to relate to God as gendered beings?

If each of us were asked to answer the question, "Is God male?" most of us would say, No. The question that follows is more difficult: "What is he then?"

The fact that the God of the Old Testament is aniconic suggests that male God images and female Goddess images are not appropriate. Yet metaphors of God are male and female—the father who carried me (Deut 1:31), the mother who dandled me on her hip (Isa 49:15–16; 66:12–13), the she bear who protected me as one of her cubs (Hos 13:8), the midwife who brought me forth from the womb (Ps 22:9–10), the warrior who protected me (Exod 15:3), the lover who wooed me (Song).

Does Jesus being the image of the invisible God make God male? No, humans have to be one sex or the other. Does the fact the Jesus calls God Father make God male? No, we understand that this is an image also. Jesus is showing us a way of relating, demonstrating the possibility of intimacy. Describing God in words is less possible than demonstrating how to relate to such a God—one who relates to us in love and intimacy, concern and compassion.

In both the Old and New Testaments metaphors for God abound. It would seem that the prohibition of concrete images is more about limiting God, than forbidding mental images. Humans think in images, in metaphors. A forbidding of metaphors or mental images would cause us to think of God as an amorphous mass, a force, an impersonal energy. If we are to live in relationship with God—as the Bible and, even more so, Jesus, clearly invite us to do—we will have images, human images, anthropomorphic images, and animals (the lion, the lamb, being under your wings, a hen gathering her chicks, a dove). Images are not wrong, they are just limited. If I only think of God as the Lion of Judah, I miss seeing the Lamb. If I only see God as the parent of a small child, I miss seeing God as one who calls me to adulthood. If I only see God as male I miss seeing her as female.

What does that pronoun "her" do to my thinking? Why is it so much less acceptable for most of us than "him"? We have grown up with God

---

7. W. Cantwell Smith, *Faith and Belief: The Difference Between Them* (Oxford: Oneworld, 1998).

and male pronouns. We are used to male images of God. They are not wrong—just limited. God is so much more than we can ever imagine. We are so afraid to imagine amiss. As if God were not constantly interacting with us to reveal the reality of who God truly is. God is more concerned than we are, that we are in relationship, that we know God as God is, relationally, experientially. We have to decide whether it is "unbiblical" to call God "her"; that is, "unbiblical" in the sense that it goes against what the Bible actually means.

GOD AS FATHER

Each of the images of God is a picture of a relationship. Each invites a response from us, an ability to relate to God in the way that image implies. Although God as Father is present in the Old Testament, Jesus relating to him as Daddy must have been challenging to many of his hearers—as it challenges many of us today. Creator God yes, even Loving God, possibly even Father God—but Daddy? A Daddy who picks me up, and kisses my face. A Daddy who lifts me by my outstretched arms and throws me in the air, catching me with laughter. Such an image demands a response of trust from me, a relationship in which I am loved and held—calling forth a response of love and receptivity from me.

When I was a child my father was a nurturing father to me, holding me and telling me stories, so coming to God as Father, as Daddy, was not difficult for me. But I have met many people for whom it has been difficult. Terri's father was alcoholic. When she lived with us for a time and saw my husband interacting with our little children, she was struck by the reality of what a loving father looked like. She began to be able to relate to God as Daddy for the first time. Another woman, Jan was sexually abused by her father from as far back as she could remember. When he died her Sunday School teacher took her under his wing—and sexually abused her as well. Needless to say her ability to relate to God as Father was badly affected.

Most of us did not have experiences as bad as Terri and Jan's. Happily most of us had "good enough" parents,[8] good enough in the sense that they were human, they made mistakes, but their hearts were for us. Nevertheless many of us still have reservations about letting God

---

8. D. W. Winnicott, *The Maturational Processes and the Facilitating Environment* (London: Hogarth, 1965).

get as close as a loving, playful Daddy might want. What is our hesitation? We may cite the formal church experiences of our childhood. We may explain our preference for a more "respectful" relationship with God. The reality is that our reservations are less likely to be "philosophical" than psychological. Our distancing is more likely to be about some residual hurts from childhood. Jesus modelled for us a relationship with a God who he called Daddy. If we are unable to enjoy the intimacy of a relationship like that, it is likely that some left-over childhood hurts or hindrances remain.

Remembering childhood experiences of our fathers may help us to recognise whether there is unresolved hurt or distancing from a father figure. A child's tender heart is easily hurt but God can bring healing in the present as we bring the reality of the pain of that memory into the present. Many people find healing for childhood experiences as they have their own children. As I notice my own overflowing love for my child I can be present to the experience of love—and dare to believe that this is also God's love for me. Many men who have experienced hurt from their own fathers have been able to revisit the love of the Father, in their own experience of being a father, and discovering from the inside the overwhelming love of a daddy for his child. This is true Connected Knowing—knowing from within a relationship.

The experience of receiving the love of God as a loving father is pivotal for many people in their relationship with God. Recently I spoke to Sue who had completed a six month experiential training program. The second week of the training was teaching—and then ministry—about "the Father-heart of God." "It was essential for the rest of the program to have meaning for me," Sue told me. "Discovering God's love for me in that way meant I could go on to understand the other teaching and so to minister to the children we then visited." Over and over I have seen people healed in this way. It is the experience of this relational knowing which changes the perspectives of our intellectual knowing. People are thus enabled to touch other people with God's love. Bruce Thompson, counsellor and long term missionary, explains that a revelation of God's Father-heart is foundational to the rebuilding of our lives in response to, and in relationship with God.[9]

Our relationships with our own fathers become a window through which we view "fatherhood." If that experience is destructive, the win-

---

9. B. Thompson, *Walls of My Heart* (Euclid: Crown Ministries, 1989).

dow is distorted, and our perception of fatherhood and intellectual conceptions are consequently distorted. Our relationships with authority figures will be shaped by early experience. Our default expectations of male authority figures will be that they are distant, critical, emotionally absent, etc. unless we experience powerfully different relationships, or receive healing. These experiences will carry over to our relationship with God the Father unless we consciously re-pattern our thinking and emotional reactions.

Traditionally we have thought that if we teach of a loving Father God people will believe this as truth. It is only more recently that psychology has demonstrated that we unconsciously bring childhood images and overlay these on to other teaching. Occasionally someone meeting God for the first time will know that he is a loving caring Father—in contrast to their own experience of an abusive or absent father, but this tends to be the exception, or, even then, the childhood experiential relationship is the default position that surfaces at times of stress, for example when God seems to be absent or a crisis happens. Then the person finds they have to work through the childhood reactions hidden under the surface of a seemingly healthy relationship with a good God.

Implicit in our perceptions of God as father will be our reactions to that relationship with regard to our gender. If I was able to relate to my father well as his little girl, it is fairly easy for me to imagine myself climbing on to God's lap and receiving his love. If however he did not know how to relate to me as a teenager or a young woman it is harder for me to relate to a male father God as a young woman, aware of my sexuality and my own developing sense of the world. If a boy was disciplined harshly by his father it is harder for him to come to the presence of God without that underlying expectation of a male to male criticism, some sense of himself not measuring up as a male or a man.

Some people might find psychological insights around these ideas to be pathologizing, feeling as though they cannot escape the inevitable negatives of growing up in a fallen world. The good news is that facing our fallenness, bringing our wounds into the healing presence of God, of a truly loving father, brings healing—a real "person-to-person" relationship and the ensuing humility of being a loved child of God, an heir of the kingdom, a co-heir with my brothers and sisters.

GOD AS LOVER

What of other images of God? The Song of Solomon has challenged Christians through the centuries with its explicit metaphors and lover-beloved relationship. Here gender becomes starker. As a woman it is easy for me to identify with the Shunammite—the beloved. It has been a healing experience over the years to identify with her and to allow the words of the lover, to be God's words to me. "You are all fair my love; Arise my love, my fair one and come away. How beautiful you are my darling, how beautiful you are." To receive the love of God the Lover until I can respond, "I am dark but comely; his banner over me is love, I am sick with love" (Song 1:5, 15; 2:4, 10; 4:1; 5:8). I cannot—and need not—separate my womanhood from the relationship. I am the beloved. My Lover's love is for me. I am wooed and held, and wed. I am made whole. His love for me gives me a rich sense of self which includes my femininity and my sexuality.

Relating to God in Jesus calls me into the imagery of a relationship of one human with another. This may be experientially different for a man than for a woman. If I am a man imagining myself in Palestine during Jesus' lifetime, I can relate to Jesus as a man who calls me into life, into ministry, into responsibility. Or, as a woman I identify with the women who followed Jesus. I can put myself into Martha's story, into her sister Mary, or into the other Mary—of Magdalene. As a woman I imagine journeying as Mary Magdalene did through the Gospel stories. Catching his eye after a healing, exchanging a look, or a conversation after some particularly challenging interaction. I imagine myself by the tomb in Joseph of Arimathea's garden; the wrenching sobs of a woman who has lost the man who meant everything to her. And then he is there with her—and her world lurches into another form. She is in his arms, never to let him go. Gently he holds her, and tenderly tells her she does not need to cling to him, he is not yet "going to the father," disappearing from her grasp.

This placing of ourselves into a Gospel story is one of the ways to receive healing, to be transformed by our God. It follows the Ignatian method of imagining ourselves present.[10] I identify with one of the characters and imagine what it would be like to be there. What do I see, hear, smell, feel? What is the experience like for me? How does Jesus respond

---

10. For more information on this meditation practice see S. Pritchard, *The Lost Art of Meditation: Deepening Your Prayer Life* (Milton Keynes, UK: Scripture Union, 2003).

to me? What is it like to be in his presence? The story of the woman at the well illustrates this process.

> I see him sitting there. In the shade, still, watching.
> I become conscious of my self. My body. I swing it a little.
> I lower my bucket and glance at him. He meets my look and asks for a drink.
> There is something in his eyes. Some promise of such richness.
> Forbidden of course. But worth pursuing.
> The old longing in my heart.
> The longing for someone who would meet me. The real me. Fully.
> There is no man, I know. But I still hope.
> And make the play for it. "Who are you a Jew who would ask?"
> Flirt a bit. Draw him on. Engage him.
> I take him my bucket and pour water into his hands. He thanks me and drinks.
> I watch him. In his look is such a self-containment. Such a wholeness.
> I know he will not be tempted by me. Is not. Yet he is not afraid to give.
> He responds to me and lets the playacting fall ignored.
> He drinks and says, "If you knew who I was you'd ask me for a drink."
> I'm asking; oh, I am asking. But how to meet that look?
> So I continue my act.
> "Well give it to me so I wouldn't have to come here and draw water."
> Draw him along. Keep him talking.
> And on one level I'm not acting. I want this life he has in his eyes. I want to know how to get it. And I'm free for the taking if he'd only have me. Which he won't, of course. Because if he's as great as he seems he'll see my brokenness and not want me.
> And he does—"Go and call your husband."
> But I'll try for a little longer. "I have no husband." Take me. I'm free.
> I'll give you all I've got for what you've got.
> I'm yours for the taking and I'll give it all for that life you have in your eyes.
> He knows what I mean. He looks at me deeply. He doesn't draw back from me.
> The promise is there in his hands. If only.

He looks at me, and without judgement, still holding out the promise he says—

"You're right you've had five husbands and the one you now live with is not your husband."

Statement —I know you.

So he knows my brokenness and my need. He sees through me.

And wonder of wonders he does not draw back. Oh, if only I could have this man.

Indeed he would be living water to my soul.

I do not know how to get him. He plays a game I do not know.

Try another tack. Keep him in reach a little longer.

"Sir I can see you're a prophet."

Well something—you're something to do with what my inner heart longs for.

Talk about that. Tell me the Answers—tell me something I can feed on for a while.

He talks and I do not hear him. I watch his lips and his eyes and know that I long for something that is beyond my reach: physically, spiritually. I am one who longs for spiritual answers but cannot attain to them—who would even believe I wanted them.

I give myself physically to receive whatever life I can get.

But this man, he knows something, he is in touch with the Real. It's not hard to see that. And he takes me seriously. He talks to me as if I was someone who was real too.

He's not sidetracked by my banter.

He looks into my eyes and my spirit is drawn to him.

I dare to let him see my real longing. "I believe in the Messiah." I want to know him.

"I am he," he says.

I am stunned yet believing in the same instant. I stare at him, my bucket forgotten. The men coming up behind me ignored. If anyone could be, it's him.

He looks into my eyes. Gentleness and truth. Promise of life forever. Living water. It really could be true.

I am caught in his look. Caught by the promise. Known for who I am, yet free to come.

I meet his look. My heart is held. Held yet free.

For once I can give my heart. Yet freely.

My whole being says Yes.

When I wrote this story I identified with this woman using her sexuality to reach out to Jesus, to flirt with him—he must have noticed that this is what she was doing! Yet he accepted her—and responded to the deeper need she was expressing—the need of her yearning heart for intimacy, for spirit-to-spirit connection. And, further, he identified himself as the Messiah to her—something he did to only a few—and only those who were ready to hear. As I identify with her, and place myself in the story, so I receive healing from a God who knows my sexuality, my longing—and accepts both. Here is a God who knows me at my most vulnerable, the reality of my gender, the reality of my sexuality, the depth of my need—and responds to me, to all these parts of me, and is known by me in return. Engaging with the stories in this way allows me to know God experientially.

GOD AS LOVER—MEN'S RESPONSES

For women, the relationship with God as lover is straightforward in terms of my feminine to God as masculine, but how are men to respond to this image? There are several possibilities.

If we see the images of God as being less about the image-object and more about the nature of the relationship, then we identify with the intimacy, the heightened self-awareness, the depth of longing. The metaphors communicate to us not so much God as *male* Lover but rather my relationship with God can be as intimate, as enlivening, as erotic, as a Lover-beloved relationship.

C. S. Lewis suggests that we are all "female" in response to God.[11] That is, God is the great Masculine, ever the initiator, the Protector, the Lion—and his church is his bride. We are all responders to his masculine, receptive to his active, loved in response to his loving. As a woman it is easy for me to accept this, and some men are able to make this step, while others find it more difficult. James Nelson explains,

> Our male biology will not change, and it will continue to give a different cast to both our sexuality and our spirituality from that which women's bodies give to theirs . . . it seems related to the desire to penetrate and to explore the mystery of otherness, a desire important to human fulfilment. At the same time, this

11. C. S. Lewis, *The Problem of Pain* (1940; reprinted, San Francisco: Harper, 2001) 44. "Our role must be always that of patient to agent, female to male, mirror to light, echo to voice."

needs balance through the development of a more receptive and vulnerable male sexuality that will form the grounding for a more receptive and vulnerable masculine spirituality.[12]

John of the Cross gives us a beautiful example of this receptive and vulnerable masculine spirituality in his *Dark Night of the Soul*. He talks of the beloved finding her Lover, of his head upon her breast. He allows himself to identify with the beloved in response to the Lover, utilising the feminine pronoun. And from his language and imagery it is clear that he experienced God's presence in this interchange profoundly.

> Oh guiding night!
> O night more lovely than the dawn!
> O night that has united
> The Lover with His beloved,
> Transforming the beloved in her Lover.[13]

Another Christian mystic who clearly experienced intimacy with God was Julian of Norwich, the thirteenth-century English spiritual mentor, who easily moved between genders in her descriptions of the Trinity. "Also the almighty truth of the Trinity is our Father. For he made us and keeps us in him. And the deep wisdom of the Trinity is our Mother, in whom we be all enclosed, and the high goodness of the Trinity is our Lord, and in him we are closed, and he is in us. All mighty, all wisdom, and all goodness; one God, one Lord, and one goodness."[14]

Julian does not try and explain how God is feminine and masculine—she simply uses the image of Jesus as mother, mixing the genders as though they are indeed only images, and the coming to God, the quality of the relationship is the whole point. Other mystics through the centuries have done similarly—not letting the compartments of the human mind hinder them from coming into God's presence, knowing God relationally, intimately.

Another perspective on God as lover is gained from men who have been confronted with their own sexuality, and homosexuality.

---

12. J. B. Nelson, *The Intimate Connection: Male Sexuality, Masculine Spirituality* (Philadelphia: Westminster, 1988) 13.

13. John of the Cross, "The Dark Night," in *The Collected Works of St. John of the Cross*, translated by K. Kavanaugh (Washington, DC: Institute of Carmelite Studies, 1979).

14. Julian of Norwich, *Showing of Love*. These quotes are found on the Westminster website: http://www.umilta.net/westmins.html.

Some people may find it difficult to accept that homosexual men can engage with this imagery—indeed to fear their own responses because of this association. Homosexual friends have told me of the power of identifying Jesus as Lover, accepting them in their maleness and their sexuality—and wooing them to deep intimacy, their relationship with God deepened by their experiencing of God in this way.

For many men both these perspectives are problematic. Nelson explains that for some, these ideas seem to imply that a man has to let go his masculinity. "Furthermore, a male God penetrates us. But to be penetrated by anyone or anything, even God, amounts to being womanized. It seems tantamount to a man's degradation, literally loss of grade or status."[15] The poet William Everson was able to face that possibility by seeing beyond the "annulling" to the transformation, "Annul me in my manhood, Lord, and Make me woman-sexed and weak, if by that total transformation I might know Thee more."[16] The challenge for men is to be able to come into the presence of God, bringing with them their masculinity and their sexuality, and finding the intimacy of the Lover.

In answer to my questioning a friend about this, he told me:

> Firstly, I am a man, husband, father, son, brother of Christ, disciple of Christ, man among men and brother to/of many, and there is a "homo-erotic" aspect to this (although I've chosen not to enter into a homosexual experience with anyone). I seek to explore and penetrate the mystery, spiritually and sexually. My spiritual modus operandi reflects my sexual design. However, secondly, there is another side to me that says I surrender, I am receptive, penetrate me, take me. I am learning to wait for the mystery (sometimes) rather than always be out there hunting it down! And then, thirdly, there are times when the question of gender all but disappears in favour of simple shared humanity. Not that I become neutered, or anyone else for that matter, but at times it ceases to matter.[17]

Some men sidestep this imagery—or come as close to it as they can—by seeing God as brother, as friend, as mate, as comrade. They can identify with Jesus' disciples and imagine walking with him along the shores of Galilee or the streets of Nazareth—in the deep intimate con-

---

15. Nelson, *The Intimate Connection*, 45.
16. W. Everson, *Earth Poetry* (Berkeley: Oyez, 1980).
17. Personal communication with Noel Giblett.

versation of close friends. This is powerful imagery. It is not the same as a Lover-beloved intimacy but it can be powerfully healing and inspiring.

Whatever our image of God is—we are the complement of that image—the opposite and corresponding partner in the relationship. If Jesus is Friend, I am friend to him—not servant, not bond-slave. "I came not to be served but to serve" (Mark: 10:45). "I no longer call you servants . . . I call you friends" (John 15:15). It is God himself who elevates us to this relationship of equals—who calls us to be mature men and women of faith, co-heirs of the kingdom. Finding how to come to God with the intimacy of a lover, a true partner with him is a deeply liberating and healing experience.

GOD AS MOTHER

For many of us, because of our gender, our sexuality, our various experiences, engaging with God as Lover may be challenging—even though clearly biblical. What of discovering the God who is also Mother to us? Again our gender, our childhood experiences, our beliefs about the feminine, will help or hinder our relating to God in this way, and will influence our theological perspectives.

If we have had difficulty with our mothers or other female authority figures, then feminine images are difficult; even as the male images are difficult for those who have struggled in their relationship with their father. Or it may be that we simply have never realised that a feminine image of God is orthodox. Or, if we are catholic, we may have been taught to pray to Mary as the acceptable female image, instead of finding God as Mother.

Julian of Norwich seems to be able to respond to God very easily as Father, Mother, Lover. Many of us have not found it so easy. Many women, like me, have somehow absorbed society's devaluing of women, and so devalued our own feminine. For many of us it was easier to imagine God as Father, or to come to Jesus as Lover. Personally for me it felt as though a feminine representation of God was more likely to condemn. I realised this most specifically when I saw my own criticism of myself as a mother. In the course of some profound retreat work I wrote to God, deliberately choosing to accept God as Mother, and articulated what came:

> And so then I come, Mother God to you—fallen human mother that I am—and say here I am, as you know me to be, naked and not covering myself—coming as a very human mother—to you, the only Divine Mother, the only Perfect One—the one who comes in such humility that you kneel at my feet, and hold me to your breast, that I may feel your heart beat, and know your love outpoured for me, forever outpoured, forever giving, forever in travail, forever in self-giving. This is my God, the One who weeps in self-giving Love.

I have found that my image of God influences the way I can relate—just as my images of different people influence the way I relate to them. Coming to God as Mother enabled me to experience myself as feminine in the presence of God's feminine. This is not the same as saying that God is goddess. It is acknowledging the feminine in God as we acknowledge the masculine, the Lover, the Protector, the Nurturer. Bringing particular struggles I have to God as Mother allows me to experience those difficulties in a different way.

James Nelson, in his examination of what it means to be aware of his maleness in God's presence, explains the ambivalence many men experience when facing the possibility of God as mother. "To embrace the 'feminine' in God is to embrace the promise of that deep nurturing presence and immanence that we so need. But it also raises our unconscious anger at the mother who abandoned us and pushed us out into a man's world where the clues and expectations about our own deepest meanings were hard to find. It is all very confusing in the heart of a man's heart."[18]

Each of us is on a journey of awareness of what it means to be gendered, and what that means in the presence of God who we experience through our own lived reality.

THE ONGOING JOURNEY

For some of us, the idea of changing an image of God, or the nature of our relationship with God, is challenging. We find it difficult to admit that our previous ideas may have been limited. Or we misinterpret the idea that God is unchanging, to think that therefore my image of God must be unchanging. Research in epistemic development has shown that the position of most maturity is a position which admits not knowing,

---

18. Nelson, *The Intimate Connection*, 45.

which admits that faith is engagement with God in an ongoing developing relationship. Anselm's "faith seeking understanding" is true in this context of God-image, and God-relationship maybe more than any other. I seek your face oh God—and as I seek your face I come to know you little by little. To use C. S. Lewis's revelation, we cannot know God face to face, till we have faces.[19] It is the unfolding of my self-knowledge, and my relational knowing which will lead me to intimate face-to-face relationship. It is a seeking which, in Rizzuto's phrase, "demands exquisite attention to the experience of the [person]."[20] May we each find the God who pays such exquisite attention to each one of us.

---

19. C. S. Lewis, *Till We Have Faces: A Myth Retold* (1957; reprinted, Orlando: Harcourt, 1980).

20. Rizzuto, *The Birth of the Living God*, 211.

8

Relationality—Getting to the Heart of It

A Response to Irene Alexander

JOYCE CARSWELL

INTRODUCTION

IRENE ALEXANDER'S COMPREHENSIVE PAPER reflects a growing shift towards relationality as a way of knowing, and outlines some implications for exploring God and self as gendered from this perspective, defined as the relational centre. Her paper begins with the observation that traditionally theology and most academic writers have used the "masculine" (so called) epistemology of careful exegesis and rational thought. The benefits of this approach for objective academic rigor are noted, but alongside are placed "feminine" ways of knowing as different, though arguably equally valid and valuable. As Alexander notes postmodernism has brought a revaluing of personal experience, and provided this is carefully contextualised and owned it has become part of an acceptable academic epistemology. In a similar vein Hazel Johns notes that traditionally Universities have valued a cognitive rational approach to learning, which has brought challenges for counsellor education, with its higher emphasis on self-awareness, connectedness, subjectivity, empathy and intuition.[1] This more experiential, subjective and connected way of knowing also fits a biblical framework through a narrative approach to

---

1. Hazel Johns, *Balancing Acts: Studies in Counselling Training* (London: Routledge, 1998) 5.

the text, one which brings a storied and experiential focus to knowing God, (as opposed to knowing about God) from the relational, personal and unique perspective of the engendered self.

Alexander begins by laying groundwork for ways of knowing described as masculine and feminine, before exploring the implications of this for the relational centre of exploring God and gender. A helpful distinction is made between knowing, in a relational and intimate sense, and knowing *about*. Implications of this are thoroughly unpacked, covering ways of knowing, women's ways of knowing, knowing and gender, how gendered experience consciously or not affects images of God for men and women and the relational implications of this. In response I plan to engage with her paper in expanding the idea of the relational centre as a way of knowing; knowing and relating to God, others, and self.

From both a theological and psychological perspective, we thrive in healthy life-giving relationships, and it is the breakdown of relationship that brings vulnerability, alienation, and a turning from others to the self for protection. Paradoxically, healing, reconciliation, and restoration to community also come through relationships. The way through this in both cases is a return to relationships, including facing vulnerabilities and defences, building trust and being reconciled and integrated (or *re*integrated) into community.

Relationality can function as a matrix for holding concepts from several related disciplines, such as theology, psychology, anthropology, and sociology. Self-awareness, including our awareness of spirituality, emerges in a relational process, shaping perception of self and others as we impact on and are impacted by them.

THE REVIVAL OF THE RELATIONAL PERSPECTIVE

The shift towards exploring and valuing relational ways of knowing and being may be seen, as noted, in theology and psychological theory and practice. Three relational ways of knowing related to theology are explored, followed by recent developments in counselling theory and practice.

Biblical Narrative

Biblical narratives are described by Jacob Licht as sacred history, with the purpose of mediating God's self-revelation to humanity. Licht notes the "readability" of these narratives reflecting common experience, not aesthetic theory. These are stories of everyday life, not idealised, but instead showing the ups and downs of individuals, families and communities as they relate to God and one another.[2] There are parallels here with the current market for reality TV, with its mundanity and sometimes compelling awfulness. There seems to be a long standing fascination with what people do in daily reality at both personal and social levels.

Material for biblical narrative is carefully selected and interpreted, keeping as close to the truth as possible, bringing together historical and or more mythical material, and a storytelling style of narrative. There are two functions of this selectivity, to engage with material at an emotional level, and also to state moral values, of how life is to be lived well.[3]

Such narrative is both inviting and evocative. This is demonstrated in Jesus' use of parables and metaphors, which engage the initial audience and the reader at an experiential level that can sidestep argument and defensiveness, then present a challenge, more difficult to walk away from once emotionally engaged. A further Old Testament example of this is David's encounter with the prophet Nathan, over David's' behaviour with Bathsheba as David is drawn into the story and responds emotively, only to find it is a story about him, bringing a response of repentance (2 Sam 12).

Robert Alter proposes that narrative in the Hebrew Bible be regarded as historicalized prose fiction, which accommodates anomalies and contradictions. This style is developed and nurtured in deliberate contrast against the epic genre of the surrounding pagan world, where the enactment of the epic functions as a form of sympathetic magic.[4] In contrast, Alter asserts that, "Prose narration, affording writers a remarkable range and flexibility in the means of presentation, could be utilized to liberate fictional personages from fixed choreography of timeless events and thus could transform storytelling from ritual rehearsal to the delineation of the ways and paths of human freedom, the quirks and

---

2. Jacob Licht, *Storytelling in the Bible* (Jerusalem: Magness, 1986) 9.

3. Ibid., 18–19.

4. Robert Alter, *The Art of Biblical Narrative* (New York: HarperCollins, 1981) 25.

contradictions of men and women as seen as moral agents and complex centres of motive and feeling."[5]

A narrative approach has therefore the ability to use stories of individuals and communities to carry ways of knowing at levels that resonate with the lived realties and idiosyncrasies of life, holding paradox, without having to reduce or explain this away.

The Social and Relational Trinity

Trinitarian theologian Colin Gunton contends that current thinking about the significance of persons being embedded in relational matrixes can be traced to careful exegesis of the trinitarian concept of God as three-persons-in-relationship.[6] The pursuit of a doctrine of the Trinity did not arise from abstract philosophical enquiry, but from the attempt by early church fathers to bring together three separate but related types of evidence about God: as one God, as thee persons representing God, and as the triune God, who is three persons in one.[7] Differences of understanding can be noted in the approach of western and eastern thinking around this, the former with a focus on the unity of God, and the latter with God's relational "three-ness." For the West this unity was contained in the substance of God, but for the east unity was not seen as a fixed or static "thing," but a unity existing in the dynamic relationship between Father, Son, and Spirit. The historical development of the doctrine of the Trinity continued down these two separate paths, with significant consequences for what it means to be a person. The eastern approach retained the relational focus of being as communion, with God and others; the western increasingly moving on what to Moltmann describes as an extreme individualism, where every person is a self possessed centre of action setting itself apart from other persons.[8]

In commenting on the rise of the concept of the self, Stanley Grenz notes a previous drawing away from the idea of people as connected and relational, culminating in the enlightenment with its linking of a person with reason and mastery, and on to the "triumph" of psychology over

---

5. Ibid., 25–26.

6. Colin E. Gunton, *The Promise of Trinitarian Theology* (Edinburgh: T. & T. Clarke, 1991) 23.

7. Millard J. Erickson, *Theology Today* (Grand Rapids: Baker, 1985) 322.

8. John J. O'donnell, *The Mystery of the Triune God* (London: Sheed and Ward, 1988) 105.

theology in the arrival of the self-sufficient modern therapeutic self, a self assumed to be "the arbiter and focal point of meaning, values, and even existence itself." However Grenz notes that this modern concept of self is now under attack from several quarters, including regaining the idea that humans are interdependent and connected social beings, embedded in relational matrixes.[9]

Beyond the modern concept of self Grenz identifies the postmodern self, a storied and socially constructed self, in a web of relationships, looking to these for identity.[10] As Grenz notes, a significant part of our being created in the image of God is a special enjoyment of community with God as we respond to his love. Grenz contends that this enjoyment of fellowship is not a privatised individual experience, but is intended to be a shared reality in community.[11] In summary, a social and relational approach to trinitarian theology—of God's being as a union and community of persons—parallels an understanding of persons embedded in interdependent relationships rather than as autonomous individuals.[12]

Feminist Theology

A further strand of relationality and a deep valuing of the other is found in feminist theology. Feminism emphasises that women and men are equal in dignity as human beings, and the realm of the personal and relational is highly valued. Anne Clifford asserts that feminist concerns address changes that act not just for women, but also for men, in restoring full human dignity to those affected by burdens of oppression through gender, race, or class.[13] Thus Clifford quotes Joann Wolski Conn's definition of feminism as, "Both a coordinated set of ideas and a practical plan of action, rooted in women's critical awareness of how a culture controlled in meaning and action by men, for their own advantage, oppresses women and de-humanises men."[14]

---

9. Stanley Grenz, "The Social God and the Relational Self," in *Personal identity in Theological Perspective*, edited by R. Lints, M. S. Horton, and M. R. Talbot (Grand Rapids: Eerdmans, 2006) 71–74.

10. Ibid., 77.

11. Stanley Grenz, *Created for Community*. 2nd ed. (Grand Rapids: Baker, 1996) 79.

12. Todd H. Speidall, "A Trinitarian Ontology of Persons in Society," *Scottish Journal of Theology* 47 (1994) 283.

13. Anne Clifford, *Introducing Feminist Theology* (New York: Orbis, 2001) 16.

14. Ibid., 17

In tracing the historical development of pneumatology LeRon Shults notes the contribution of women's experience. He writes "feminist theology in general is characterised by a retrieval of biblical metaphors that evoke traditional feminine imagery of connecting, nurturing, embracing and so forth ... calling all Christians towards a spiritual maturity that balances independence and vulnerability."[15]

This balancing is compared by Catherine LaCugna to the concept of *perichoresis*; that is being-in-one-another; permeation without intrusion or confusion.[16] Such relationships entail a genuine valuing and accommodation of the other. La Cugna contends that this way of approaching relationality has the potential to counteract forces destructive to genuine community, be they sexist, racist, or related to exploitation of one class of people by another.[17] Seeing people this way helps to overcome stereotyping and objectification of both individuals and groups of people. Miroslav Volf asserts that cultures and tradition (including gendered expectations and roles) are not able to be reduced to homogeneous integrated wholes; this does not do justice to the differences that exist within them, and such conflation is likely to privilege the dominant voices within communities, as other voices are lost.[18] The same point may be made for valuing different ways of knowing to bring out the richness and potential for all members of community, and their varied ways of knowing and carrying that knowing in their communities.

The Relational Turn/Return in Psychology

As with theology, similar trends can be seen in a relational turn in psychological theory and practice. In tracing the development of relational therapy Jeffrey Magnavita distinguishes five theoretical inter-related strands that have come together. These are the intersubjectivity of the dyadic relationship, by this Magnavita means an I–Thou relationship, as opposed to a distanced expert approach on the part of the therapist. The

---

15. F. LeRon Shults and Steven J. Sandage, *Transforming Spirituality* (Grand Rapids: Baker, 2006) 45.

16. This term is used of the Trinity to express a mutual containing or interpenetration, both containing and making room for, mutual movement as well as indwelling. Thomas F. Torrance, *Trinitarian Perspectives* (Edinburgh: T. & T. Clark, 1994) 141.

17. Catherine M. LaCugna, *God for Us: The Trinity and Christian Life* (San Francisco: HarperSanFrancisco, 1993) 271, 273.

18. Miroslav Volf, *Exclusion and Embrace* (Nashville: Abingdon, 1996) 208–10.

second development is that of triadic therapy, a relational systemic approach that sees the individual in a familial and interdependent matrix. The third component is the centrality of relationships in women's development, and the fourth is the therapeutic alliance, seeking to identify what the core relational skills are that enhance this. Finally, there is a shift from clinical and pathologizing ways of viewing problems to seeing these as embedded in relational contexts.[19] This is not to discount such tools as the DSM 4 (Diagnostic and Statistical Manual) but to realise that different ways of viewing people and belief structures can bring different views, and more importantly different outcomes, as family systems and cultural beliefs, including spirituality are included in information gathered, assessments made and interventions planned.

Related to this in the New Zealand context there is a need to consider indigenous models for well-being and mental health. Such models are holistic, with a rich oral tradition, including stories and metaphors, with the rich cultural nuances these carry. Such an example is the Te Whare Tapa Wha model developed by Mason Durie, and the Samoan Fonofale model. The Whare Tapa Wha model may be compared to the four walls of a house, these being Taha Wairua, with a spiritual focus, taha Hinengaro, a mental focus including communication thinking and feeling, taha Tinana, related to physical growth and development, acknowledging that mind and body are not separate entities, and taha Whanau, a focus on extended family, caring, sharing and belonging as part of relational systems. The spiritual aspect is of significance to ways of knowing, as it focuses on faith, and this being embedded in wider communion, recognising that health is "related to unseen and unspoken energies."[20] This is an embodied way of knowing.

The Samoan mental health model Fonofale has significant similarities to the above model and begins with the family as a strong foundation. This model has a roof, conveying shelter, including the metaphorical protection of the culture from outside worldviews. The house is supported by spiritual, physical, mental, and an others post, which includes gender and sexuality.[21] In outlining this model Seilosa Skipps-Patterson

---

19. Jeffrey Magnavita, "Introduction: The Growth of Relational Therapy, JCLP/In Session," *Psychotherapy in Practice* 56 (2000) 1003–4.

20. Mason Durie, Whaiora: *Maori Health Development* (Melbourne: Oxford University Press,1998) 69.

21. Seilosa Skipps-Patterson, Hawaiki-Leilei, "Journeys to Wellness," in *Penina*

acknowledges that she works best with Samoan clients when being intuitive and connected, allowing clients to bring their encultured selves and ways of knowing into the counselling room.[22]

Relational Schemas as Ways of Knowing

The significance of relational schemas in forming ideas about God is noted by Alexander. Peter C. Hill and Todd W. Hall assess the value of these in processing both one's image of God and self.[23] They note that individuals live most fundamentally in relationship, and for people of faith that relationship includes some relation to the sacred. In the Judeo-Christian context, in both the Old and New Testament concepts of both God and self are embedded in relationship and it is imperative to consider both within this relational matrix.[24] They contend, "The fundamental premise is that the self exists in relationship and that, for the religious or spiritual person, ones image of the sacred helps to ground the sense of who one is."[25] A positive correlation is proposed between the knowledge of God and the extent to which people are wanting and willing to engage with God in relationship.

Different approaches to ways of knowing privilege different sets of data for analysis. In researching concepts of God, Hill and Hall note a difference in focus between study of God as concept and God as image. Knowledge of God as concept is formed from external sources—perhaps from parents, Sunday school—ideas which cast God as an external construction, rather than as internally constructed and experienced image of God. The latter lends itself to a more relational and experiential way of knowing.[26] In a similar vein Steven Sandage notes that God images also draw on part experience and knowledge, but while God concepts are intellectual concepts of God, God images draw on more intuitive internal working models. These God images "draw on affectively loaded relational experiences and attachment processes with parents and care

Uliuli, edited by Philip Culbertson, Margaret Nelson Agee, and Cabrini 'Ofa Makasale (Honolulu: University of Hawaii Press, 2007) 137–39.

22. Ibid., 139.

23. Peter C. Hill and Todd W. Hall, "Relational Schemas in Processing One's image of God and Self," *Journal of Psychology and Christianity* 21 (2002) 365.

24. Ibid.

25. Ibid.

26. Ibid.

givers."²⁷ Sandage gives an as an example people who experience patents as distant having a tendency to project this on to God, who is then perceived as distant. The opposite would apply, of affective relationships of warmth trust and nurture being projected on to God. Whilst not fully determinative of spiritual experience, Sandage identifies a strong link between God images and spirituality.

In the context of relational counselling Stephen Paul and Geoff Pelham write that "relations between people are the basis of social and individual life and relational concepts are used to understand human life in all its complexity."²⁸ This includes the spiritual, or relationship to God, and awareness of ourselves as gendered beings, as outlined by Alexander. What does it mean to be a woman or man in any given community, including a community of faith, and what material is privileged as the main source for meaning making?

Joann Allen and Joan Laird note that

> the story of the world is HIStory. History as narrative [or story] in every culture has been created and told largely by men about men. Different cultures provide us with "both public and private stories that carry powerful prescriptions for gender role performance which will shape and constrain our lives in important ways." Stories for both women and men can serve as powerful constraints on people's identities, life choices and relational experiences. Many of the images portraying men in the media show them as "emotionally inadequate, aggressive and physical, and these images, often overdrawn, can shape our consciousness about masculinity. This can serve to reinforce the story that masculinity is defined through separateness and individuation and autonomy, and femininity through attachment and connectedness."²⁹

Such descriptions create binary distinctions that skew both men and women's development and associated ways of knowing, which are incapacitating for all concerned. Carol Gilligan proposes that traditional approaches to human development trace the development of the male

---

27. Le Ron Shults, *Transforming Spirituality*, 168–69.

28. Stephen Paul, Geoff Pelham, "A Relational Approach to Counselling," in *Integrative and Eclectic Counselling and Psychotherapy*, edited by Stephen Palmer and Ray Wolfe (London: Sage, 2000) 110.

29. Joann Allen, Joan Laird, "Men and Story: Constructing New Narratives in Therapy," in *Feminist Approaches for Men in Therapy*, edited by Michele Bograd (New York: Harrington Park, 1991) 75–86.

child, where the process of separateness and autonomy, along with logical and rational thought is seen to be the healthy norm. However adolescent girls highly value connectedness, and a more fluid and relative way of knowing, that takes relational impact into account. Such knowing has not always been valued as a strength, but as a deficit, or sign of immaturity.[30]

Adolescence is an important time linked to a sense of identity, including gender identity. Following Eriksons' stages of psychosocial development Gilligan notes the stages subsequent to stage one, (trust vs. mistrust) are seen to track the male norm.[31] As Rolf Muss notes, each item of the personality is linked to the others, and they depend on what is assumed to be the proper development and sequencing of the preceding stages.[32]

Gilligan proposes that for girls Erikson's model doesn't describe their experience. In this model boys are expected to resolve the crisis of industry vs. inferiority and move on from this secure base to finding their identity and becoming adult. This is associated with separation, autonomy, and industry, and the development of intimacy is seen to be part of the following stage, intimacy vs. isolation. However Gilligan contends that for girls the sequencing is different, pairing intimacy and identity together, in other words identity is associated with intimacy and connectedness, not separateness and autonomy.[33]

There are consequences for both genders through separateness and autonomy being upheld as the healthy norm, including repression of self-awareness that may not fit this conventional wisdom. For girls, there may be a sense of dissociation as they discount former beliefs of efficacy, and for boys a sense of disconnection from fuller ways of being in the world as interdependent. Gilligan concludes that societally defined roles assigned to males and females have a very significant impact on behaviour, but notes the difficulty of differentiation without an accompanying

---

30. Carol Gilligan, *In a Different Voice* (Cambridge: Harvard University Press, 1993) 11–14.

31. The stages being trust vs. mistrust, autonomy vs. shame and doubt, initiative vs. guilt, industry vs. inferiority, identity vs. identity confusion, intimacy vs. isolation, generativity vs. stagnation, and finally integrity vs. despair.

32. Rolf E. Muss, *Theories of Adolescence* (New York: Random House, 1988) 53–54.

33. Carol Gilligan, *In a Different Voice*, 12.

judgment of "better" or "worse."[34] There are long-term consequences for both women and men with this discounting of fuller forms of self-identity and ways of knowing. Disconnection for men may include the sometimes lonely burden of expectation to express nurture and relationality through the traditional role of primary "procreator, protector, and provider" whether he feels adequate to the task and fulfilled by it or not.[35] For women wanting to pursue academic interests in postgraduate academic circles, a sense of acceptance may also mean a sense of distancing from previous senses of self, of losing the distinctive voice associated with the relational centre that Alexander refers to. This is summed up poignantly in the following quote from research on women in post graduate theology programmes. "I remember when I was studying for my Ph.D.—I would bypass the table of women . . . to get to the table of men where I felt they were talking real stuff. And I have thought about that so many times, and I have felt ashamed, and have wished I could do that better . . . But part of coming home to myself is being able to say, I don't ever want to pass that table again. In my own experience, to bypass the table is to bypass a part of who I am."[36]

In writing about the importance of relationships, Jean Baker Miller asserts that, "it seems increasingly obvious that our societal models inevitably cannot be models of what it is to be fully human, but models of what you should be to be members of a dominant group."[37] Miller envisages a different model, not based on serving others from a subordinate position, but "in which everyone learns to participate in relationships that are growth-fostering for all the people involved, that is, mutually empathic and mutually empowering relationships . . . Growth fostering relationships have to be mutual, or, more accurately, moving toward mutuality." This is languaging that mirrors the *perichoresis* of mutual valuing, love, empathy, and reciprocity inherent in God, viewed through the lens of the social/ relational Trinity.

In defining traditional psychological and philosophical views of the self, Judith Jordan describes modern views of the self as being object

---

34. Ibid., 14.

35. Philip Culbertson, *Counseling Men*, Creative Pastoral Care and Counseling Series (Minneapolis: Fotrress, 1994) 25.

36. Nicola Hoggard Creegan and Christine D. Phol, *Living on the Boundaries* (Downers Grove, IL: InterVarsity, 2005) 77.

37. Judith V. Jordan, *Women's Growth in Diversity* (New York, Guilford, 1997) 29.

rather than subject, reified, and primarily agentic, as relatively independent, using "supplies from others to support its well being and growth." This self is described as competitive, territorial, and exercising power over others, at the expense of connectedness and community, contrasted to the self as relational, connected focusing on process, interaction, and mutual influence.[38]

The difference in emphasis may also been noted in women's academic writing and research. As an example, writing with respect to integration of psychology and theology Terri Watson et al, note there is not a significant amount of research by women, but that while women's' voices have been largely silent, change is happening gradually. Watson also examined the content of articles on integration, finding that in general women moved from praxis to theory, rather than undertaking abstract uncontextualised research.[39] This seems to relate to the more "feminine" ways of knowing and the source of the desire to know identified by Alexander.

What then is the significance for the above of the relational centre in exploring God and gender? In reviewing recent developments in psychoanalysis and of attachment theory Todd W. Hall identifies a common core of implicit relational meaning, "implicit meanings in which our spiritual stories are embedded and enacted."[40] He describes Christopher Bollas's concept of "unknown thoughts," a deep form of relational knowing that is not formed in thoughts or words. Neuroscience and research on emotions have provided support for this way of knowing. Hall writes, "There is now strong support for the idea that we are hardwired for two ways of knowing and that we are hardwired for stories." Hall defines these two types of knowing as explicit verbal knowledge that is conscious, linear, existing in images and words, and knowledge that is implicit, gut-level knowledge, "carried in our bodies, emotions and stories."[41] Hall describes the latter as implicit relational meaning, as "unthought knowing." Through storying this

---

38. Ibid., 29–30.

39. Terri Watson, Shelley, Burdine Prevost, Sally Faries, Fumi Para-Mallam, "Gender Differences in the Integration Literature; a Content Analysis of JPT and JPC by Gender and Integration Type," *Journal of Psychology and Theology* 29.1 (2001) 52–61.

40. Todd W. Hall, "Psychoanalysis, Attachment, and Spirituality, Part 11, The Spiritual Stories We Live By," in *Journal of Psychology and Theology* 35.1 (2007) 32.

41. Hall, "Psychoanalysis, Attachment, and Spirituality," 32–33.

implicit knowledge may be articulated and expressed,[42] and brought to bear on stories about self others and God.[43]

This has implication for both men and women especially those who experience dissonance between "head" and "heart" knowledge; between knowledge *about*, compared with intimate relational knowing *of* God and of gendered self. As Alexander, in drawing from a range of sources, has skilfully demonstrated, it can bring enlightenment, affirmation, and hope for change where this is sought, but it also allows for both some sense of mystery and gestation, and of emerging knowing, at implicit and explicit levels.

---

42. Ibid., 32–34.

43. The idea of unthought knowings echoes the writing of mystics of the fourteenth century, such as Julian of Norwich, and the unknown author of *The Cloud of Unknowing*. Clifton Wolters describes an enduring timelessness and reality, a longing desire and love for God, and a sense of mystery. Author unknown, *The Cloud of Unknowing*. Translated by Clifton Wolters (Middlesex, UK: Penguin, 1961) 9, 25.

9

Is There a God in This Text?

Violence, Absence, and Silence in 2 Samuel 13:1–22

Miriam Bier

INTRODUCTION

Narrative criticism has observed the superb literary artistry of the composers of biblical narrative, and identified literary techniques by which biblical narrators elicit agreement from their readers, such that the narrative perspective is considered equivalent to God's perspective. This identification of the narrative voice with the voice of God becomes problematic, however, when the governing point of view being expressed by a text is morally or theologically dubious. This chapter addresses the insidiousness of equating the voice of the narrator with the voice of God in 2 Sam 13:1–22, and suggests that to do so posits a God who is violent, absent, and silent as far as Tamar is concerned. The interplay between narrative perspective, moral judgement, and divine perspective will be explored, to conclude that ultimately, Tamar's own voice does illuminate the text, hinting at a narrator's and hence divine indictment on Amnon. Tamar is then, however, forcibly silenced and dismissed, leaving disarming ambiguity for readers trying to make sense of her tragedy.

NARRATIVE POINT OF VIEW

The impression conveyed by the text of biblical narrative, by a combination of rhetorical factors, is that the narrator "presents not just his own human point of view but the point of view of the Lord."¹ As an initial definition, point of view is "the position or perspective from which a story is told." In literary theory various facets of point of view have been delineated.² Berlin distinguishes between the "perceptual" point of view (determined by which character is viewing events); the "conceptual" point of view (the attitudes, conceptions, and worldview being expressed); and the "interest" point of view (determined by which character is benefiting from the outcome of the story).³ Berlin's conceptual point of view is similar to Upensky's ideological level—the "point of view according to which the events of the narrative are evaluated or judged"⁴—and to Powell's evaluative point of view—the "norms, values, and general worldview that the implied author establishes as operative for the story."⁵

In biblical narrative, it is the narrator who expresses and communicates the governing conceptual, ideological, or evaluative point of view.⁶ This is the perspective that is transmitted to readers and guides their interpretation of events.⁷ Accordingly, the narrator's point of view is considered to represent God's, such that "the narrator tells the story from God's point of view *because he is a spokesman for God*."⁸ The narrator's voice is thus seen as the "voice of the one and indivisible truth,"⁹ the voice of God Godself.

This becomes a problem, however, when reading those stories that seem, from the narrator's perspective, to permit and perpetuate violence

1. Sidney Greidanus, *The Modern Preacher and the Ancient Text: Interpreting and Preaching Biblical Literature* (Grand Rapids: Eerdmans, 1988) 207. Berlin, sensibly, is not quite so convinced, allowing only that "one often *gets the impression* that the narrator is reflecting the way God would evaluate events if he had been the one telling the story." Adele Berlin, *Poetics and Interpretation of Biblical Narrative*, Bible and Literature Series 9 (Sheffield: Almond, 1983) 148 n. 28, emphasis mine.

2. Berlin, *Poetics*, 46.

3. Ibid., 46.

4. Ibid., 55.

5. Mark Allan Powell, *What is Narrative Criticism?*, Guides to Biblical Scholarship (Minneapolis: Fortress, 1990) 24. These three terms—conceptual, ideological, evaluative—will hereafter be used interchangeably.

6. Berlin, *Poetics*, 55.

7. Tremper Longman III, *Literary Approaches to Biblical Interpretation*, Foundations of Contemporary Interpretation 3 (Grand Rapids: Zondervan, 1987) 88.

8. Greidanus, *The Modern Preacher*, 207, emphasis mine.

9. Meir Sternberg, *The Poetics of Biblical Narrative*, Indiana Literary Biblical Series (Bloomington: Indiana University Press, 1985) 128.

toward women. The Hebrew Bible contains stories that do not just *record*; but in fact appear to *condone* violence against women in order to advance the stories of their male lead characters. That is to say, while there is clearly a narrative indictment of the violence against Tamar, and a clear negative evaluation of that violence, it remains that this violence stands, predominantly unchallenged and unproblematized, in the biblical text; and ultimately serves a male-driven plot. Do these narrative perspectives necessarily represent God's point of view? What effect does adhering to the narrative perspective and equating this with the voice of God have on women (and sympathetic others) reading the Bible?

The story of the brutal, politically motivated rape of Tamar by her brother Amnon in 2 Sam 13:1–22 is one such story. Equating the voice of the narrator with the voice of God in this episode raises disturbing questions for twenty-first century female readers. In this narrative Tamar is violated by one brother who rapes her, another who uses this rape as a political opportunity, and a father who, while not exactly complicit, keeps silent when it counts.

Further violence is perpetrated by the (presumably male) narrator's use of Tamar's story to serve the greater narrative, and by generations of male interpreters who have seen significance in Tamar's story only insofar as it advances the plotlines of her father's and brothers' stories. In 2 Sam 13:1–22 the interest point of view revolves around the male characters, and the conceptual point of view allows for a woman to be the object of violence in order to see the outworking of God's providence in the greater narrative. But what about Tamar? Is this her story at all? And, even more disquieting, where is God in all this? Silent? Absent? Even violent?

CONTEXTS

According to the narrative perspective, Tamar's story appears as an episode in the lives of her father David, and her brothers, Absalom, and Amnon. To what extent does Tamar's story play a part in these male stories?

Tamar's story is David's story. In the canonical context 2 Sam 9–20 and 1 Kgs 1–2 trace the unravelling fortunes of David's court.[10] Tamar's

---

10. J. P. Fokkelman, *Reading Biblical Narrative: An Introductory Guide*, translated by Ineke Smit (Louisville: Westminster John Knox, 1999) 139.

story appears closely after the account of David and Bathsheba (2 Sam 11–12) and is thus understood to comprise part of the disaster wrought on David's family as punishment for his adultery (2 Sam 12:7–12).[11] Read in this context, it looks as though Tamar is "scandalously incidental to the story."[12] Does Tamar's experience contribute merely "to the outworking of his wrongdoing and (even more horrifyingly) to the achievement of Yahweh's purpose" in punishing David?[13]

Tamar's story is also Absalom's story. Within the immediate context of 2 Samuel, chapters 13–19 trace Absalom's escalating rebellion and attempts to gain power.[14] In the very next episode (2 Sam 13:23–39) Absalom will use Tamar's rape to justify killing Amnon, thereby removing the major competition for the throne.[15] Indeed, Brueggemann contends that the story *only* makes sense in the context of Absalom's revolt, and may be considered a "prologue to the account of Absalom's rebellion."[16] In addition to its significance for David's story, Tamar's story is therefore "a component of Absalom's history."[17] Is Tamar's story thus included in the narrative for "the primary purpose of justifying Absalom's later murder of Amnon"?[18]

---

11. Burke O. Long, "Wounded Beginnings: David and Two Sons," in *Images of Man and God* (Sheffield: Almond, 1981) 26–34; Shimon Bar-Efrat, *Narrative Art in the Bible*, translated by Dorothea Shefer-Vanson, JSOTSup 70 (Sheffield: Almond, 1989) 282; Yairah Amit, *Reading Biblical Narratives: Literary Criticism and the Hebrew Bible*, translated by Yael Latan (Minneapolis: Fortress, 2004) 127; William H. Propp, "Kinship in 2 Samuel 13," *CBQ* 55 (1993) 39–53. Keefe eloquently argues that these consequences for David's family are also to be read as consequences for the nation Israel, with Tamar's rape symbolic of the deterioration within the established order of the royal family and thus the nation, Alice A. Keefe, "Rapes of Women/Wars of Men," *Semeia* 61 (1993) 79–97.

12. John Goldingay, *Men Behaving Badly* (Carlisle, UK: Paternoster, 2000) 257.

13. Ibid., 257.

14. A. A. Anderson, *2 Samuel*, WBC 11 (Dallas: Word, 1989) 286; Fokkelman, *Nar-rative Art*, 101; with this as the prologue, Walter Brueggemann, *First and Second Samuel*, Interpretation (Louisville: Westminster John Knox, 1990) 172. According to Brueggemann, this entire sorry story can only make sense in the context of Absalom's revolt; Brueggemann, *First and Second Samuel*, 176.

15. Long, "Wounded Beginnings," 30.

16. Brueggemann, *First and Second Samuel*, 172.

17. Fokkelman, *Narrative Art*, 101.

18. Pamela Cooper-White, *The Cry of Tamar: Violence against Women and the Church's Response* (Minneapolis: Fortress, 1995) 5; Eryl W. Davies, *The Dissenting Reader: Feminist Approaches to the Hebrew Bible* (Burlington, VT: Ashgate, 2003) 59.

And Tamar's story is Amnon's story. Amnon seeks to humiliate Absalom by humiliating his sister Tamar, as part of his own bid for the throne.[19] According to this view, the rape of Tamar is politically motivated, demonstrating the extent to which Tamar is merely a pawn in the power play between her brothers. The narrative does make clear, however, that committing this outrage disqualifies Amnon from the throne.[20] He receives his just desserts in the outworking of chapter 13. But although it is clear that the narrator does not approve of Amnon's actions, the story is still cast as a story about *him*. Does Tamar's violation only feature then, in order to demonstrate how Amnon's attempts at "self-assertion over against Absalom and his family" will ultimately lead to his own downfall?[21]

All these contexts are drawn together in the wider struggle for succession that moves to its conclusion 1 Kings 2.[22] The reason for including *this* story in chapter 13, according to male readings, is to "explain the reason for the power struggle which subsequently ensued between the male members of the family."[23] But what about Tamar? What is *her* story?

TAMAR'S STORY?

At the beginning of 2 Sam 13 four characters are identified by name and the scene is set, "David's son Absalom had a beautiful sister whose name was Tamar; and David's son Amnon fell in love with her" (13:1). From the outset Tamar is placed between Amnon and Absalom in the very structure of the verse. This indicates the way in which she becomes a source of conflict between them, and situates her story in the context of *their* stories.[24] Note that while Amnon and Absalom are qualified as

---

19. Brueggemann, *First and Second Samuel*, 171. From a biblical point of view, rape is considered a violation of a man's (usually husband or father) sexual property, Sandie Gravett, "Reading "Rape" in the Hebrew Bible: A Consideration of Language." *JSOT* 28.3 (2004) 279–99; cf. Propp, "Kinship in 2 Samuel 13," 41. Amnon's motivation for the rape could thus have included a political power play to make Absalom a "whore's brother," Amit, *Reading Biblical Narratives*, 128. This fits with the designation of Tamar as Absalom's sister—i.e. his sexual property—rather than as David's daughter, as his.

20. Mark Gray, "Amnon: A Chip Off the Old Block? Rhetorical Strategy in 2 Samuel 13.7–15." *JSOT* 77 (1993) 39–54.

21. Brueggemann, *First and Second Samuel*, 177.

22. Ibid., 172.

23. Davies, *Dissenting Reader*, 59.

24. Phyllis Trible, *Texts of Terror: Literary-Feminist Readings of Biblical Narratives*, OBT (Philadelphia: Fortress, 1984) 38.

sons of David, Tamar's designation is not "daughter of David" but rather "sister of Absalom," a step removed from the king.[25]

The narrative then turns and follows Amnon, who is said to love Tamar so much that "he made himself ill," because he was unable to "do anything to her" (13:2).[26] He and his crafty friend devise a scheme that will enable Amnon to be alone with her, for which purpose readers are not yet told. Amnon will pretend to be ill. When the king, his father, comes to see him he will request that his sister Tamar be sent to make some food for him, to sustain him during his illness (13:3–6). Everything goes according to plan. David is duped and Tamar is duly sent to her brother's house, ostensibly to "prepare food for him" (13:7). Tamar is to this point depicted as none other than willing sister, dutiful daughter and innocent assistant. Note too, that by now Absalom, introduced as a main character in the first verse, has disappeared from the story and Amnon has become the major protagonist.

When Tamar arrives, as bidden, at Amnon's house, the narrative lingers and all eyes are on her as the process of preparing, baking and serving bread are described in minute detail. Tamar is in Amnon's "sight," a common motif throughout the narrative, and "voyeurism prevails" as the readers, too, have their gaze fixed on Tamar (13:8).[27] Tension builds as details, requests, responses and repetitions delay the climax of the story and increase the building tension in the narrative.[28]

Finally, Amnon is alone with Tamar and his intentions toward her become clear. He commands her "come lie with me, my sister" (13:11). Tamar now takes centre stage, refusing Amnon and making her objection loud and clear.[29] With an articulate and intelligent argument she appeals to social and moral custom "in Israel," to her own "disgrace," and to his shame as a "wicked fool" in order to try and prevent him from forcing

---

25. Cooper-White, *The Cry of Tamar*, 5. It is also Absalom who will later avenge her, rather than David, Bar-Efrat, *Narrative Art*, 241.

26. There is a clue that something is odd: what exactly might Amnon want to "do" to "his sister"? The narrative thus builds suspicion and suspense.

27. Trible, *Texts of Terror*, 43.

28. Charles Conroy, *Absalom Absalom!* Analecta Biblica 81 (Rome: Pontifical Biblical Institute Press, 1978) 21.

29. Cf. the other two major rape cases in the Hebrew Bible, Dinah (Gen 34) and the unnamed woman (Judg 19).

her to "lie" with him (13:12).³⁰ She then reasons that the king would allow him to have her if he only went about it properly (13:12).³¹

Tamar protests, however, to no avail. In a series of quick actions Amnon "refused to listen to her, and since he was stronger than she, he raped her" (13:14).³² It then becomes apparent that his "love" was no love at all. His lust now satisfied, he can no longer stand the sight of her and commands her to "Get out!" (13:15). Tamar is, however, not so easily dismissed. She refuses to leave, reminding Amnon that he is now obliged to marry her to prevent her from suffering further shame (13:16; cf. Deut 22:28–29).³³ As a virgin she had been a commodity, but she will be condemned to a life of disgrace if he sends her away.³⁴ In her eyes, so

---

30. Davies, *Dissenting Reader,* 58. "wicked thing"(נבלה, *nblh*) is also translated "senselessness" or "disgraceful folly" and has the sense of a "disruption of and violation against the order of community life" (Keefe, "Rapes of Women," 82).

31. Esther Fuchs, *Sexual Politics in the Biblical Narrative: Reading the Hebrew Bible as a Woman,* JSOTSup 310 (Sheffield: Sheffield, 2000) 212. The legitimacy of this claim has been questioned. Elsewhere marriage between half siblings is forbidden by law (Lev 18.9; 20:17; Deut 27:22). Was Tamar just buying time, giving a "panicked catalogue of reasons for Amnon to desist?" Robert Alter, *The Art of Biblical Narrative* (New York: Basic Books, 1981) 73. Or perhaps custom and law were two different things—if the king himself had broken the rules for his own sexual gratification, he would hardly withhold it from his son. Conroy argues convincingly that the "prohibition of marriage between brother and half-sister was not recognized in the urban setting of Jerusalem in David's time." Conroy, *Absalom Absalom!,* 18 n. 3, On the basis that this text comes from a later standpoint than that of the Decalogue; cf., Gen 20:12. Goldingay also suggests that "there is indeed little indication that the Torah ever shaped Israel's life in practice." Goldingay, *Men Behaving Badly,* 260. Bar-Efrat points out that Tamar does not appeal to a prohibition of incest in her argument, suggesting the crime is not a violation of her as sister but of her as a woman. Bar-Efrat, *Narrative Art,* 264; cf. Fokkelman, *Narrative Art,* 103. Propp notes the ambiguity—Tamar claims it would be permissible to marry but the narrative's constant use of brother/sister language, suggests something seriously wrong in the brother/sister relationship. Propp, "Kinship in 2 Samuel 13," 42; cf. McCarter, who claims the brother/sister language indicates incest, P. Kyle McCarter, *II Samuel,* AB 9 (Garden City: Doubleday, 1984) 328.

32. TNIV. The verbs used in the Hebrew leave no doubt that this is rape. The Piel ענה (*'nh*) is traditionally rendered "humbled" but the fact that Amnon had to use his strength to overcome Tamar (חזק *ḥzq*) in order to forcibly lie with her (שכב *škb*) defines the act as rape, Gravett, "Reading 'Rape,'" 280; Keefe, "Rapes of Women," 82. Anderson notes further that ענה (*'nh*) indicates an act of power of strong over weak, Anderson, *2 Samuel,* 287.

33. Propp, "Kinship in 2 Samuel 13," 42.

34. Cooper-White, *Cry of Tamar,* 8.

the narrator tells us, throwing her out would be far worse than raping her to start with.[35]

And again, Amnon does not listen. Tamar is forcibly removed from Amnon's house and his violence is complete (13:17–18). Not only has he physically and emotionally assaulted Tamar, she is now to be socially ostracised as well.[36] Tamar has ceased to be a sister or even a person in his sight. She is merely an object to be discarded.[37]

Tamar laments her shame openly until her brother Absalom reappears in the narrative, offering shallow words of consolation and cautioning her to say nothing because "he is your brother." After his absence from the narrative, Tamar is now taken in to her brother Absalom's house where she remains "a desolate woman" (13:19–20). Tamar's plight does not go unnoticed by the king, but David, although "furious," does, and says, nothing (13:21).[38]

SILENCE

Instead of responding and dealing with such gross violence and injustice within his own family, King David is now, ironically, impotent. He speaks out neither on Tamar's behalf nor against Amnon's despicable actions. Anderson makes the astute observation that David is "so compromised by his own past action he can do nothing."[39] David is silent: Is God also silent?

Biblical narrators seldom give overt value judgements or opinions about characters in the biblical texts.[40] However, this "rarity of explicit judgements by the narrator should not obscure the fact that a good nar-

---

35. Brueggemann, *First and Second Samuel*, 175.

36. Keefe, "Rapes of Women," 91.

37. Bar-Efrat, *Narrative Art*, 266; Davies, *Dissenting Reader*, 60; Long, "Wounded Beginnings," 28.

38. Fuchs, *Sexual Politics*, 220; cf., Dinah—Jacob, her father, also does nothing (Gen 34). LXX fills in the detail that he took no action against Amnon because he was the beloved firstborn. Bar-Efrat, *Narrative Art*, 273. A more subversive reading questions whether David is furious because of what had been done to Tamar, or because of the "violation and devaluation of his (sexual) property." Cooper-White, *Cry of Tamar*, 8; cf., Davies, *Dissenting Reader*, ?.

39. Anderson, *2 Samuel*, 289.

40. Bar-Efrat, *Narrative Art*, 277. In 2 Sam 13:1–22 there is in fact have some direct description of characters: Tamar is "beautiful" and Jonadab is "crafty," Fokkelman, *Biblical Narrative*, 151–52.

rative can convey a very definite attitude without making explicit statements at all."[41] Moral evaluations of characters may be inferred from characters' words and from their actions. Narrators may convey their own evaluative stance to readers through the characters' direct speech and by the use of emotive words when describing their actions.[42]

Consequently, although this narrative may not contain explicit moralising, "the pleading of Tamar is a more effective judgement" on Amnon than any editorial comment.[43] The narrator's choice of verbs at the climax, along with Tamar's own words, *do* judge Amnon's actions and clearly depict him in a negative light.[44] In this way "the narrator really conveys his judgement on what happened."[45] Tamar's words thus "function literarily as a massive indictment of Amnon."[46] Through Tamar's own voice, the narrator expresses an evaluative view of Amnon such that the reader now has an "indisputably negative" view of him.[47] Tamar's plea in verses 12–13 presents the narrator's evaluation that Amnon is indeed a "scoundrel."

Again, the moral position of the narrator can be drawn from the text through Tamar's claim after the rape in verse 16 that rejecting her after violating her is "worse and more reprehensible than the rape itself."[48] It was earlier noted that in biblical narrative the narrator is, rightly or wrongly, understood to speak for God, representing the divine point of view. In 2 Sam 13, if the narrator's moral standpoint is expressed through Tamar's own words, could it be that her words also voice *God's* judgement on the matter?

Unlike her counterparts (Dinah and the unnamed woman in Judg 19) Tamar *is* given a brief platform from which to voice her reproach.

---

41. Conroy, *Absalom Absalom!*, 23 n.16.

42. Bar-Efrat, *Narrative Art*, 34, 41.

43. Brueggemann, *First and Second Samuel*, 177; Conroy, *Absalom Absalom!*, 23 n. 16.

44. Bar-Efrat, *Narrative Art*, 277.

45. Conroy, *Absalom Absalom!*, 24.

46. Anderson, *2 Samuel*, 287.

47. Bar-Efrat, *Narrative Art*, 264.

48. In accordance with Deut 22:28–29, a rapist is obligated to marry the victim and thus ensure her security and status in society, Bar-Efrat, *Narrative Art*, 267. Davies astutely notes that Tamar's appeal to this convention reveals the extent of her powerlessness in a patriarchal society—she is forced to appeal to a law that ultimately protects the interests of men, Davies, *Dissenting Reader*, 59.

As Cooper-White observes, "Tamar is possibly the only rape victim in Scripture to have a voice."[49] With this awareness of narrative technique, it is clear the narrator's sympathies lie with Tamar.[50] Readers are accustomed to, consciously or unconsciously, submitting to the narrator's biases and consequently readers too are drawn to sympathise with Tamar. She has been presented only in a positive light, beautiful (13:1), an obedient daughter (13:8), a dutiful sister (13:10) with a clear moral position (13:12–13). The narrator elicits sympathy for Tamar as her grief (13:19) and desolation (13:20) are undeserved.[51] But to what effect? Conroy maintains that in this narrative, "the outstanding point here is the way in which the reader's sympathies are alienated from Amnon and gained for Tamar (*and therefore for Absalom*)."[52] Could it be that all this sympathy garnered by the narrator serves to elicit sympathy not only for Tamar, but ultimately for Absalom? Once her complaint has been voiced and silenced, Tamar is subsumed by Absalom, living in his house with no further voice or action of her own, while the narrative continues telling *his* story.

ABSENCE

Absalom is named at the beginning of the narrative, suggesting that he will be a key player in the ensuing drama as it unfolds. Curiously, however, after the initial introduction, Absalom does not act in the story until verse 20, where he reappears as the consoling elder brother who will go on to enact vengeance on Tamar's behalf.[53] In the central section of the narrative, when Tamar is at her most vulnerable, Absalom is nowhere to be found. Absalom is absent: Is God?

It is, perhaps, significant that while God *is* frequently a character in Hebrew narrative, God is *not* a character in *this* story. Although there is often an implicit acknowledgement that God is in the background of every biblical account, in this narrative the "presence of God is ambigu-

---

49. Cooper-White, *Cry of Tamar*, 3.
50. Brueggemann, *First and Second Samuel*, 177.
51. Conroy, *Absalom Absalom!*, 23.
52. Ibid., 23; emphasis mine.
53. I am suspicious of Absalom's motive here. He may be consoling, but his words read as Goldingay rightly designates, "spectacularly useless male advice." Goldingay, *Men Behaving Badly*, 268.

ously rendered and thus not easily identified."[54] Indeed, Fuchs points out that in contrast to the preceding and subsequent narratives, the character of Yahweh is entirely absent from 2 Sam 13:1–22. This absence of the character God allows the text to "underplay God's absence from the represented events."[55] Fuchs further contends that "any reference to God in these contexts is likely to elicit the question why God has not intervened on behalf of the raped woman, either as redeemer or as avenger."[56]

But is God really absent from this story? Jürgen Moltmann's *Theology of Hope* proposes that in the crucified and resurrected Christ, God reveals Godself as a God who "suffers with."[57] Is it too much of a stretch to suggest that God is *not* absent from 2 Sam 13, but is present as the God who "suffers with" Tamar? Is it valid to read Tamar's story retroactively and see, in Jesus crucified, a God who identifies with Tamar as the object of violence? Is this fair to the text, which, although Christian Scripture, also stands independently as *Jewish* scripture?

Christian biblical interpretation has been criticised for tritely imposing christological frameworks on such difficult texts, and for uncritically subjecting all suffering to the cross. Phyllis Trible asserts that "to subordinate the suffering of ... women to the cross is spurious ... to seek the redemption of these stories in the resurrection is perverse."[58] Yet if Christ is indeed the central figure of our faith, is it not appropriate to search the Scriptures, even those of the Hebrew Bible and find episodes where "women, not men, are suffering servants and Christ figures"?[59] I suggest that Christians can *only* begin to make sense of the violence suffered by individuals in the Hebrew bible when they read with the (admittedly anachronistic) knowledge that God is a God who "suffers with."[60]

But this reading too, is problematic. The context of 2 Sam 13 suggests that the rape of Tamar is part of the outworking of God's punish-

54. Gray, "A Chip off the Old Block," 52.

55. Fuchs, *Sexual Politics*, 222.

56. Ibid., 222.

57. Jürgen Moltmann, *Theology of Hope*, translated by James W. Leitch (London: SCM, 1967).

58. Trible, *Texts of Terror*, 2.

59. Ibid.

60. This does not, however, solve the difficulty of God's apparent absence during Tamar's plight for Jewish readers.

ment of David for his adultery with Bathsheba (2 Sam 12:10–11). If God is the *agent* of this punishment, and God is *with* Tamar as she bears the brunt of this punishment, there is therein a great paradox. The God who is providentially working out punishment in the life of David works violence against the God who "suffers with" Tamar. How can it be that God works violence against God? This same criticism is levelled at traditional transactional models of the atonement, that see the need for God to work divine violence on Jesus on the cross, and this is a difficulty that will not easily be resolved.

Perhaps the absence of God as a character from the narrative at this point removes God from complicity in the episode. Alternatively, a Christian reading might attempt to read in Tamar's story the presence of a God who "suffers with" her. Could this reading, however, further perpetuate violence against Tamar by seeking the redemption of her story in the cross, when for Tamar herself, there was no resurrection?

VIOLENCE

Amnon is violent towards his sister Tamar, using her to satisfy his own lust, and then rejecting her. There is no doubt that the narrative perspective works to "lay a heavy charge against Amnon."[61] There is, from the narrator's perspective "no doubt as to his culpability."[62] Throughout the text Amnon is "unambiguously characterised as a sly, corrupt, and ruthless character."[63] Readers leave the narrative feeling an intense antipathy toward Amnon. Amnon is violent. Is God?

In the context of succession to the throne, the narrator allows Tamar to be abused in order to advance the plot. Is God complicit in this use of violence against Tamar? The narrative perspective will not excuse readers from concluding that the events of 2 Samuel are the outworking of God's purposes in punishing David, and of God's providence in excluding candidates from succession to the throne.[64] The violence this works against an innocent daughter and sister begs the question: where is "this same God of providence for *Tamar?*"[65]

---

61. Amit, *Reading Biblical Narratives*, 130.
62. Davies, *Dissenting Reader*, 58.
63. Fuchs, *Sexual Politics*, 202.
64. Cooper-White, *Cry of Tamar*, 14.
65. Ibid.

Gray is right to ask how long "a holy God of justice (can) insinuate God's self in the machinations of a regime plunging headlong to squalid immorality in all its varied private and public forms?"[66] And indeed, God does appear to be implicated here. The repeated use of violence against God's children throughout history leads the Jewish scholar David Blumenthal to conclude that "God, as portrayed by our holy scriptures and as experienced by humans throughout the ages, acts, from time to time, in a manner that is so unjust that it can only be characterised by the term 'abusive.'"[67] In 2 Sam 13:1–22 it is a woman who experiences this abuse such that from the narrative point of view "this God of the children of Israel seems transfixed by his chosen 'son'(s), oblivious to his chosen 'daughters.'"[68] Does this text thus posit a God who is at most ambivalent, and at worst abusive, as far as women are concerned?

CONCLUSION

The narrator of 2 Sam 13:1–22 draws the reader into the text to the extent that Tamar's rape is "not merely a narrative fact, a device of the plot, but an experience of woman's pain shared intimately with the reader."[69] As a woman, I cannot help putting myself in the picture with Tamar. As a feminist, I rage against the injustice perpetrated against her by Amnon, Absalom, David, and generations of (male) interpreters who have valued her story only so far as it advances the plot of the stories of her father and brothers. As far as Tamar is concerned, it certainly looks as if God may be violent, absent, and silent. Is there a God in this text, or do we indeed have the fearful prospect of divine "silence, absence and opposition" as far as women are concerned?[70] Tamar's voice, though strong, is quickly subdued. David is silent. Absalom is absent. Amnon is violent. Where is God?

---

66. Gray, "A Chip off the Old Block?" 53.

67. David R. Blumenthal, *Facing the Abusing God: A Theology of Protest* (Louisville: Westminster John Knox, 1993) 247 and passim.

68. Gunn and Fewell, *Narrative in the Hebrew Bible*, 88.

69. Keefe, "Rapes of Women," 92.

70. Trible, *Texts of Terror*, 2.

10

In Whose Interests Do We Read?

A Response to Miriam Bier

Tim Meadowcroft

Miriam Bier begins with a scenario familiar to many readers of these contributions—the assumption that the Bible is the word of God in that God caused it to be written in the form in which it has been received. She ends by asking of the particular text in question—2 Sam 13:1–22 on the rape of Tamar—"Where is God?" This is not a question that one might expect to have to ask of a text which God has supposedly caused to be written. Yet it emerges under Bier's treatment as a perfectly fair question. And it is a question that for her could not be more acutely personal, impinging as it does on both her own faith commitments and her sense of solidarity with her gender.

She chooses not to answer her own question, and I do not plan to be enticed by Bier's silence on God's silence into doing so either. Instead, I will highlight various angles of inquiry that are raised by her experience of the narrative of the rape of Tamar. I will do so under the following heads: sociological, political, literary, hermeneutical and theological. As I do so, I find myself retuning again and again to the question, in whose interests do we read?

SOCIOLOGICAL

Under this heading, by means of a personal illustration I make a preliminary comment on one aspect of the dynamic that underlies this enquiry. Over the years I have noticed in myself a refreshing sense of freedom when doing exegesis with Catholic readers of Scripture. Such readers seem to me to be able to critique, wonder, and worry about the text, remarkably free of concerns about respecting the interests of the text. This is in stark contrast to the evangelical protestant context in which I do most of my reading, wherein there is a simmering anxiety as to the consequences of reading badly or untruly.

I have wondered about the irony that I feel more freedom in my treatment of the text in a Catholic context than in my protestant evangelical one. I suspect this is because I have a particular view of the unique nature of the authority of Scripture that places constraints on what I may say about the text. For my Catholic colleagues, authority is differently conceived, and so there is freedom at least in the matter of reading Scripture.

And the nature of this freedom and constraint is a sociological one, in that the question of authority is closely related to the question of belonging. If I critique the authoritative text too strongly, my belonging within my interpreting community is quickly called into question because I am questioning the very thing that holds the community together. And I want to belong. Again, for my Catholic colleagues, questioning Scripture does not so readily entail the matter of belonging, for the authority that holds the interpreting community together is not in question.[1] For somebody such as Bier, torn between dissatisfaction with aspects of the text and commitment to a way of reading and regarding that text, the challenge is not merely a theoretical one, nor does it only or primarily relate to the individual quest for intellectual or spiritual integrity (although her quest is that). It entails the more visceral matter of her (and my) belonging or not to a particular interpreting community. This is one aspect of the interest that is brought to the story of the rape of Tamar.

POLITICAL

It is not the only aspect of Bier's interest, but it does highlight that all readings are personal and hence, to a greater or lesser extent, interested. In that sense the process of reading is inevitably "political" in that it has to do with the interactions of the various interests that readers bring to

---

1. There are local and particular nuances that I am ignoring, and I am conscious of the idea of the magisterium. But I express what has been my observation and experience.

the text. This phenomenon is primarily illustrated in this treatment by the interest of gender. There are other aspects of the politics of reading the rape of Tamar, or any other biblical text for that matter, that might emerge, but in Bier's treatment gender is paramount.[2] This is the case partly as a result of the subject matter, as it is a story acutely about relationships between the sexes. It is also the case in the nature of the concerns of the particular reader to whom I am responding, for Bier brings questions to this particular text that are most likely to have been posed by a woman. It would not have occurred to me to worry about Tamar after the event in the way that Bier worries about her. Of course, I deeply regret what happens to Tamar while it is happening and I think that the men of the story are churls and I would try not to behave in the same way if my father were a king with many wives who between them had produced many half-siblings. But then I move on with the plot and immerse myself in the important masculine matter of the Davidic succession, forgetting completely about Tamar as I do so.

In this connection, Bier makes an important observation that could have been made more of but only appears parenthetically, "according to male readings." This aside alerts me to the fact that the various attempts at ameliorating the silence of God, as referenced by Bier, are male ones. These male attempts may also be rejected by other male commentators, but it is Phyllis Trible's voice to which Bier turns to express her own sense of the "perversity" of the situation. It is Trible who allows Bier to "rage against the injustice perpetrated" on Tamar by the other male characters and, possibly, by the narrator and even God.

And yet this intensely interested involvement with the story by Bier has another side to it, for she, as well as "raging" about Tamar, is also "desperate to find a redemptive element" in the text. As well as her gendered interests, Bier brings to her reading an interest in the integrity of the text, and perhaps also the integrity of God, and this too must be satisfied somehow, but as yet has not been.

LITERARY

Despite that, Bier does hint at some subversion in her own reading. Notwithstanding her *angst* at the fact that God appears to be absent

---

2. For a provocatively counter-intuitive example of reading similar texts out of a different interest see John E. Goldingay, *Men Behaving Badly* (Carlisle, UK: Paternoster, 2000).

and silent in the face of Tamar's suffering, she "contends that Tamar's own voice illuminates the text." This is the case in a limited sense. As possibly the only rape victim in Scripture to have this much of a voice, Tamar admonishes Amnon. And her personal qualities are presented in a uniformly positive fashion. Tamar is not alone in being a woman who subverts her patriarchal surrounds. Rebekah's performance in Gen 24 suggests her rather than Isaac as the inheritor and purveyor of blessing in the line of the patriarchs (Gen 24:60). Esther ironically takes more and more control of a king who has just banished her predecessor for being insufficiently submissive. Naomi and Ruth leverage their limited assets, albeit in an unorthodox fashion, to take control of their circumstances and ensure the eventual birth of Obed and all that would flow from that.

Even so, Bier knows that the subversion of Tamar still leaves her with a problem. In fact, I would suggest, two problems, both arising from the interested nature of her reading. The first is that it is not always the case that a woman in the narrative is able to subvert. The concubine of Judg 19 has no voice. The daughter of Jephthah is granted a brief, one might almost say a compassionate, reprieve, but is fundamentally a victim (Judg 11:34–40). Dinah's perception of the nature of her encounter with Shechem is not considered as her brothers wreak their terrible revenge (Gen 34). Where are the voices of these women? This is precisely what is reflected in Bier's anguished final sentence.

This leads into the second problem, which is that Bier's objections arise from reading beyond the story itself. Were Bier able to confine herself to the discrete pericope, she could relax knowing that Tamar is vindicated by the narrative perspective of the story itself, in that the narrator expects us to notice that Absalom and Amnon and David are indubitably cads. But she reads in the context of the wider succession narrative, and in the wider reading she discovers that Tamar is merely a tool in the apparently more significant question of who should succeed David. The heart of Bier's objection, as I read it, is not the fate of Tamar but the subservience of Tamar's story to a wider patriarchal agenda. The aggrieving silence of God is not so much silence as acquiescence in another voice.

HERMENEUTICAL

And this is where the matter gets interesting (using the word in its technical sense), because the problem is that Bier's interests and the interests of the narrative have diverged. I suggest that is the heart of her objection to the story. Bier wants to see an affirmation of the interests of women in the text, and a concern for their well-being; the wider text apparently does not. There are two aspects to her objection, I think. The first is that if the text is seen to be concerned about particular women in its stories, then it may be presumed to be concerned about other women, including the women who read the text. The reader longs to find herself in the story, but at moments like the rape of Tamar, she experiences only terror, as Phyllis Trible has so ably discerned.[3]

The second aspect is that the perspective of the text is presumed by Bier to express the perspective of God. There are different ways of articulating the mechanics and theology of this, and there are differing levels of awareness on the part of readers about how this dynamic between God and the text may work, and for most it is at the level of unexamined assumption, but for a believing reader somewhere and somehow the question of God in the text will be informing the reading.[4] Therefore if the interests of the reader do not seem to cohere with the interests of the text, then the interests of the reader perhaps also do not cohere with the interests of God. For a person whose religious quest is to know the mind and heart of God, this too is a "land of terror."[5] The very revelatory instrument that is supposed to draw the believer forward in her quest, the Scriptures, instead repels and diverts.

The first aspect outlined above relates to the question of whose interests should prevail when there appears to be a clash of interest in reading, such as is illustrated by Bier's response to the Tamar story. In this case the interests of the narrative within which the encounter be-

---

3. Phyllis Trible, *Texts of Terror: Literary-Feminist Readings of Biblical Narratives*, OBT 13 (Philadelphia: Fortress, 1984).

4. R. Walter L. Moberly, *The Bible, Theology, and Faith, A Study of Abraham and Jesus* CSCD 5 (Cambridge: Cambridge University Press, 2000) 45, refers to this as "the question of God in and through Scripture."

5. Trible, *Texts of Terror*, 5. Mary Daly, *Beyond God the Father: Toward a Philosophy of Women's Liberation* (Boston: Beacon, 1973), is a sustained evocation of that terror. For a more measured description of the feminist dilemma, see Phyllis A. Bird, *Missing Persons and Mistaken Identities: Women and Gender in Ancient Israel*, OBT (Minneapolis: Fortress, 1997) 248–54.

tween Tamar and Amnon is set are repugnant to the reader; it is felt that the expression of priorities by the narrative is in some way deficient or unworthy. But who says that is the case? Who decides whose priorities should prevail? Is it possible that, by insisting on the interests of the reader, we have shut the door to the possibility that Scripture may challenge or guide?

When Scripture is read from the point of view of religious commitment, it is assumed in some sense to be a "revelatory text."[6] Therefore it is a text that may contradict or challenge, and a text whose interests demand our attention. Is it possible that Bier is being asked to submit her own interests to those of the text, even at points where that is most uncomfortable? Or is it mistaken to think of the text as a monolithic entity in this way? Perhaps it is rather a chorus of voices, some of which are out of tune and need to be discerned as such.[7] Others, however, draw us into the chorus, even at points where we would rather remain outside.

If this is valid, then it also confronts a related complication, that the clash of interest that drives Bier's response to 2 Sam 13:1–22 is not only a clash between the text and the reader; it is also a clash of interests within the soul of the reader herself. But it is not simply the case that one interest is worthy and one is unworthy. Bier brings two interests to her reading, each arguably as valid and important as the other. She has an interest, strongly expressed, in the integrity and usefulness of the biblical text, and at the same time she has an understandable interest in justice and a place to stand for her gender. If the two are to find a way of working together, then the different voices must be distinguished somehow.

One way to advance this is the sledgehammer approach; to simply smash one of the interested parties and take one of two options. The first is to insist on the importance of the question of succession in 2 Samuel, silencing the voices of those who want to read and speak on behalf of the women in that story and other stories. This approach is cautious of an ideological reading of Scripture.[8]

---

6. The phrase in the title of S. M. Schneiders, *The Revelatory Text: Interpreting the New Testament as Sacred Scripture* (Collegeville, MN: Liturgical, 1999).

7. Using a different metaphor entirely, Brueggemann proposes in a similar direction when he speaks of the "counter testimony" of Scripture. See W. Brueggemann, "The Hiddenness of Yahweh," in *Theology of the Old Testament: Testimony, Dispute, Advocacy* (Minneapolis: Fortress, 1997) 333–58.

8. David J. A. Clines, *Interested Parties: The Ideology of Writers and Readers of the Hebrew Bible* GCT 1 (Sheffield: Sheffield Academic, 1995) 23–25, identifies ideology

The second option has two manifestations. The first is a monolithic rejection of the authority or importance of the biblical text *per se*. If we no longer have to worry about defending the text then we have declared that the reader's interest is paramount and that of the text may be ignored. This is one of the feminist responses to the patriarchy of Scripture.[9]

The second manifestation is more subtle, and addresses not the matter of the text in all its time and culture-boundedness, but the reliability of the text. Does the narrator express a reliable perspective on events that he or she is relating, and, furthermore, can the perspective of the narrator, reliable or not, be broadly taken to be that of God? The first part of that question is a literary matter, and it is generally agreed amongst readers of the biblical text from a literary perspective that the narrator of the biblical is reliable in the technical sense. Where the narrator is not to be trusted, this is normally clearly signalled.[10] There does not seem much headway to be made in contesting the literary point.

But how about the second part of the question? Philip Davies has articulated the possibility that the God who owns the narrative, or is at least conveyed in it, may not be trusted.[11] If Davies is right, Bier's problems have been solved, for she can simply reject the silent absent God of her narrative and move on to construct a scenario in which the victimization of Tamar receives a just response. If Davies is not right, then God,

---

with interest, whereas I am here distinguishing the two. For me, ideology implies a predetermined need for Scripture to speak in a particular way, while interest entails whatever it is that a reader brings to his or her reading of Scripture. One may lead to the other but they are not quite the same thing.

9. This is the position that Mary Daly appears to have come to in *Beyond God the Father*, to the extent that the authority or otherwise of Scripture does not receive a mention. This is a move beyond the position taken in her earlier *The Church and the Second Sex* (London: Chapman, 1968), wherein she still acknowledges that "The equal dignity and rights of all human beings as persons is of the essence of the Christian message. In the writings of Paul himself there are anticipations of a development toward realization of the full implications of this equality" (p. 32). At this stage the problem is still the church's interpretation of Paul rather than Paul per se.

10. Note for instance the case of Dan 4 where Nebuchadnezzar takes over the narration.

11. P. R. Davies, *Whose Bible is it Anyway?* JSOTSup 204 (Sheffield: Sheffield Academic, 1995) 113, concludes from the story of the near sacrifice of Isaac that, "The story says to them: do not trust a deity. He or she or it almost certainly does not trust you, and has no reason to tell the truth." Moberly, *Bible, Theology, and Faith*, 170-83, responds to Davies' highly suspicious reading of the story.

along with the narrative that expresses God, remains a problem. Either way, at the end of hermeneutics we are left with the question of God.

THEOLOGICAL

This raises the possibility that we are being asked to read and interpret the text in the light of God. After all, as Goldingay has so exhaustively and convincingly demonstrated, the Bible is the story of God, understanding that genitive construction as both subjective and objective.[12] It is a story about God and it is a story by God.[13] It is a story that must be read theologically. In that respect, it is heartening to see the recent interest in the theological reading of Scripture, and the spate of treatments of that approach.[14] Each commentator brings his or her own emphasis on theological reading, but they have in common the recognition that Scripture must be read in the light of what God is like. Several subsequent moves are necessary to pull this off.[15] The first is to recognize a necessary conceptual distinction, however expressed or understood, between the literary artefact that is the text and the word of God that comes by reading the text. The second is to make a further distinction between the particularity of the text and the truth towards which the text points. In other words, the text bears the limitations of its humanity but the God of the text does not. And a third move is to suppose that, notwithstanding its particularly, the text shows us enough of God for us to be able to hear when the story itself strikes discordant notes within God's story.[16] For the Christian reader the culmination of the story is the word made flesh

---

12. John E. Goldingay, *Old Testament Theology: Volume One: Israel's Gospel* (Downers Grove, IL: InterVarsity, 2003).

13. See T. J. Meadowcroft, "Method and Old Testament Theology: Barr, Brueggemann, and Goldingay Considered," *TynB* 57 (2006) 52–53.

14. I think for example of Moberly, *The Bible, Theology, and Faith*; F. Watson, *Text, Church and World: Biblical Interpretation in Theological Perspective* (Edinburgh: T. & T. Clark, 1994); C. R. Seitz, *Word Without End: The Old Testament as Abiding Theological Witness* (Waco, TX: Baylor University Press, 2004); and the recent advent of the *Journal of Theological Interpretation*.

15. A theology of reading Scripture, for which my brief comments cry out, is well beyond the brief of this response.

16. While her comments are perhaps more hermeneutical than theological, E. F. Davis, "Critical Traditioning: Seeking an Inner Biblical Hermeneutic," in *The Art of Reading Scripture*, edited by E. F. Davis and R. B. Hays (Grand Rapids: Eerdmans, 2003) 163–80, explores this possibility around the proposition that "no biblical text may be safely repudiated as a potential source of edification for the church" (164).

in the person of Jesus, and so all such readings inevitably become in some sense or other christological.[17]

For a reader such as Bier (and me), these distinctions are enormously risky. Much can go wrong on the human side of the encounter with God in God's story. It would be much easier if the Scriptures could simply be asserted as the full and final agent of revelation, rather than as merely "revelatory," to appropriate the terminology used by Schneiders. Nevertheless, it does seem to me that we have no choice but to take the risk,[18] because of the incarnation of God in Christ.[19] God becomes known to humanity by participating in the human experience, not by issuing propositions as a *deus ex machina*.

This is foreshadowed by the nature of the text of the Hebrew Bible, which constantly holds together the paradox that God both authors the story and functions as a character alongside other characters in God's own story. God's participation is evocatively expressed in the first book of the canon: "God [walked] in the garden at the time of the evening breeze" (Gen 3:8). For the Christian this dynamic reaches its culmination in the person of Jesus, in whom God took on all that it means to be human. And so Bier is entitled to be enraged by the rape of Tamar because she knows enough of God to know that God is also enraged, even though God appears to have other things on God's mind at this moment.

However, this brings us back to the matter of interest. For, even in so reading we also know enough of God to know that our reading interests and the interests of God may diverge at certain points, for in Scripture we meet a God who is occasionally inscrutable. Jesus comes to bring not peace but a sword (Matt 10:34); he asks us to sell all that we have and give to the poor (Luke 18:22); he calls for us to hate our nearest and dearest (Luke 14:26). We are accomplished at interpreting our way around these difficult sayings or "texts of terror," yet our interpretive competence

---

17. This is expressed in almost as many ways as there are interpreters. See for example the varied approaches in M. A. Rae, J. E. Goldingay, C. J. H. Wright, R. W. Wall, and K. Greene-McCreight, "Christ in/and the Old Testament," *JTI* 2 (2008) 1–22.

18. Schneiders, *Revelatory Text*, 186–97, in a reading of John 4:1–42 illustrates the risk and possibility of approaches "employed by feminist biblical scholars in the effort to liberate the text from its own and its interpreters' ideological bias and women from the oppressive effects of that bias" (183).

19. For further, see T. J. Meadowcroft, "Between Authorial Intent and Indeterminacy: The Incarnation as an Invitation to Human-Divine Discourse," *SJT* 58 (2005) 199–218.

does not finally answer the charge that sometimes the interests of God do not coincide with the interests of the reader, and the rationale for God's perspective remains inscrutable. Sometimes we are driven at the end of a long disheartening process, like Job, to acknowledge, "I have uttered what I did not understand, things too wonderful for me, which I did not know" (Job 42:3).

Perhaps Bier is right that God is unaccountably silent and absent during the rape of Tamar. And perhaps that is because sometimes God is unaccountably silent and absent.

11

Being Masculine in My Disabled Male Body

S. J. Immanuel Koks

SHOULD I FEEL INFERIOR because most women are physically stronger than I? Should I be wrecked with guilt because I may not be able to provide for my family the way other men my age can as I do not have the same earning potential? I must answer yes, if I accept the complementarian mindset, believing men and women, though equal, have different roles based on their sex.[1] On the other hand, should I be apologetic that, due to my disability, I am unable to job share in many areas of home life that have traditionally been considered feminine roles? I must if I adopt radical[2] egalitarianism, which is that there should be no distinction between the roles men and women adopt. This leaves me just as guilt-ridden as the woman in my life would have to adopt some traditional roles. In what follows I show that a biblically-based model of masculinity frees me from this guilt.

I consider two prevalent traits in contemporary complementarian literature about masculinity being a warrior and being the head[3] of a household. I find them lacking for three reasons. First, they are scriptur-

---

1. John G. Stackhouse, *Finally Feminist: A Pragmatic Christian Understanding of Gender*. Acadia Studies in Bible and Theology (Grand Rapids: Baker Academic, 2005) 19.

2. I have added the word "radical," because there are egalitarians who do not wish to iron out all the natural distinctions between people (especially between the sexes), they simply do not want those distinctions to remain grounds for discrimination. I sit in this more moderate egalitarianism. See ibid., 17–18.

3. Usually interpreted as leader and provider.

ally unsustainable. Second, they do not embrace the need to live authentically as individuals in community. Third, they contribute to the societal barriers for men with disabilities. Instead of seeking scriptural ways to separate masculine roles from feminine roles, I simply ask, what would it look like for me to refrain from being a warrior and seeking to be the leading head, and yet remain true to scripture?

A key concept of the debate around gender is sex-role theory. This argues that depending on the sex of an individual they will take on different roles. In the case of men, they are providers, protectors, strong and athletic.[4] Women take on complementary (hence the word complementarian) roles of home makers, soft-spoken, dependant, and passive.[5] Critics have correctly noted that not all individuals fit these moulds.[6] This is especially true for disabled men who may be unable to fulfil the traditional masculine roles. Thus sex-theory must be rejected. However I do not go as far as Landau who argues that men and women should share the same roles in the home and the workplace.[7] She asserts that wives should not work part-time in order to support home and children while husbands work fulltime, rather both should have equal opportunities to pursue careers.[8] However her solution is itself an external ideal, which takes no thought for the individuals involved.

Rather than attempting to construct an alternate set of roles for disabled men, which invariably isolates some men when they are unable to perform those roles, I argue that masculinity arises out of living authentically as a male individual in community. Roles must be negotiated from a position of authentic living, not social constructs. I remain egalitarian because I do not hold that sex itself dictates different roles (even if they are complementary) or that roles should privilege men above women.[9] However traditional roles are not bad, in and of themselves. Conversely I do not judge negatively the adoption of non-traditional

4. Mary Stewart Van Leeuwen, *After Eden: Facing the Challenge of Gender Reconciliation* (Grand Rapids: Eerdmans, 1993) 226.

5. Ibid.

6. Ibid., 227. Critics have also correctly noted that while the rhetoric of equality may be found in the sex-theory, invariably the women's roles have been deemed inferior to men's roles. Van Leeuwen, *After Eden*, 228.

7. Reva Landau, "On Making 'Choices,'" *Feminist Issues* 12.2 (1992) 47–72.

8. Ibid.

9. Though I realise that my western culture still has a long way to go before this is fully realised.

roles. Whatever roles one adopts they must be authentic, reflecting a true sense of personal identity in relationship with others, rather than an attempt to meet a societal role.

To live authentically is to live in the paradox of autonomy and relationship. We are unique individuals, yet the biblical statement "it is not good for man to be alone" (Gen 2:18) remains true. As the first account of creation records, we were created in the image of God. Adam and Eve were different people, called to reach out over the boundaries of those differences and embrace each other in relationship (Gen 1:27).[10] The sense of one and many reminds us of the triune God, whose image we bear; three persons who have their own identities, Father, Son, and Holy Spirit, who are completely united in relationship. This image in us has been marred by the fall. The result is a deeply unauthentic life. We are unable to realise our individual potential as we remain hamstrung by sin, and those we love often bear the brunt of our sins and we get hurt by theirs. Paul the Apostle shows that in Christ[11] we are new creations (2 Cor 5:17). We see true authentic living modelled in the incarnate Christ. So authenticity means imitating and living in Christ, who, through the power of the Spirit, enables us to become who we are created to be as unique individuals living in rich relationship with others.[12]

MY EXPERIENCE OF MASCULINITY

My childhood, teenage and young adult experiences of masculinity where mixed. My father modelled many traditional masculine traits. However, due to the divorce of my parents and his alcoholism, he was often absent. My stepfather appears bound by the traditional roles he has been exposed to in his church involvement, but these do not sit comfortably with him. My mother, on the other hand, is a natural leader, but also cognitively adheres to complementation roles. My church during much

---

10. In his "Drama of Embrace" Volf shows that embrace involves holding the other in their difference while maintaining one's own difference. Miroslav Volf, *Exclusion and Embrace: A Theological Exploration of Identity, Otherness, and Reconciliation* (Nashville: Abingdon, 1996) 141–45.

11. This is not the forum for a robust explanation of the mystical union which believers have with Christ.

12. This paragraph is a syntheses of thinking which draws heavily on Christopher J. H. Wright, *The Mission of God: Unlocking the Bible's Grand Narrative* (Downers Grove, IL: InterVarsity, 2006), 421–34; and D. M. Ackermann, "Becoming Fully Human," *Journal of Theology for Southern Africa* 102 (1998) 13–27.

of my life has been fiercely patriarchal, with women only allowed a small role in the worship music or flowers at church.

As a boy with Cerebral Palsy I could not participate in the rough and tumble games my brother, peers, and youth group were involved with. As is normal for children, many did not reach out to me on the sidelines. So I struggled with feelings of rejection and aloneness. I had an adventurous spirit, and in my teenage years went through a "cowboy stage"[13] to use Eldredge's terminology. I had many opportunities to test my physical strength at outdoor camps or on my recumbent tricycle. I was able to give expression to some of my mechanical interests by developing recumbent tricycles.

Gerschick and Miller describe three strategies their research participants use when engaging with society's masculine norms:[14] reliance—adoption of the norm, often in a "hypersensitive" manner; reformulation—redefinition of societal norms in one's own terms; rejection—renunciation of societal norms and even masculinity, or at least a personal construction of masculinity.

So in many respects I still relied on societal norms, though I did reformulate them in some ways. In this chapter I reject societal norms as they are imposed on men with disabilities. The key here is the imposition of norms. I find that some norms, while in a redefined form, sit comfortably with me. For example, I find expression of my adventurous streak, in the adventure of following God's lead in my life though I do not know what form that will take, or pushing myself academically.

MUST I BE A FIGHTER?

Bly, Moore, Gillette, and Eldredge insist that there is a warrior dimension to masculinity. Citing the way war defines history, Moore and Gillette argue that warriorhood is an integral part of who we are as men.[15] Biblically, they argue that David was a mighty warrior and that the Hebrews were a

---

13. John Eldredge, *The Way of the Wild Heart* (Nashville: Nelson, 2006).

14. Thomas J. Gerschick and Adam Stephen Miller, "Coming to Terms," in *Men's Health and Illness: Gender, Power, and the Body*, edited by Donald F. Sabo, David Gordon (Thousand Oaks, CA: Sage, 1995) 187.

15. Robert L. Moore and Douglas Gillette, *King, Warrior, Magician, Lover: Rediscovering the Archetypes of the Mature Masculine* (San Francisco: HarperSanFrancisco, 1990) 76–77.

warrior people, following a warrior God.[16] As we are in God's Image we should imitate him in this.

Eldredge says that God is a warrior, citing the song Israel and Moses sung after God's defeat of the Egyptian Army (Exod 15:3).[17] He also cites Jeremiah and Isaiah as they refer to God as a warrior.[18] Then he argues that Israel's passivity meant spending forty years wandering in the wilderness, when they should have gone on the offensive and taken the Promised Land.[19] He argues that the fall was caused in part by Adam's failure to stop Eve.[20] To cement his position even further, he argues that Jesus acted as a warrior, when he made a whip and drove the money changers out of the temple (John 2:13–17).[21]

The problem with this line of argument is that it fails to ask: is God's primary identity that of warrior, or is his wrath a response that is invoked by a sin? The story of Scripture and humanity is better conceived of as the story of God's desire to restore peace. In it we find God seeking shalom—the restoration of wholeness.[22]

Aggression is said by all of these authors to be central to Warriorhood. Make no mistake disabled men can be aggressive. Eddie, one of Tom Shakespeare's subjects, explains how he acted aggressively when he was at school:

> I was involved in a lot of fights outside school, although I would never fight a disabled person. A lot of people took the piss out of me, and my brothers had taught me from an early age about fighting. I was in a position where people would take the piss out of me and I would fight back . . . I gave people good hidings! It wasn't a problem that I was in a wheelchair, in fact it was an advantage. I couldn't do anything, and then they would come closer, and then

---

16. Ibid., 78.
17. Eldredge, *The Way*, 139.
18. Ibid., 140.
19. Ibid., 144.
20. Ibid., 145.
21. Ibid., 140.
22. G. Lloyd Carr, " šālēm," in *Theological Wordbook of the Old Testament*, edited by Robert Laird Harris and Gleason Leonard Archer (Chicago: Moody, 1999). Wholeness is not simply the absence of ailment or impairment; rather it is the ability to grow towards ones potential in all aspects of one's life (physical, social, emotional, intellectual and spiritual.) see John Sturt and Agnes Sturt, *Created to Be Whole: Becoming the Person You Were Meant to Be* (Guildford, UK: Eagle, 1998) 15.

> I would smack them in. I would put myself into a position where I knew someone would attack me, and then I would hit them, and feel justified in hitting them.[23]

But is aggression really what God desires of men? Is aggression a legitimate part of Christian masculinity, regardless of whether the man has a disability or not? In the Genesis story the penalty for disobeying God, and eating from the tree of the knowledge of good and evil, was said to be death (Gen 2:17.) Cain's slaughter of Abel arose out of a sinful heart. The messianic age prophesied by Isaiah is characterised by the absence of war. In the New Heavens and New Earth I find the absence of death and sin (Rev 21:4, 8.) War will have no part in it. This leads me to question the very notion that masculinity and aggression are inextricably linked. It is contradictory to believe that the fullness of humanity is seen with the absence of war, and yet believe that to be masculine requires me to be aggressive.

What these authors fail to account for is that aggression without God often failed. Consider the incursion into the Promised Land after God had told Israel they would have to wait forty years. It was a dismal failure (Num 14:37). Contrast this with the victories the people had under Joshua when God was with them (e.g., Josh 11:16–23). Consider the cowardice of the people when confronted by Goliath, when compared to David's courage. What made the difference? David was doing his fighting in the strength of the Lord, not his own strength. It is clear that aggression outside the will of God was always doomed.[24]

The theme continues in the New Testament, when Paul, referring to the Love of Christ, says, "Who will separate us from the love of Christ? Will hardship, or distress, or persecution, or famine, or nakedness, or peril, or sword? . . . No, in all these things we are more than conquerors through him who loved us' (Rom 8:35,37). In another place, after recounting times of blessing and times of trial in the name of Christ, Paul says, "I can do all things through him who strengthens me" (Phil 4:13). The theme is the same—strength to face my battles is not found within me but in God.

---

23. T. Shakespeare, "The Sexual Politics of Disabled Masculinity," *Sexuality and Disability* 17.1 (1999) 53–62.

24. I don't claim to understand why God chose to use such aggressive tactics in the Old Testament. Nor do I wish to imply that he may use his people today in aggressive manners.

Also problematic is the link between physical prowess, warriorhood and masculinity. Moore and Gillette say, "Warrior energy is concerned with skill, power, accuracy, and with control, both inner and outer, psychological and physical."[25] Yet as a disabled man, I find myself lacking in many of these areas, especially physically. I am not alone. Many of Shakespeare's respondents also struggle with the notions that masculinity demands strength.[26] Respondent Jeremy has rejected this notion, but articulated where his lack of strength has an effect on him, in everyday life.

> Because my disability means that most women are stronger than me, like when it comes to opening a train door, so I would like to think I am not as sexist as an able-bodied man is, because if, like, I couldn't open a bottle, I would get who ever [sic] was with me, a woman or male friend to do it. So the strength thing doesn't relate to me; most women are stronger than me. I never actually thought about the masculinity thing, it's never to come into it, because I just assume that most people are stronger than me anyway.[27]

Discipleship, however, lets me express the positive aspects of warriorhood, even in my disabled body. Like a warrior, a disciple can have a transcendent cause. I am empowered by God's Spirit to bring and proclaim the gospel (Matt 28:18–20). I must be passionate for my cause and, like a warrior, be willing to undergo hardship for it. Verses such as Matt 5:11 and the book of Acts, reveal that Christian discipleship is a life of struggle at times. Like a warrior, I must be aware of my frailty[28] and surrender my life to Christ and not seek its preservation (Luke 8:35). Disciples, like warriors are discerning,[29] and assess situations quickly and clearly.[30] A theme in the book of Proverbs is the necessity of discernment, the ability to read life and the world around us.

The cause of the kingdom is not furthered by aggression. N. T. Wright brings out that in Christ's time there were three mindsets about

---

25. Moore and Gillette, *King, Warrior, Magician, Lover*, 83.
26. Shakespeare, "Sexual Politics of Disabled Masculinity," 60.
27. Ibid.
28. Moore and Gillette, *King, Warrior, Magician, Lover*, 82.
29. Ibid., 80.
30. Ibid., 83.

the establishment of the kingdom of God.[31] The first was to remove yourself from the world in the hope that the kingdom would be established through your isolated community, as the Qumran community did.[32] This was not the model of Jesus. He sent his disciples into a world that hated and persecuted them, just as it had hated and persecuted him (John 17:18, 15:18–25), however he promised to be with them (Matt 28:20). Pharisees worked a second way, seeking to bring the kingdom by collaborating with, and appeasing, the establishment in the hope that this would create an environment of peace.[33] But the example of the apostles was to be so passionate for the gospel that no one could make them stop proclaiming it. The more the authorities said stop, the more powerful the proclamation became.[34] Zealots, promoted a third way, armed uprising against the Romans.[35] Yet Jesus condemned even anger, let alone outright violence against an enemy (Matt 5:21–26). Instead Jesus told the disciples to turn the other check, to go the extra mile, and to pray for their enemies (Matt 5:38–48).

The events in the Middle East in the last few years,[36] in Northern Ireland[37] during the last century, and in much of western history, show that the kingdom of God is not advanced when mixed with military combat. The kingdom is advanced by passionate men and women who are strengthened by the Spirit living in them and who are totally committed disciples of Jesus.

Can we adequately reshape warriorhood into discipleship? A possible critique may be the frequent use of militaristic language to talk about the disciple's life as they challenge the powers of Satan.[38] Arnold correctly argues that we are living between two ages: "the present evil age" and "the age to come/kingdom of God."[39] He also makes clear that

---

31. Which the Jews of Jesus day interpreted as liberation from Rome.

32. N. T. Wright, *The Challenge of Jesus: Rediscovering Who Jesus Was and Is* (Downers Grove, IL: InterVarsity, 1999) 37.

33. Ibid.

34. E.g., Acts 5:40–42, 6:8—7:53 (story of Stephen), Acts 12:1–17.

35. Wright, *Challenge of Jesus*, 37.

36. Bush and Blair both claimed that they felt led into the war in Iraq by God.

37. Catholic and Protestants fighting over land.

38. See Clinton E. Arnold, *3 Crucial Questions About Spiritual Warfare* (Grand Rapids: Baker, 1997) 22–23.

39. Ibid., 20–21.

victory is ours because we are in Christ.[40] He goes on to argue that because the two ages are in conflict, we must engage in spiritual warfare.[41] Again he has a point, however the question is, Should our self-identity be as a warrior?

Because the victory of God has not been fully applied as it will be after Christ's return, we who are in Christ sometimes must assertively engage with the malevolent forces of sin and darkness that still seek to exert rule over this earth and our lives. However, this is only possible, not because we possess prowess as a "spiritual warrior," but because we are united with Christ. Through the power of the Spirit which is mediated to those in Christ, we find strength to engage, not from ourselves but from God. Because we are in Christ we can participate in the victory he won on the cross. We are not fighting to establish a victory;[42] we are merely following Christ as he furthers his reign on the earth through us. The apostles assertively pursued the advance of the gospel and exercised the authority Christ gave them before he left. However while they acknowledged the battles they faced, they did not take on the identity of warriors. They were followers of "the way" (Acts 19:9, 23). That is, followers of Jesus. They were disciples not warriors.

Pursuing the kingdom requires discipleship not warriorhood. As a disciple I can doggedly pursue the kingdom, just as a warrior pursues what they believe to be right. As a disciple I risk everything, including my life (Luke 9:24), just as a warrior must risk theirs. As a disciple I must work hard to conform my life to Christ's,[43] in the same way a warrior must be disciplined. The disciple's life has few certainties, but just like a warrior's life, adventure is a given. However, I need not feel less of a man because I lack the physical strength of a warrior. Discipleship demands inner strength and fortitude. Warriorhood always involves destruction and only sometimes leads to a tense cessation of hostilities. Discipleship involves constructing a better life in Christ, and always leads to shalom. A disciple's life is not characterised by passionless passivity. A true dis-

---

40. Ibid., 24.
41. Ibid., 22–23.
42. Arnold agrees Christ is the source of our strength and victory see Ibid., 40.
43. I am not saying we do this on our own, or that our works somehow supersede the gracious work Jesus does in us. What I am saying is that it does take effort to yield to that inner working.

ciple's life displays a determined intentionality, given vibrancy by the Holy Spirit.

LIVING IN A LOVING RELATIONSHIP WITH A WOMAN

Promise Keeper Stu Weber writes, "Men must develop a thorough, biblical, manly love. Now what is that? In a word, headship. It is leadership with an emphasis upon responsibility, duty, and sacrifice. Not rank or domination."[44] But was this kind of leadership really what Paul was talking about when he called men the head?

To start, consider 1 Cor 11:2–16.[45] Note first, this passage is about the way men and women should look during gatherings of the *ecclesia*. Fee correctly points out that it is difficult to argue that Paul is referring to leadership within the marriage, when the context is not about authority, but relationship.[46] The second thing to note is that the Greek society functioned by maintaining honor and shaming those who would threaten that honor.[47] The way a woman looked in this society reflected on her husband[48] and was a matter of much concern.[49] It is also clear from verse 6 that Paul did not want any unnecessary shame brought to women, through culturally inappropriate appearances.[50] Paul offers

---

44. Stu Weber, *Tender Warrior* (Sisters, OR: Multnoma, 1993) 97.

45. In this Passage the word γυνή is translated both "woman" and "wife" depending on the way the translators felt the context was leading. The Greek can mean both. The same situation is true for ἀνήρ which is translated "man" and "husband." See Richard B. Hays, *First Corinthians*. Interpretation (Louisville: Westminster John Knox, 1997) 185. In this paper I adopt a consistent translation throughout, that is "woman" not "wife," and "man" not "husband." As it would apply to equally to singles who were as well as married people who were active members of the community, which is something Paul is in favour of (see 1 Cor 7:32–35).

46. Gordon D. Fee, *The First Epistle to the Corinthians*, NICNT (Grand Rapids: Eerdmans, 1987) 502.

47. Mark Strom, *Reframing Paul: Conversations in Grace & Community* (Downers Grove, IL: InterVarsity, 2000) 67.

48. Sarah B. Pomeroy, *Goddesses, Whores, Wives, and Slaves: Women in Classical Antiquity* (New York: Schocken, 1995) 182–83. As cited in Anthony C. Thiselton, *The First Epistle to the Corinthians: A Commentary on the Greek Text* (Grand Rapids: Eerdmans, 2003) 802. Hays says it reflected on all the men in the congregation, see Hays, *First Corinthians*, 185.

49. Raymond F. Collins, *First Corinthians*, SacPag 7 (Collegeville, MN: Liturgical, 1999) 396.

50. Thiselton, *First Epistle to the Corinthians*, 828.

guidance on how women can express concern to male believers who are close to them. He also requires that men have the same regard for their sisters in Christ. To cement the need for mutual care in the way one appears, Paul says that both men and women are dependent on each other (verses 11–12).

Malphurs insists that Paul upholds "the created order of things" in 1 Cor 11:7–9 [51] where men were given the leadership role.[52] However, he fails to discuss the fact that men's leadership over woman[53] was part of the curse God proclaimed on Adam and Eve (Gen 3:16.) In the first account of creation, Adam and Eve were created together, and together given dominion over creation (Gen 1:27–28). In the second account, Eve was created from Adam, after Adam could not find an equal partner[54] in the animal kingdom (Gen 2:19–22). Adam was not looking for someone to lead, but rather he wanted a companion, someone to be alongside him, an equal to help him in his tasks. Any notion that Adam was given the leadership over his wife role from creation, is reading this presupposition into the text.

Having established that neither the creation, nor this passage, demands that we understand the husband's role as exercising authority over their wives, how do we understand Paul's use of "head" in verses 3–5? One approach has been to resolve the controversy about the word, *kephale*— "head." Traditionally, it has been understood in terms of leadership and authority.[55] Recently it has been argued that the word means source.[56] However, if Paul's metaphor of head was the locus of honor or shame then this line of argument does not lead much further.

Paul wants the Corinthians to understand the parallels between the divine relationship between the Father and the Son, and our human relationships. The question is, does this correspond to a hierarchy,

---

51. Aubrey Malphurs, *Biblical Manhood and Womanhood* (Grand Rapids: Kregel, 1996) 42.

52. Ibid., 42–44.

53. Leadership is a God given skill which men and women both posses—to one degree or another depending on the individual—and can exercise towards the other gender. The issue here is not leadership as much as the assertion that, because of their gender, men must lead their wives.

54. The Hebrew *'ēzĕr* means *helper*, it does not denote any sense of following while the other leads. Indeed God is called a *'ēzĕr* in Deut 33:29.

55. Thiselton, *First Epistle to the Corinthians*, 812.

56. Ibid., 814.

as Malphurs argues? God, then Christ, then men, and lastly women.[57] Malphurs then insists that women should submit to men in everything, regardless of whether the men are righteous or not.[58]

There are two reasons why this view is unsustainable. First, the context itself is about not shaming others. I consider a far more likely scenario to be that the women are realising their liberation in Christ, and are intent on exercising it.[59] Paul is simply saying, don't forget the relationship you have with others. Don't forget the way that, due to societal norms, your actions can reflect negatively on them.

The second has to do with the relationship between the Father and the Son. Theologically we run into trouble if we insist that God exerts authority over the Son. This is sub-ordination, which is shown to be false in verses such as Phil 2:6, where we see that the Son is equal to God in his divinity though he divested himself of it in his incarnation.

Is there another way of understanding headship? Consider who Christ is. He is the Son of God. He reveals the Father to us. He is our savior, saving us so we can enter into relationship with God. He is the Lamb of God. He is the suffering servant of God. While not denying the distinctiveness of the Son, he is who he is because so much of his identity derives from his relationship with the Father. Christ was always intentional in passing the glory and honor to his Father in what he said and did. In the same way, as a Christian man, I must be deliberate in giving Christ the glory and honour in my words and actions. Therefore the man's headship of women in this context means that woman should give honor to men, through their actions. Why? Because part of her identity lies in her relationship with men.

The concept need not feed patriarchy when understood in the light of several realities for Paul. First, the patriarchal society he lived in meant that when a wife's appearance, in a worship service, dishonored her husband it *socially* dishonored him. Second, the mutual need and dependence man and woman have for each other (verses 8–9, 11–12) radically upended the social order that declared a woman the possession of the husband. Third, Stackhouse correctly identifies that Paul was pragmatic.

---

57. Malphurs, *Biblical Manhood and Womanhood*, 132.

58. Ibid., 133.

59. Gordon D. Fee, "Gender Issues: Reflections on the Perspective of the Apostle Paul," in *Christian Perspectives on Gender, Sexuality, and Community*, edited by Maxine Hancock (Vancouver: Regent College, 2003), 66.

He saw the spread of the gospel as paramount,[60] and regarded public shaming of men as hampering the spread of the gospel. The pragmatism meant he phrased this passage to solve the immediate problem, of men being shamed, rather than address and ideal of mutual honor. Fourth, only a few paragraphs later Paul expounds the idea of giving honour to those considered least honourable (1 Cor 12:22–26). Fifth and perhaps most importantly, for Paul, being in Christ meant there was no gender distinction (Gal 4:26–28). If he believed that the men and women were new creations in Christ, why then would he demand that they maintain a relationship that is not based upon their new found equality?

Let's consider Eph 5:21–33 which talks about headship within a marriage. Note carefully that this section on marriage is predicated on the concept of mutual submission.[61] Both the husband and the wife are called to submit to each other.

Paul wanted to explain marital relationships in terms of the metaphor of Christ and the church. Here Christ loved the church so much he gave his life for her. He did this so that he could present the church to himself in splendor, without a spot or wrinkle or anything of the kind—yes, so that she may be holy and without blemish (Eph 5:27). The effect of this remodelling of the people who make up the church is that they come into their true identity in him, they become fully restored. This is of incalculable value to them. The church, however, has to yield to this process, which can at times be painful and difficult. It must submit to him.

This closely parallels a husband's role. He has to love his wife, with a love that extends to being willing to give his life for her. He is told to imitate Christ in nourishing and caring for his wife. What will be the effect of this nourishment and care? She will blossom and grow. This will be of mutual benefit. If she rejects that care, she will not grow. Thus submission in this context is not about power, but a willingness to grow.[62]

---

60. Stackhouse, *Finally Feminist*, 42.

61. There is some debate whether Paul started a new thought in verse 21 or 22. Reading the passage in context, it appears that Paul changes the thought between 20 and 21 because he moves from discussing the celebration of the Spirit's work in verses 18–20 to submission in 21ff. In addition, verse 22 lacks a verb, this must be borrowed from verse 21, linking the two together. See Robert G. Bratcher, *A Handbook on Paul's Letter to the Ephesians* (London: United Bible Society, 1982) 139.

62. To be clear, the submission is not so much to the husband will, but to the painful process of making the sacrifices required for growth.

A practical example of this may be a wife who has had a dream and a gift to write. However, to maintain a certain lifestyle, she considers not returning to University to complete a Masters in creative writing. As an empowering head, the husband might encourage his wife to return complete the qualification. They both understand that this would mean a drop in their standard of living for a period, but agree this is the best thing for her to do. In this context submission may mean accepting and enduring the next few years of a lower income, which could involve a period of painful adjustment for both of them.

What then, in this context, does the concept of head mean? It is one who does whatever he can to facilitate the growth of the other. It is one who enables full expression of the identity and brilliance[63] of the other. This is consistent with Paul's other use of the head/body metaphor in Eph 4. Being in the body, of which Christ was the head, enables each person to express their individual gifting. The effect of this expression is to build the body (verse 12), to unify the church (verse 13), to enable each member of the church to mature (verse 14) and to grow up into Christ (verse 15) who is the head. When the church is functioning well it will enable us to be who we really are in Christ. Our true identity will be revealed, because our head is Christ. For Paul, who we are (new creations, reconciled to God and each other), and what we do (good works created before the foundation of the world, in Christ Jesus 2:10), are a function of our union with Christ. When we live with him as our head, we fulfil the reality of the identity we were meant to have. Returning to our passage, husbands, like Christ, are to empower those they love.

If the empowered is always sceptical and antagonistic towards the empowerer, how can they realise the fullness of the liberty they are given? If, on the other hand, the empowered respects and trusts the empowerer, freedom is likely to come much more easily. That is why submission of the empowered is crucial for this to happen. It is not a removal of control, but an acceptance of freedom.

Now, in interpreting this passage, must the onus of headship rest entirely on the shoulders of the man? Or asked another way, should a woman fulfil the role of a head? Would it be right for the wife to love her husband, Yes. Should she do whatever she can to see her husband

---

63. Brilliance means displaying the gifting and full expression of the way a person images God to shine through. It is not necessarily intellectual achievement, see Mark Strom, *Arts of the Wise Leader* (Sydney: Sophos, 2007) 103–4.

flourish and grow? Yes. Would the wife's support of her husband include supporting and loving herself? Yes. Is it proper for a wife to nourish and care for her husband? Yes. Should she seek to become one with him? Yes. In doing all this would she be reflecting what Christ does for the church? Yes. If she fulfilled all these things, which we have seen she should, then she is also fulfilling the role of head. Therefore, we have established that headship should be empowering and mutual.

However Fee argues that the mantle of leadership remained on the husbands in this passage.[64] The key point to remember, however, is that men in that culture had the power to make the radical changes needed for the home to come under the rule of Christ. Under Christ's rule, we find mutual submission and women being empowered to come into the fullness of who they are meant to be. For Paul, this meant coming into a place of radical equality with men. As with the slavery, the trajectory of scripture is towards equality. Therefore as we apply the biblical ideal of equality in our increasingly egalitarian society, we must promote the concept of mutual headship.

With mutual headship, the celebration of uniqueness, talent, and gifting is shared. In this culture, each needs to submit to the liberating efforts of the other, while being conscious of not taking advantage of the gift of freedom. That's why the passage starts with mutual submission, which is essential if mutual empowering is to be effective. Scanzoni and Hardesty explain mutual submission this way: "It was not to be a submission rooted in fear or grudging duty but rather 'as to the Lord'—a response of love, joy, and delight because of Christ's self-giving love for us which calls for our self-giving love in return."[65]

Mutual headship has powerful ramifications for disabled men seeking to live well in bodies which mean they are unable to fulfil societal norms of masculinity. Volf argues that our culturally conditioned, and therefore fluid, gender identities are still founded on the "stability of the sexed body."[66] Oh, that it were so simple. The reality that this essay addresses is that my body is very different to other males. My gender identity is shaped by my body, which does include maleness but also disability. The power of mutual headship is that both parties invest in

---

64. Fee, "Gender Issues: Reflections on the Perspective of the Apostle Paul," 73.

65. Letha Scanzoni and Nancy Hardesty, *All We're Meant to Be: Biblical Feminism for Today*, 3rd ed. (Grand Rapids: Eerdmans, 1992) 149.

66. Volf, *Exclusion and Embrace*, 174.

finding ways to express our true identities. If I marry a woman who loves to cook, then I should feel free to allow her to express this, not guilty because I can't share half this load. If I marry someone who does not enjoy cooking so much, well maybe we will be valued customers of the local take-away. If the woman I marry is physically stronger that I, then I should not feel inner conflict when I ask her to open a jar.

Does this mean that I can place all the pressure of the household on my wife? No! It simply means that we can find ways to work together to achieve the best outcome for the household, in a way that allows us both to be authentic to who we are as unique individuals. We do not need to allow externally prescribed roles to dictate how we live. Rather we need to negotiate a way of living that we both feel free to express our authenticity.

In Ephesians, Paul is calling men to empower their wives to live authentically. But in 1 Corinthians Paul is reminding wives who are relishing their freedom, to live that life in a way that honours their husbands. As a disabled man, I find this is incredibly liberating. Living well this way means I can rightfully expect to be respected and regarded with due dignity. Living well when I get married means I must accept the call to respect and dignify my wife. More than that, I am called to empower her to become more and more true to who she is as a person. Instead of seeking power, this way of life demands I give it away.

CONCLUSION

I have grappled with the tensions of understanding masculinity while living in a disabled body. I have rejected the roles espoused by my conservative Christian heritage. In particular I find the demand that men be warriors untenable. Instead I have shown that following Jesus demands that we jettison this idea. I must become a shalom-seeking disciple who seeks the peaceful kingdom for myself and for those around me. The wholeness that comes with shalom will bring me into a state of peace with my true identity. An identity found in Christ.

The other problematic notion is that to be the head means that the man is the leader in the home. I have shown that if I am to follow Jesus, who is my head, I must seek to empower those around me to live authentically—true to who they are. At the same time I can expect to be treated with dignity and respect as I seek to live authentically.

While it is true that authentic human life is equally the aim of women, demanding that authentic life is the same for both genders denies the difference God created between genders. However any social construction of different gender norms denies the uniqueness of individuals. Rather than imposing an external norm I have argued that a liberating concept of masculinity is to live authentically within a male body while empowering others to live authentically in theirs. Important ways to achieve this, regardless of gender, come growing as disciples of Christ and reflecting his headship through mutually empowering each other to grow into the fullness of our union with Christ.

12

Heads and Bodies

A Response to Immanuel Koks

CHRIS MARSHALL

IMMANUEL KOKS HAS WRITTEN a sensitive and perceptive essay on the difficulties he has faced as a disabled man in coming to terms with his masculinity in a cultural context in which conceptions of manhood are so heavily focused on men's physical attributes and strength. His account is yet another indication of the extent to which all dominant communities (in this case, able-bodied people) instinctively assume that their particular experience of reality corresponds with the way things are for everyone else. Feminists have long complained that men typically regard their experience of the world as generically human rather than distinctively male. The same kind of criticism can be levelled at the able-bodied population in general.

Over the past generation or so, and in virtually every major academic discipline, including theology, there has been a flurry of interest in the category of the "body" and in the significance of embodiment for human identity. However, the body in question has usually been assumed to be the fully functioning body of the autonomous, secularist, western individual. Able bodiedness has been tacitly accepted as "naturally" human, with the result that the distinctive consciousness of the disabled has been excluded from view. This is where, as Immanuel notes, the disability sector has something in common with advocacy movements, such as feminism or queerism. Like them its existence constitutes an implicit protest against the false universalizing of one form of human experience, even where that experience is common to the vast majority of the population.

Of course, it is never comfortable, especially for Christians, to be told that how one sees the world, as a member of mainstream society, is partial and provisional, and often exclusionary. But it is important to be constantly reminded that there are innumerable people who do not fit our paradigm of normality, yet who are still fully formed human beings, of equal value, worth and dignity as every other "normal" person.

In this connection, I was personally prompted by Immanuel's essay to reconsider one of the ways I have articulated the meaning of gender equity in the Christian community. I have long been committed to the principle of sexual equality, and have done my best in my teaching and writing to elaborate the biblical and theological justification for such equality. Paul's remarkable assertion that "in Christ Jesus there is neither Jew nor Greek, slave nor free, male and female" (Gal 3:28) is still, I believe, the best brief statement we have on Christian egalitarianism. In discussing this passage with students, I take pains to emphasize that the reality Paul is talking about in Gal 3 goes far beyond some abstract notion of "spiritual equality." Undoubtedly the apostle accepted the precept of spiritual equality of Jews and Gentiles, slaves and citizens, males and females before God. But he pushes on to insist that this spiritual equality must play itself out on the ground in the way believers interact with each other in the day to day life of the church. The spiritual principle must be translated into corresponding social practices or it is not true Christian equality.

That is why, in the previous chapter of the letter to the Galatians, Paul recounts an episode in which he had accused Peter of rank hypocrisy after Peter had withdrawn from table fellowship with Gentile believers in the church of Antioch (Gal 2:11–21). Paul explains that Peter, though a Jew, had for a long time lived like a Gentile (v. 14), by which he means he had suspended those Jewish purity laws that had previously prevented him from sharing food with Gentiles. Now as a Christian believer he felt free to eat with Gentile believers, and to share the Eucharist with them, as a tangible outworking of the spiritual oneness that existed between Jews and Gentiles in Christ. But for some reason, following a visit to Antioch by "certain men from James" (v. 12), he faltered on this commitment. He was persuaded by the delegation to re-erect the barriers of ethnic distinction and religious privilege he had formerly torn down. Others followed suit, including, Paul says in pained astonishment, "even Barnabas" (v. 13)!

Paul was livid. How could Peter and Barnabas possibly revert to the old hierarchical and separatist norms in view of what Christ had achieved through his death and resurrection? It was a scandalous failure of nerve on their part. For them to abandon the common table, Paul thunders, was to nullify the grace of God, deny the truth of the gospel, commit transgression, and render the cross of Christ of no effect.

Such an impassioned theological defence of the everyday social practice of sharing food between believers proves, I stress to students, that for Paul spiritual equality was not quite enough. What the gospel actually demands is a *social* equality between Jews and Gentiles, as well as between slaves and free persons, and between males and females.

To reinforce this point, I have tended to characterise Paul's position on equality as an equality of opportunity, the freedom for all believers, irrespective of their race, class, or gender, to have the same opportunity to exercise whatever gifts or ministries God has given them. This is quite different to the so-called "complementarian" account of equality, which argues that men and women, whilst of equal spiritual worth and value, have distinctive social roles to play in church, home, and society. Roles that involve leadership or pedagogical authority over the gathered community are not equally available to both sexes but only open to men. Under such an arrangement, no genuine equality of opportunity can exist, for one part of the community is necessarily privileged over the other part. For that reason I consider the complementarian approach to be tantamount to a replication of Peter's grave error at Antioch, which Paul would probably have us denounce with equal vehemence.

But Immanuel alerts me to a difficulty with construing Christian liberty as equality of opportunity. It places a heavy burden on those who, for reasons of physical disability, are unable to contribute equally in many aspects of life. The problem with "equality of opportunity" discourse is that it assumes people start from the same position and have the same potential. Of course, this is false. Individuals are never equal in talents, gifts, or strengths or fortune, and therefore people can never have equal opportunities in life. The notion, much beloved of free market economics, of a level playing field where everyone can compete on equal terms is a damaging and dangerous illusion. It disregards both the natural inequalities that exist between individuals and the systemic injustices that lock some people out of the game entirely.

Immanuel makes the point that disabled people do not have the same opportunities available to them as the able bodied people, so that for the disabled to ground their gender identity in freedom to participate fully in every dimension of life is problematic. In this connection, I think it is significant that Scripture roots human equality, not in our potential to achieve equal outcomes in life, but in our intrinsic constitution as creatures made in God's image as male and female. Accordingly there remains an important sense in which human equality, including gender equity, *is* primarily a *spiritual* reality, something that is gifted to us by grace independently of anything we can do or deserve or achieve in life. It cannot be translated without remainder into the idea of equality of opportunity. It is, more fundamentally, an equality of intrinsic spiritual worth.

Having said that, it is still the case that the message of Gal 2–3 is that equality of worth and of salvation in Christ *requires* transformation of social patterns in the direction of a genuine equality of opportunity. Not in the sense that everyone must have exactly the same chance to do exactly the same things in life (which is impossible), but in the sense that everyone should have the same opportunity to achieve their own created potential in every sphere of life without arbitrary limitations being imposed by race, class, or sex. Masculine or feminine identity is not determined by specific gender roles, nor defined by particular physical attributes, but resides in the totality of the individual person, who is free to express his or her created identity in every field of life in accordance with their individual gifts, talents, and abilities. A disabled man is no less a man for lacking certain physical capacities, such as brute strength. His masculinity is expressed in and through everything he is, and everything he can (and cannot) do, as a unique individual male, something that is true of every person in different ways.

This is a good reason why the image of a warrior is an inadequate or inappropriate metaphor for characterizing masculine identity. Immanuel rightly raises two objections to it. First it validates male aggression as a legitimate part of Christian masculinity, and second it presupposes the possession of a certain physical prowess that is not true of every man, whether disabled or not. He also notes, and this for me brings us closer to the heart of the problem with the warrior image for Christian conceptions of masculinity, that Jesus explicitly condemns the anger, belligerence and violence that warriors specialise in (Matt 5:21–48). It is surely significant that Jesus makes comparatively little use of warrior imagery in his teaching, especially compared to servant or family imagery. Moreover when he summons his followers to love their enemies, turn the other cheek, and go the second mile, he is effectively cutting masculine aspirations to warriorhood off at the knees.

Certainly Jesus engaged in conflict with his opponents, but the combat was exclusively spiritual and moral in nature, not physical. Certainly the warrior attributes of courage, commitment, and sacrifice have an important role to play in Christian living. But these attributes are not unique to warriors, and they are certainly not the exclusive province of men. It is also helpful that Immanuel reminds us that Paul's central metaphor for Christian experience is not warfare but union with Christ, and union is a profoundly relational, even erotic, image, quite unlike that of domineering warriorhood. In a world bathed in blood, and in a New Zealand society disfigured by domestic violence, we need fewer warriors, not more, and it behoves Christian men in particular to disown the warrior ideal in favour of the self-giving servant figure commended and enacted by Jesus.

This brings me to the much contested question of "headship," though the term itself is wrongheaded (!) since it presupposes the phenomenon it seeks to prove. Yet it is questionable whether theologically any such thing as headship exists. It is true that the New Testament occasionally uses the metaphor of "head" to designate the place of men in relation to women and husbands in relation to wives. But whether it is justified to turn a metaphor into an ontological reality called "headship" is quite another matter. Be that as it may, in the tired old debate between complementarians and evangelical egalitarians, much has ridden on the interpretation of *kephale* in 1 Cor 11:2–16 and Eph 5:21–32. Immanuel reviews the standard options of "leader," "source," and "locus of honor," and offers a richly relational interpretation of the metaphor in which hierarchical ordering plays little role. I think he is on exactly the right track here, though when he speaks of headship ideally being a shared reality I think he verges on over-working a limited metaphor.

What is notable in all this discussion about the meaning of "head" and "headship" is the extent to which it misses the most obvious implication of the metaphor. Heads cannot exist without bodies, and bodies cannot live without heads. The interdependency of heads and bodies is made quite explicit in Eph 5, and is implicit in 1 Cor 11 as well. Let me comment briefly on each passage.

Eph 5 is one of the profoundest discussions of marriage we possess, and it is a travesty to restrict its meaning to the question of who should be boss in the relationship. Marriage is the most intimate of all human relationships, and in a truly loving, and truly Christian, marriage, issues of authority and obedience should have no place whatsoever. Some argue that every community needs leaders, and so marriage, as a small community of two people, requires its own CEO. But biblically marriage is *not* a little community. It is, as verse 31 states, a "one flesh" relationship in which two people become so united in love and devotion to each other that the life-experience of each becomes the lived-experience of both. To be in a one-flesh relationship means that what happens to my partner happens to me, and what happens to me, happens to my partner, and both our lives are fundamentally shaped by our experience of each another, and by the common experience of our marriage. That's why verse 28 calls on husbands to "love their wives *as they do their own bodies*," so intertwined do the couple become.

This image of husband and wife being "one flesh" or "one body" (cf. 1 Cor 6:16) is the key, I suggest, to appreciating the use of "head'" for the husband. The husband is likened to a head in verse 23 and his wife is likened to a body verse 28 in order to show that the union between husband and wife is as life-giving and inviolable as is the relationship of the physical head to the physical body. A body cannot exist without a head, and a head cannot exist without a body. Both are indispensable. They need each other equally for life to exist; they are totally interdependent and inseparable. So it is with marriage. It is significant that when the text speaks of Christ as head, it expressly identifies the church as his body (v. 23, cf. v. 30). Heads and bodies go together. And it is the existential union of the two, as one flesh, that is the central emphasis of the text, not the hierarchical ordering of the chief executive over his subordinates.

In 1 Cor 11:2–11, the word "body" is not used as a counterpart to head, since the entire focus of the discussion is on what members of the congregation were doing with their literal heads. But when Paul says that "the head of woman is man" (v. 3), the implication again seems to be one of intimacy, interdependence, and inseparability, such as exists between heads and bodies. Paul unpacks this relationship of mutuality further by alluding to the creation narratives, in which woman was created by a rib taken from Adam's body and presented to him as his perfect reflection, in contrast to the animals, who belong to another order of being entirely (vv. 8–9; cf. Gen 2:18–25). Paul knows all too well that as a result of the entry of sin into human experience, the creational duality of the sexes has occasioned hierarchical domination (cf. Gen 3:16). So, having stressed the goodness and permanence of the sexual distinction gifted in creation, he hastens to explain that "nevertheless, in the Lord, woman is not independent of man or man independent of woman, for just as woman came from man, so man comes through woman; but all things come from God" (vv. 11–12).

This counts, alongside Gal 3:28, as one of the most profound egalitarian assertions in all of Scripture. It is an exquisite insight, rarely, if ever, used in the Christian gender debate. Paul makes it unmistakably clear that the relationship of men and women "in the Lord," that is, in the Christian community and in the sphere of Christ's lordship (which includes marriage), recovers the equality and mutuality intended in creation. This equality and mutuality is disclosed in two instances of creation: in the *original* creation of the human species, where woman was taken out of the body of man, and in the *continuing* creation of human beings, where every man who has ever existed has come out of the body of a woman. Paul may not develop the head-body relationship as fully here as in Eph 5. But he certainly alludes to body-opening and birth-giving in order to underscore the oneness and equality of men and women in creation and now recovered and reaffirmed in Christ.

Immanuel concludes his essay by characterising masculinity as "living authentically within a male body, and empowering others to live authentically in theirs." This attractive definition wisely avoids using social mores or cultural clichés to identify the core of being male. What then are the differences between masculinity and femininity? This needs further research, Immanuel suggests, but we should be cautious about making generalisations beyond the most obvious biological differences. Perhaps this too is wise, though the experience of raising children suggests to me that gender distinction is more pervasive than simply biological or anatomical differences.

To finish, let me mention two insights from the biblical tradition that may have something to contribute to the perplexing question of how to define gender difference. One comes from the creation narrative in Gen 1, where the curious shift from the singular noun to plural pronouns says something profound about sexuality. "God created humankind in his image, in the image of God he created him, male and female he created them" (Gen 1:29). The divine image is both shared equally by male and female, and manifest in and through our sexual difference. This means that we can never pinpoint the essence of manhood or womanhood in isolation from the other. I cannot be a man apart from the reality of woman. I can only know what it means to be masculine by being in relationship with the feminine dimension of human existence, and vice versa.

In a very real sense, then, my identity as a man is gifted to me by women, those other divine image bearers who are like me in every respect, yet also disturbingly unlike me, who are bone of my bone and flesh of my flesh, yet who stand opposite me in order become my sole true companion (Gen 2:18–23). Whatever it is that particular cultures or historical periods judge to be characteristically masculine or feminine (and it fluctuates enormously), it is always determined by men and women in relationship to each other. Sexuality is negotiated in dialogue with the sexual other. It cannot exist on its own.

The second insight comes from Eph 5. The author concludes his discussion of marriage by quoting Gen 2:4–5, "For this reason a man will leave his father and mother and be joined to his wife, and the two will become one flesh" (v. 31). He then expostulates. "This is a great mystery, and I am applying it to Christ and the church" (vv. 31–32). The mystery here is not, as is often assumed, the relationship of Christ and the church, but rather the one-flesh relationship of husband and wife, which Paul *applies* to Christ and the church. At the end of the day, sexuality and sexual intimacy is a mystery, in fact "a *great* mystery," so mysterious, in fact, that it is a worthy analogy for the divine fellowship that exists between Christ and his people. Mysteries are there to be experienced, not to be explained away. No gender theory will ever be up to the task of penetrating the mystery of our creation as male and female, as jointly and severally bearers of the *imago Dei*, and made for unique relationship with one another and together with their Creator.

13

Divine Masculine and Feminine in Judeo-mystico

A Tree of Life

YAEL KLANGWISAN

INTRODUCTION

I AM NOT THE first person to yearn to see God. I imagine swimming through the vast recesses of foggy blackness and perhaps coming upon, as John, a crystal sea, a vision of the molten throne and the Ancient One. So I approach this study with curiosity and desire, but also with trepidation and nervous awe. As the sages once warned via a tale: "Four entered Pardes[1] . . . Ben Azzai, Ben-Zoma, Acher ('the other one') and Rabbi Akiba. Ben-Azzai having looked, died; regarding him the scripture says, 'Precious in the sight of the Lord is the death of his pious ones'; Ben-Zoma, having looked, was injured; regarding him the scripture says: 'Hast thou honey, eat no more than is sufficient for thee, lest thou be filled therewith and vomit it.' Acher cut off the plants. Rabbi Akiba went out unhurt."[2] According to the Talmud, questing to look on God can result in death, insanity, or atheism, but for the pure of heart there is new life and wisdom (Matt 5:8).

But in what space might Judaism and its mystical stream dialogue with the Christian theologian? Judaism and Christianity share the larger

---

1. The Garden (Heaven).

2. H. Sperling, "Jewish Mysticism," in *Aspects of the Hebrew Genius*, edited by Leon Simon (London: Routledge, 1910) 150–51.

part of their sacred writings. Conceivably both Judaism and Christianity share the same God. But from the Christian perspective this is the rub. These are those who could not conceive that the Messiah was that young Jewish prophet who died nailed up on a tree outside Jerusalem in the early first century. This is a great stumbling block, and so what is truly fascinating is that those streams of Judaism that continued to look for Messiah have developed theology that in certain areas makes strangely harmonic parallels with New Testament writing. It seems that the extrapolations of the Jewish mystics based on the Hebrew bible have found themselves in a similar space albeit using sometimes vastly different language, imagery and vantage points.

The Jewish mystics, the great kabbalists, were zealous men.[3] They were mature, being at least forty years or more, and had first studied the Law of Moses over the course of several decades, memorized it, and sung it, even rising through the night to continue their study. They had most of all proved themselves in its observance.[4] For this amazing commitment to sacred scholarship, their writings and reflections are worthwhile reading. They saw Torah as their life's vocation; to trace every nuance, link every possible verse, count numeric values for every word and line, to formulate, to anticipate. They incorporated every kind of study and method into their quest for deeper knowledge of the Hebrew Bible: linguistic, mathematical, scientific, statistical, philosophical, astronomical, abstract, and mythological. The results of their studies, though regularly fantastic, were the stuff of genius. Christian groups often hold Kabbalah with deep suspicion but the cabalistic charlatans, magicians, occultists, and popular kabbalists of the current century are not the same. This Kabbalah is the work of medieval Jews earthed in *Torah* and yearning for relationship with *YHWH*.

In contrast to the rabbinic stream, the kabbalists believed that an otherworldly journey to God could be conducted through deep study of Torah, unlocking its vaults. This journey they described as walking through the halls of heaven.[5] Some of these extra-biblical tales of mortal

3. To this point in my study I have not come across any female kabbalists from this period.

4. Note the legend regarding Rabbi Abba in Genesis portion of the Zohar. It was believed that at midnight God enters the Garden of Eden (drawing on Ps 119:62, "midnight I will rise and give thanks to You for Your righteous judgments"). Gershom Scholem, *Zohar: The Book of Splendour* (New York: Schocken, 1949).

5. "In My Father's house are many mansions; if it were not so, I would have told you. I go to prepare a place for you," John 14:2.

journeys to paradise—*The Garden*—are antique, such as the apocalypses and the books of creation. Some journey narratives are ancient. Several vignettes from within Scripture allude to an out-of-this-world ripping of the fabric of time and space. Some biblical personalities cross the abyss to the Other. The rapture of Enoch, Isaiah's vision, and Elijah's fiery *merkavah* ride are examples of mysteries from biblical books that fascinated these esoteric circles of study from first century Jerusalem and on into the synagogues and yeshivas of medieval Spain, Baghdad, and Safed.

These typically Jewish mystical meditations and experiences of the Divine surfaced in the writings of the Jesus movement. Consider the strange story of 2 Cor 12:2-4 narrated by Paul, the Messiah's man to the Roman world: "I know a man in Christ who fourteen years ago ... was caught up to the third heaven. And I know that such a man ... was caught up into Paradise (Eden) and heard inexpressible words, which a man is not permitted to speak" (MKJV).

This small New Testament reference alone begs exploration for the possible influence of both apocalyptic and mystical knowledge of the late Second Temple period. Paul uses the language of mystical convention of the time and his cosmological worldview of multiple heavens and the location of Eden/Paradise in the third heaven matches 1 Enoch.[6] The great medieval mystics inherited this same worldview.

Jewish mystical traditions were handed down through the centuries, developing in complexity, often profundity.[7] These traditions found themselves crystallized during the medieval period around the turn of the first millennia AD. The thirteenth century work, The *Zohar*, Book of Splendour, is the most famous exposition of many of these ideas.[8]

The *Zohar* itself is written in conventional form, a commentary on the books of Torah. It is pseudoepigraphic, locating itself in first century Palestine and, to suit this context, written in the language of first century Palestine, Aramaic. The Aramaic while very good, betrays a medieval Hebrew at work, and is most probably the product of the Spanish

---

6. Leif Carlsson, *Round Trips: Otherworldly Travellers in Early Judaism and Christianity*, translated by Judy Breneman, 19 vols., Lund Studies in History of Religions (Lund: Lund University, 2004) 19:74.

7. Each generation of kabbalists used the language and systems of philosophy of their times in their speculation of the Godhead. The work of the great kabbalists is genius both theologically and philosophically.

8. D. S. Russell, *Divine Disclosure: An Introduction to Jewish Apocalyptic* (Minneapolis: Fortress, 1992).

kabbalist Moses de Leon who obviously drew on the mystical literature available in his time.[9] Leon romantically attributed his writing to the first century Palestinian Rabbi Simeon ben Yohai. Gershom Scholem describes Leon as a genius of homiletics, and it is true that his writings are profound, imaginative and fascinating.[10]

Sefer Ha-Bahir,[11] the book of 'illumination', is contemporary to *Sifra-Zohar*. It was written or at least redacted by Isaac the Blind in France in the twelfth century. Both *Zohar* and *Sefer Ha-Bahir* drew from *Sefer Yetzirah*, a much earlier work from the second century AD.[12]

The conception of the Godhead in *Sefer Ha-Bahir* and *Sifra-Zohar* complements but also challenges Christian conceptualizations especially in the area of gender. Of particular interest is the Jewish mystical notion of the Godhead as a unity of male and female akin to marriage, monogamous, committed sexuality as a divine virtue akin to spirituality, and masculinity, inherently and equitably bound to femininity. This definitively contrasts with the traditional Christian notion of the Godhead as a masculine triune, celibacy as a divine virtue and heaven/paradise as the domain of men.[13] The Jewish mystical conception of God is vastly more inclusive and egalitarian than the traditional Christian notion, and rests on a significant biblical rationale, primarily Gen 1:26–27: "And God said, 'Let Us make man in Our image, after Our likeness'... And God created man in His image; in the image of God He created him. He created them male and female" (MKJV).

In this chapter we will explore the concept of God from the perspective of the Jewish mystical stream, and in particular that of Moses de Leon in *Sifra-Zohar*. We will trace the masculine-feminine paradigm of the Judeo-mystico God culminating in an exploration of the principal divine feminine, *shekinah*.

9. Daniel C. Matt, *The Zohar: Translation and Commentary*, vol. 1 (Stanford: Stanford University Press, 2004) xix.

10. Scholem, *Zohar*.

11. The name "The Bahir" comes from Job 37:21. The book is considered one of the oldest kabbalistic texts. Aryeh Kaplan, *The Bahir: A Translation and Commentary* (Lanham, MD: Rowman & Littlefield, 2004).

12. Gershom Scholem, *The Origins of the Kabbalah*, edited by Zwi Werblowsky, translated by Allan Arkush (Princeton: The Jewish Publication Society/Princeton University Press, 1987).

13. Elaine Pagels, *Adam, Eve and the Serpent: Sexual Politics in Early Christianity* (New York: Vintage, 1988).

Sifra-Zohar begins in the beginning in the black depths of *eyn sof*.

IN THE BEGINNING

> In the beginning (Gen 1:1)—when the will of the King began to take effect, he engraved signs into the heavenly sphere [that surrounded him]. Within the most hidden recess a dark flame issued from the mystery of *eyn sof*, the "Infinite," like a fog forming in the unformed—enclosed in the ring of that sphere, neither white nor black, neither red nor green, of no color whatever. Only after this flame began to assume size and dimension, did it produce radiant colours. From the innermost center of the flame sprang forth a well out of which colors issued and spread upon everything beneath, hidden in the mysterious hiddenness of *eyn sof*.[14]

In the beginning we have, from the kabbalists, recognition of the undelimitable-ness of God, the hidden centre that evades all, *eyn sof*. As known in the *Zohar*, *eyn sof* is the "Uncaused Cause" or the "Cause of Causes" and literally means "without end."[15] The *Zohar* puts forward a philosophical and mystical concept of God as a series of wheels, spheres or worlds. The *eyn sof* is the origin and terminus and cannot be known and while concealed is not confined. There is nothing created that is outside of it.[16] Out of this unknowable origin comes YHWH in all the various aspects, a rainbow of light-filled colors. In the realm of light God allows God to be known, to be seen.

> Before anything emanated, there was only *Eyn Sof*. *Eyn Sof* was all that existed. Similarly, after it brought into being that which exists, there is nothing but it. You cannot find anything that exists apart from it. There is nothing that is not pervaded by the power of divinity. If there were, *Eyn Sof* would be limited, subject to duality, God forbid! Rather, God is everything that exists, though everything that exists is not God. It is present in everything, and everything comes into being from it. Nothing is devoid of its divinity. Everything is within it; it is within everything and outside of everything. There is nothing but it.[17]

---

14. Scholem, *Zohar*. 3 and *Parashat Be-Reshit 1:15a* in Matt, *The Zohar*. 107.

15. Daniel C. Matt, *The Essential Kabbalah: The Heart of Jewish Mysticism* (San Francisco: HarperSanFrancisco, 1996).

16. This is not unlike the Maori conception of Io.

17. "Nonduality." Matt, *The Essential Kabbalah*, A text from *Elimah Rabbati* by Moses Cordovero (1522–1570).

Eyn Sof, in the Jewish mystical system is neither male nor female. *Eyn Sof* simply is.

The Ten Sephirot

God is first and foremost the living God who speaks: *Yehi Ohr!* (Gen 1:3).[18] From out of the core of *eyn sof* comes a lightning flash of light, an unfolding of an illuminated, audio-visual, divine language; a multimedia, communicative act.

The *sephirot*[19] are the sacred names, aspects or hypostases of God but are also conceived as the ten words, *middot* or *logoi* that enabled and outworked creation.[20] These *sephirot*, unlike the *eyn sof* are creative forces, energies, potentialities. In the *Sefer haBahir* they are called "kings," "crowns" and in other places "voices," "faces," and "garments." They are independent yet interconnected in a structured and complex framework called the *sephirotic tree*, the Tree of Life which stretches from heaven towards earth.[21]

The *eytz' chaim* or Tree of Life is conceived as representing the Godhead for several logical reasons, and quite a few obscure ones. The Tree of Life was a significant feature of the Genesis depiction of Eden. It had some quality that was otherworldly yet earthed and intrinsically God.[22] In the book of Proverbs, the Tree of Life again makes an appearance, this time something connected with Lady Wisdom, but more importantly something of the "Garden" that can be accessed via the study and righteous observance of the *Torah*.

To the obscure . . . *eytz* is made up of two Hebrew letters ע and צ and these letters in the Hebrew originally were pictographs of the "eye"

---

18. "The world of divine emanation is one in which the faculty of speech is anticipated in God . . . it is the seed of all creation." Gershom Scholem, *Major Trends in Jewish Mysticism*, 3rd ed. (New York: Schocken, 1961) 216.

19. *Sephirah* is the Hebrew word for "sapphire." What is meant by this word in Kabbalah is that the pure and unified light of God is refracted as though through a cut sapphire and becomes separate rays and bands of coloured light.

20. Gershom Scholem, *On the Mystical Shape of the Godhead: Basic Concepts in the Kabbalah*, translated by Joachim Neugroschel (New York: Schocken, 1991).

21. Gershom Scholem, *On the Kabbalah and its Symbolism*, translated by Ralph Manheim (New York: Schocken, 1965).

22. Gen 3:22, "And Yahweh Elohim said, 'Behold, the man has become as one of Us, to know good and evil. And now, lest he put forth his hand and take also of the tree of life, and eat, and live forever.'"

and "the righteous one." We find these two concepts connected in Ps 34 where *the eyes of YHWH are to the righteous*.[23] At the mystical or "*sodh*" level of exegesis, kabbalists believe that the righteous are given the "eyes of YHWH" in that they are able to look into Torah, (the Tree of Life) with their right eye and understand its mysteries and with their left eye they are given creative power, power to redeem and rectify reality.[24]

The Tree of Life

"It was I that planted this tree, so that all the world could delight in it, and I engraved all within it, and called its name 'the All'; for all hangs from it and all comes from it and all need it, and all look upon it and set their hopes upon it."[25]

The Tree of Life is thus conceived from the depths of *Torah*. It is portrayed as having three pillars that stretch through the heavens down through the four worlds to earth. The pillars have names—Severity, Mildness and Mercy—and these pillars are ruled by the three highest corresponding *sephirot: binah, keter,* and *chokmah*.

Keter or "crown" is the first effect of the *eyn sof*, "the cause of causes." This first *sefirah* contained within itself the plan of the universe in the infinity of time and space.[26] *Keter* stands alone at what would be the root of this Tree of Life growing down from *eyn sof* to the earthly sphere (*malkut*). *Keter* at the head of the configuration unifies the *sephirot* as does *malkhut* at the foot. Unity to diversity to unity is the crucial concept in Jewish mystical tradition.

The pillar of mercy is active or expansive and is therefore considered as masculine in nature. The pillar of severity is responsive and considered feminine in nature. Wisdom in the mercy pillar concerns knowledge regarding the world, the Primordial Torah. *Binah*, the matching *sephirah* in the severity pillar concerns the application of wisdom in new or future contexts. Judgment or *gevurah* is referred to as feminine and responds to transgression bringing peace. Her counterpart, *chesed*

---

23. (Rav) Yitzchak Ginsburgh, *A Torah Message for the Month of Shevat: The Tree of Life* [Online] (Kabbalah and Modern Life: Living with the Times, 2006 [cited June 10, 2007]); available from http://www.inner.org/times/shevat/shevat58.htm.

24. Ibid.

25. *Sefer Ha-Bahir* S§14, M§22 in Scholem, *Mystical Shape of the Godhead*.

26. Kaufmann Kohler and Louis Ginzberg, *Cabala* (Jewish Encyclopedia.com, 1901–1910 [cited Dec. 20, 2005]); available from http://www.jewishencyclopedia.com.

or mercy is outflowing. In the sephirotic tree of life, *chesed* and *gevurah* can therefore occur at the same time.

The whole tree is a procreative force and in general considered a masculine act received and responded to, with equal force and energy, by the lower *sephirot*—"the lower waters"—in particular *malkut* (kingdom), a feminine act. In Kabbalah, YHWH works together in balance and equilibrium of both genders in the unseen dimension, in ways empathetic with the unification that occurs in marriage. This is not the penetrator-penetrated model of the Greco-Romans, so while the idea of feminine as restricted to "responsiveness" may be problematic, the idea of a system characterized by an equal interdependency of gender is positive and outworks itself positively in the marriages of authentic kabbalists.[27] According to these this syzygy of the masculine and feminine is a precondition of all the worlds.[28]

The *sephirot* were not arbitrarily chosen by the kabbalistic sages. Though vastly imaginative and often provocative in many of their speculations, these sages had immense knowledge of Scripture and developed most of their conceptions about the Godhead from patterns they discovered throughout *Tanakh*. For example, in Isa 11:2 we see the spirit of YHWH flowing out and descending on the Shoot of Jesse and in this verse we clearly see an arrangement of God-originating attributes or potentialities: wisdom (*chokmah*), understanding (*binah*), might (*gevurah*), knowledge (*da'at*), counsel (*tiferet*), and fear of YHWH (*malkut*).

From the *eyn sof* through *keter* comes *chokmah*. Together between *hochmah* and *binah*, the two wisdoms, the rest of the *sephirot* are literally birthed. *Chokmah* is an attribute that is conceived as the primordial idea or seed of *eyn sof*, the cosmic Torah but when unified with *binah* (understanding) the intent of *chokmah* is embraced. The other *sephirot* emerge from her womb so to speak and ultimately *malkut*, the sphere that touches humanity.[29] The result, according to the kabbalists is that

---

27. See *Iggeret haQodesh* on the final page.
28. Scholem, *Origins*, 142.
29. These are the ten *sephirot* in order but including *da'at* which is not a true *sephirah* Each is listed with its number of occurrences in the Hebrew Bible: *keter* the crown (the first effect) (12), *chokmah* wisdom (past) (149), *binah* Understanding (future) and fear of YHWH (40), *da'at* Knowledge (93), *chesed* (249) mercy, *gevurah* or *dun* which is power/judgment (62/50), *Tiferet* beauty/glory (50), *Netzah* endurance/victory (43), *Hod* glory/splendor (25), *Yesod* Foundation/covenant (25), *Malkhut* Kingdom/Knesset Israel/Shekinah (90).

YHWH has created the best possible world to accomplish the "purpose." This creative work of YHWH is modelled on the same procreative human process of male and female, conceiving and birthing in the human world.

The *sephirot* can be arranged or categorized in various ways. The particular arrangement considered in the *Sefer haBahir* and *Zohar* becomes much more clearly gendered and God becomes not one or two but a series of embracing gendered roles, king, queen, father, mother, husband, wife, groom and bride, son and daughter. The fascination is the name of God יהוה which neatly divides into two gendered pairs. So, in the eyes of the kabbalists, even God's name is a cooperative work of both genders.

THE MESSIAH IN THE TREE OF LIFE

Tiferet

The presence and place of the Messiah in the Tree of Life is a very interesting concept in Jewish mysticism. The Messiah in Jewish Mysticism is God. He is a tangible culmination of all the attributes of *eyn sof* but since the middle pillar is the fusion of right and left, he is most strongly associated here. In fact Messiah is called the "Master of the Middle Pillar." At the head of the pillar called "mildness" is *keter*, the crown. Messiah is considered "King of Kings" and at the right hand of *eyn sof*. He is also in the lower *sephirot*, the "Son," the "Son of Torah."[30]

Tiferet is an unusual Hebrew word signifying "glorious beauty." This *sephirah* in the sephirotic tree is central in the configuration, at a point where all other *sephirot* converge and connect. It is thus considered in the *Zohar* as embodying the central pillar. Because from *tiferet* are connections to all the *sephirot*, it is considered the mediator between the upper and lower *sephirot* and the kingdom, *malkut*. The most significant characteristic of *tiferet* is again that it embodies and unifies all the attributes of God, and is therefore a reflection or "image" of the unseen *eyn sof*. It is called the "image of God," or "*Tiferet Adam*."[31] The Messiah

30. The other aspects of Messiah represented by each of the ten Sephirot are: King of kings (Rev 19:16), Creator (John 1:1), Motherly compassion (Matt 23:37), High Priest (Heb 2:7), Righteous judge (John 5:22), Image of God (Col 1:15), Victory over death (1 Cor 15:57), Spirit of prophecy (Rev 19:10), The Righteous One (Heb 10:38), kingdom of God present before humanity (Luke 17:21)

31. Scholem, *Mystical Shape of the Godhead*. Scholem notes that *imago Dei* means to the kabbalist two things: "that the power of divine life, exists and is active also in man,

is thus the image of *eyn sof* and this is the deepest meaning of beauty, "He is the image of the invisible God" (Col 1:15 [NASB]).

Tiferet is also known by the Hebrew word *rachamim* (compassion). The central pillar is at the fusion point of the masculine and feminine pillars of the tree and a maximization of both genders. At the point of *tiferet* or *rachamim* is the fusion of the *sephirot*, *gevurah* justice to the west and *chesed* kindness to the east. *Tiferet-rachamim* thus becomes a focused kind of divine compassion. Messiah's purpose is redemptive and through his centre at *tiferet* the river of healing can flow down to the kingdom. Also coming up from earth, through him the righteous can gain access to the higher worlds. Although he is both masculine and feminine due to his position in the middle pillar, he is given a masculine conception and called the "Bridegroom" with respect to his partner. She is in balance with him and her name is the "Bride."

Yesod

"The Holy One, blessed be He, saw and considered that the world cannot exist without the Foundation. And what is the Foundation upon which the world rests? As it is said, 'The righteous is the foundation of the world.' And this is the primordial foundation which the Holy One, blessed be he, created in His world, that is called 'light', as is written, 'Light is sown for the righteous'" (Ps 97:11).[32]

The Hebrew word, *yesod* literally means "foundation," and forms the second to last connection between the illuminations of *eyn sof* and the human world. It is the last *sephirah* prior to *malkut* and through this final conduit the life-bringing river of God channels down through to the earth. It is synonymous with the name *el shaddai* and is a reservoir for pools of blessing.

Yesod is represented in Scripture as "covenant." The covenant aligns people with God. In this way *yesod* is more than just a schematic bridge. It is a conduit for peace and love from the *sephirot* above. Fused together in *yesod* these attributes become *emet*, "truth."

Yesod is quite plainly masculine in representation and contemplations on the role of *yesod* are quite earthy in Kabbalah. Even more so since *yesod* is symbolized by the male reproductive organs. Thus its chief

and that the world of God the creator can be visualized under the image of the man he created," 215

32. Sifra-Zohar, *Midrash ha-Ne'elam*. Ibid., 100.

icon in the human body is the phallus. From this proceeds the river of life, the divine seed. Its symbolism as the phallus is not meant as a perverse application. In the Hebrew worldview the primary indicator of covenant with God beside the *shabbat* was the circumcised penis. *Brit-milah* represented on the flesh of a man, the covenant between God and Israel. The human sexuality and fecundity is the guarantor of future generations. As the mystics firmly believed, infinity lay in the seed of a man and in the womb of a woman.[33] Sexuality was therefore a divine and sacred act resting on a covenant between man and woman. Man and woman become partners with the Divine in the creation of new life. From *yesod* the life-bringing force of God hovers over the lower waters and is unified with *shekinah*. The two are betrothed but harmony is not yet restored on the earth.

Because covenant is necessarily an interaction between people and God, it is a plane that some in the human world can access. Consequently many Jewish mystical traditions see *yesod* as a plane where the *zaddikim* (the righteous ones) interact with the Divine, *"the righteous is an everlasting foundation"* (Prov 10:25 [JPS]). In some traditions the righteous ones of the earth are crucial to the divine plan. They create a foundation for the world. Some of these heroes of faith are the covenant makers, Noah and in particular Abraham and the other Patriarchs. Moses was thought to transcend *yesod* and even experience *tiferet*.

The tradition discussed in *Zohar* rather sees these *zaddikim* overshadowed by a penultimate "Righteous One." This Righteous One, the *zaddik*, ultimately identified as the Messiah, is the keeper of this single path to the Most High. There is only one path to the Most High and that is through *yesod* (foundation). "What is the eighth? GOD has one righteous in his world, and He loves him, because he maintains the entire world, and because he is its foundation."[34]

Put another way, there is no way to the "Father" except through *yesod*, "the Son," who is the "Foundation of the world," "the Stone," the "Keeper of the Covenant." He is thus honoured with the title the "Life of the Universe," and described as the first born of all creation.[35] "He [the Righteous] also has in his hand the souls of all living things, for he is the

---

33. The mystics were unaware of the existence of ovum.
34. *Sefer Ha-Bahir* §39, in Scholem, *Origins*, 155.
35. Scholem, *Mystical Shape of the Godhead*, 96.

'life of the worlds.' Every act of creation spoken of occurs through him ... for he is the middah [logos] of the Sabbath day."[36]

Yesod symbolizes *shalom* in the Tree of Life. Flowing down from *tiferet*, the Righteous One or *zaddik* establishes *shalom* and harmony in the world by means of his actions. In this *yesod*-messiah is "Master of the Sabbath," the place of rest and harmony. "As the Zaddik awakens the world to repent or to fix that which is not whole, this attribute is called Peace, mediating for good between YHWH and Adonai [Shekinah], making peace between them and bringing them near to dwell together without separation or breaking up in the world; and at that hour we find that GOD is one."[37]

SHEKINAH

". . . and the woman was taken from man, for it would be impossible for the upper and lower worlds to exist without the feminine . . ."[38] The Jewish mystic could not conceive of masculinity without femininity; as man, he is the east and woman, she is the west. They meet together with equal force in equal balance. Especially in the Godhead, the masculine is incomplete without the feminine. *Yesod* (foundation) is inconsequential without *shekinah*.

The concept of *shekinah* is bound up in deep, complex, and sometimes obtuse readings of the Hebrew Bible. She is not a goddess, just as any of the sephirotic attributes are not gods. She is an element of the oneness of God. The place of *shekinah* in the Jewish mystical system is one of its most fascinating speculations.

Originally in Talmud and in the Targummim, *shekinah* is not identified as "feminine" as such. Being God's presence, the "glory" of God, she was beyond gender distinctions. *Shekinah* appears often in rabbinic texts but does not appear in Scripture (not unlike the word "Trinity"). Allusions in Scripture to a seemingly transcendant "She"[39] are available and these combined with a mystical reading of the Song of Songs produced the schema of the kabbalists. She is the indwelling of God and

---

36. *Sefer Ha-Bahir* in Scholem, *Origins*.

37. *Sha'arei Orah* 22b., quoted in Scholem, *Mystical Shape of the Godhead*, 104. Matt 4:17: "From that time, Jesus began to preach and say, 'Repent, for the kingdom of heaven is at hand.'"

38. *Sefer Ha-Bahir* S§117 in Scholem, *Origins*.

39. Such as Lady Wisdom in Proverbs 8.

according to them, is best conceived as his counterpart: Queen, Bride, Beloved, Sister, Daughter, Mother.

Chokmah is a significant feminine personification of an aspect of God in the Proverbs and belongs in the upper *sephirot*. Fulfilled in *binah* she is called "the mother." She is also called the upper *shekinah*. The kabbalists see the upper attributes of God as father and mother in the Proverbs: Prov 1:8 (JPS) "Hear, my son, the instruction of your father, and forsake not the teaching of your mother."

The *shekinah* we are discussing here belongs to and is synonymous with the "lower waters" of *malkut* (kingdom), touching earth and connected to the rest of the Godhead via the bridge of *yesod*. *Malkut* and *shekinah* are a synonymous "She." Note the following passage from Cordovero's *Or Ne'erav*: "Malkut receives solely from Yesod, through whom she receives from them all [the *Sephirot*]. Without him, she cannot receive from any of them; without her, none of the *Sephirot* can emante to the lower worlds, for she is the essence of those worlds, conducting them. These are the major channels; their facets are infinite."[40]

Malkut is kingdom. This is the last of the *sephirot*. *Malchut* shines like a ray of light into the world of humans, the earth, the fruit of creation. *Malkut* is also pictured as a gate (Matt 7:14) through which only the righteous, that is those of the *knesset* or *ekklesia*[41] of Israel may enter. She is feminine in nature because she receives from the other attributes of God and responds to them while still being part of God. She is recognized by the metaphor "the Bride," as well as "the Queen" which is also bound up in the feminine imagery associated with Jerusalem, Zion, Judah, and Israel. Even in the Psalms there are mystical allusions to her: "on your right hand stands the queen in gold of Ophir" (Ps 45:9 [MKJV]).

Much of the kabbalists' inspiration for *shekinah* is gleaned from the Song of Songs. What inspires them about the relationship between the "Divine Lovers" is their constant communication and interaction, passion for passion, love for love. They are both strong. "I am the rose of Sharon, a lily of the valleys. As the lily among thorns, so is My love among the daughters (Song 2:1–3 [MKJV])."

---

40. *Or Ne'erav* §6, (Moses Cordovero) quoted in Matt, *Essential Kabbalah*, 43.

41. See Scholem's discussion of the connection between the mystical idea of "knesset Israel" and church, "ekklesia" of the ancient Christianity in Scholem, *Mystical Shape of the Godhead*, 145.

The kabbalists also recognized the anticipative and love-unfulfilled quality of the Songs and saw in this God's intense desire for reunion with the *shekinah*. But they considered that such intense longing is evident mostly when two parties are separated or prevented from culminating their love. Could the *shekinah* possibly be separated from God?

The idea of the *shekinah* in exile is a focal concept in *Sifra-Zohar*. The *shekinah* however was not exiled due to some irreconcilable difference within the Godhead. It is for the sake of the *Knesset Ysrael*, the *ekklesia,* that she comes down.

> At times this *middah* is called Shekhinah, for it has dwelt constantly with Israel since the making of the mishkan, as it is written, "and let them make Me a sanctuary that I might dwell among them"... Hence, the Shekhinah dwelt with the lower ones; and so long as the Shekhinah was below, heaven and earth were one ... But when Adam came and sinned, the ranks were disrupted, the channels were shattered and the pools [of blessing] were cut off. There-upon the Shekhinah withdrew and the bond [connecting all things] became undone. Then Abraham, Isaac and Jacob of blessed memory came and began to draw the Shekhinah back down again ... and they made their bodies into thrones for the Shekhinah. But the Shekhinah did not come down to a fixed dwelling on earth, but only to a temporary one, and it dwelled with them [the Patriarchs] ... But Moses, of blessed memory and all of Israel together with him built the Tabernacle and the vessels, and repaired the broken channels, and put the ranks in order, and repaired the ponds, and drew live water into them.[42]

Her goal is as a bride's is, preparing for her marriage—a mystical reunion between *malkut* and *tiferet*, or in some traditions at the level of *yesod*. She is the bride and Messiah is the bridegroom. This husband-wife partnership of the Godhead is often symbolised mystically in the narratives of the Patriarchs. For example the *shekinah* is likened to Rachel, wife of Jacob. There is an unusual reference to a transcendent Rachel in the prophet Jer 31:15: "A voice was heard in Ramah, wailing and bitter weeping; Rachel weeping for her sons; she refuses to be comforted for her sons, because they are not."

In the identification of *shekinah* with the *knesset* of Israel and as bride with the goal of uniting (through marriage) with Messiah we have strong New Testament parallels. "For this cause a man shall leave his

---

42. *Sha'Arei Orah* §9 (Joseph Gikatilla). Ibid., 177.

father and mother and shall be joined to his wife, and the two of them shall be one flesh. This is a great mystery, but I speak concerning Christ and the church" (Eph 5:30–33 [MKJV]). And further, "And one of the seven angels who had the seven vials full of the seven last plagues came to me and talked with me, saying, 'Come here, I will show you the bride, the Lamb's wife'" (Rev 21:9 [MKJV]).

The kabbalists believe there is some property within *shekinah* that draws towards the righteous on earth, but that also enables the *ekklesia* to be drawn up towards God. This enabling by the Spirit of God is reminiscent in the parable of the ten wise and foolish virgins, only those with oil could enter the marriage: "Then shall the kingdom of Heaven be likened to ten virgins, who took their lamps and went out to meet the bridegroom ... the wise took oil in their vessels with their lamps ... And they who were ready went in with him to the marriage, and the door was shut" (Matt 25:1–10 [MKJV]).

It is the *shekinah*, the holy indwelling, according to the kabbalists that is the conduit between the righteous (by faith) to Messiah. She is the heart of the *ekklesia*, dwelling in their midst and within them. This re-unification with God is the goal of the *ekklesia*, restoring the *shekinah* within them to God. Thus *shekinah* dwells in a world of redemption.

> It is the way of the world that if one man wishes to take another's wife, becomes angry and does not allow it. But the Holy One does not act in this way! "This is the offering"—this is the Congregation of Israel. Even though all of her love is for Him, and all of His love is for her, [the children of Israel] take her away from Him, that she may dwell among them ... And even though they take her, they are only able to do so with the permission of her husband and his will, so that they may perform the service of love before Him. (Zohar §2, 135a)[43]

In the tradition of Zohar *Bereshit* §52 even as early as Gen 3 when humanity is expelled from the garden, *shekinah* is the provision of God that goes with them. In the midst of the community she reflects the light of the Godhead like a mirror. However the sins and neglect of the *knesset* muddy her garments. As one zealot saw in a vision,

> Upon raising his eyes, he saw above the [western] wall a figure of a woman with her back toward him; out of respect for our Creator, I shall not record the garb in which he saw her. But as

43. Ibid., 184.

soon as he saw her in this state, he fell upon his face and cried out in tears: "Mother Zion! Woe is me that I have seen you thus!" And he wept and tore his beard and the hairs of his head until he swooned and collapsed and fell upon his face and slept. Then he saw in a dream that she came and put her hand on his face and wiped away his tears and said to him: "Be comforted, Abraham my son, There is hope for thy future, and thy children shall return to their own border." (Jer 31:17)[44]

The reverse is true also, that the righteous adorn her with their righteous acts and are thus carried up in her trains. The garments of the "Bride" are made pure on the basis of righteous ones. Revelation attests to a similar notion. "And it was given to her to clothe herself in fine linen, shining *and* pure; for the fine linen is the righteous acts of the saints" (Rev 19:7–8 [MKJV]). But, as is evident also in the passage about Rabbi HaLevi's vision, she is a comforter, and active in translating the attributes of the Godhead to the *knesset*.

CONCLUSION

The kabbalistic system's concept of God based on a transcendent unity of male and female is profound and provocative. Are there lessons that can be learned from this system? Can it provoke and challenge Christianity to deepen its understanding of the representation of femininity and masculinity in the Godhead.

This final passage is from *Iggeret ha-Qodesh*, written in the thirteenth century. A Jewish mystic writes a letter about the sacredness of marital sexuality on the occasion of his son's marriage. He refutes the Christian and Jewish philosophy of the time that even marital sexuality was a necessary evil and that women were generally unwelcome in heaven. His letter is a profound reflection on the divine equilibrium that masculinity and femininity represent. The passage is beautifully affirming towards women, astonishing material to come out of thirteenth century Italy. This equitable syzygy of a man and woman within the marriage covenant is an outworking of the mystic's notions about God and takes him ahead of his time. The passage describes a holistic intimacy, involv-

---

44. A story of Rabbi Abraham HaLevi of Safed, by Shlomo Shlimel Dresnitz (seventeenth century). Ibid., 192–93.

ing all that is human: the mind, the soul, the intellect, the emotions, the senses. It is also spiritual, an echo from heaven.[45]

> The union of a man and a woman, when it is right is the secret of civilization. Thereby, one becomes a partner with GOD in the act of creation. This is the secret of the saying of the sages: "When a man unites with his wife in holiness, the divine presence is between them." Human thought has the power to expand and ascend to its origin. Attaining its source she is joined with the upper light from which she emanated. She and he become one. Then, when thought emanates once again, all becomes a single ray: the upper light is drawn down again by the power of thought. In this way the divine presence appears on earth. A bright light shines and spreads around the place where the mediator is sitting. Similarly when a man and a woman unite, and their thought joins the beyond, that thought draws down the upper light. You should welcome her with words that draw her heart, calm her mind, and bring her joy. Then her mind will be linked with yours, and your intention with hers. Speak with her in words that arouse desire, love and passionate union—and words that draw her to the awe of GOD.

The representation of the Godhead has consequence. The way people define God in terms of gender impacts the way the people define humanity, and gender within humanity. The kabbalistic system as conceived and experienced by the mystic who authored *Iggeret ha-Qodesh* has clear earthly consequence with regard to gender. In this letter, man and woman have equality as persons and agents, both are seen as welcomed by heaven and their unification via their sexuality is sacred, mutual and joyful.

---

45. Matt, *Essential Kabbalah*, 155.

14

Imaging the Triune God in Otherness and Encounter

A Response to Yael Klangwisan

DAVID WILLIAMS

AT THE CONCLUSION OF her essay, "Divine Masculine and Feminine in Judeo-mystico: A Tree of Life," Yael Klangwisan asks the question any theologically-minded Christian reader would have asked already: Can the Kabbalistic conception of God, based on a transcendent unity of male and female, provoke and challenge Christianity to deepen its understanding of the equal sharing of femininity and masculinity in the Godhead? The question seems to make two assumptions about Christian theological views[1] on the issue of gender within God: 1) that orthodox Christianity has any "understanding" of femininity and masculinity within the Godhead at all; and, that if it does, 2) its understanding needs to be "deepened." On the first assumption alone I would have to respond with No: the Kabbalistic conception of gender in God has nothing to add to the Christian conception of God, since the traditional position would not speak of gender within the Godhead, at least not in the way the Kabbalists would. But on the second assumption I would argue that the Kabbalistic conception of God, at least as presented by Klangwisan, certainly does have the potential to stoke the conversation about the being of God, and perhaps even deepen our appreciation of how the gender question can inform our understanding of God's relationality—though perhaps not in the way Klangwisan's essay anticipates. So, an apt

---

1. By "Christian" I have assumed that Klangwisan means, roughly, orthodox Christian belief.

response to Klangwisan's concluding question, to echo a popular British comedy duo, is "Yes, but—no, but!"

On the first point, I have a concern with the assumption Klangwisan seems to make on how "Christianity" works gender into its conception of the Godhead. Klangwisan describes this as the "traditional Christian notion of the Godhead as a masculine triune." She contrasts this with the Kabbalistic conception of God as a "unity of male and female akin to marriage," which Klangwisan evaluates as "vastly more inclusive and egalitarian than the traditional Christian notion." If there is such a thing as a "traditional Christian notion of the Godhead" it is doubtful that one could accurately categorise it as a masculine triunity. For one thing, the metaphors of Father, Son, and Spirit represent relational categories—they are not gender labels. Secondly, these descriptors are hardly Christian notions. They are drawn from Jesus Christ's own claim to be the Son of the Father who he knows uniquely in the Spirit. A major difference between Christian theology and the Jewish mystical conceptions of God as presented by Klangwisan is the claim of revelation in Jesus as a foundation for method. While the Kabbalists hold to an "otherworldly journey to God," a walk "through the halls of heaven," Christian theological method begins and ends with God's self-revelation in the midst of this world, in the human being Jesus Christ. It rejects such an otherworldly theological exercise as gnostic, and as an attempt to discover God via our own means. Christian theology takes its lead, and measures its discourse, against Jesus, and against the earliest, and the prior, witnesses to him. For this reason it holds to the metaphors Christ uses of himself and his God as normative, and seeks to avoid projecting other descriptors onto God. It is no surprise, then, that in a system that does not begin with God's self-revelation in Jesus we discover the idea that God is both, and equally, masculine and feminine. A theological method that begins with the phenomenological and takes an otherworldly journey to God is always at risk of viewing God in humanity's image, whether that be in the gender categories of male and female, or any other anthropomorphic category. Inclusive and egalitarian it may be, but it is not necessarily good theology.

James B. Torrance summarises the "Christian" position on gender in God this way: "The ancient church hammered out the doctrine, as in the Nicene Creed, against any sexist notions. They were clear that there is no gender in God; but, in revealing himself, God has commandeered human language and named himself as 'Father.'"[2] Father is a name, not merely a human metaphor—and, according to Torrance, certainly not a metaphor we are to project onto God. "In theology our knowledge of God as Father is derived from his self-revelation in Jesus Christ. The danger of certain extreme liberal feminists is that they evacuate the word 'Father' of all the content Jesus has put into it, and then want to dismiss the word as sexist and patriarchal—in effect accusing Jesus of mythologising."[3]

Miroslav Volf deals with the implications of projecting human categories of gender onto God in far more depth than I can do here.[4] Like Volf, I consider the equality between men and women a given.[5] I also share with Volf the view that there is a fundamental equivalence between masculine and feminine metaphors about God,[6] though with some reserve. For example, because Jesus was a man, the name "Son" is more than a metaphor. However, it should never be used to categorise God as "male." The fundamental purpose of the incarnation was to reveal God in his humanness, not in his maleness. It was in his humanity that Jesus Christ redeemed fallen humanity—his was a vicarious life of inclusion, of both male and female. It could also be argued, particularly on the basis of Col 1:15–20, that his vicarious representation was on behalf of the whole creation.

As Volf notes, most theologians would agree that God is "beyond sexual distinction."[7] Masculine and feminine metaphors are used to depict God not because God is either male or female, but because he is "personal." What "personal" means with regards to God is a huge area of discussion, and will be addressed in brief below. But Volf quite rightly points out that the fatherhood of God, and the sonship of Jesus, do not comment on God's gender, but on his relationality. I suspect that in the Judeo-mystical tradition we are witnessing what Volf describes as the ontologizing of gender in God—the assumption that gender distinc-

---

2. James B. Torrance, *Worship, Community and the Triune God of Grace* (Downers Grove, IL: InterVarsity, 1996) 101.

3. Ibid., 100.

4. Miroslav Volf, *Exclusion and Embrace: A Theological Exploration of Identity, Otherness, and Reconciliation* (Nashville: Abingdon, 1996).

5. Ibid., 170.

6. Ibid.

7. Ibid.

tion is present within God's own being, and the shaping of our social practices on the basis of that projection. But as Volf argues, according to the Genesis creation accounts men and women share their maleness and femaleness with the animals, not God. Humans "image God in their common humanity."[8] If the "equal sharing of femininity and masculinity in the Godhead" is our basis for femininity being viewed "less as passive and supplementary and more as an integral equal force: partnering and passionately responsive,"[9] then I think we are in trouble. It is not gender in God, but rather the self-surrendering love that is played out between the Son and the Father in the Spirit which gives us a more certain theological basis for mutual respect, wonder and appreciation between genders. Says Volf, "Instead of setting up ideals of femininity and masculinity, we should root each in the sexed body and let the social construction of gender play itself out guided by the vision of the identity of and relations between divine persons."[10]

Of far more value to a discussion of God's relational nature, and also to our understanding of gender distinction, formation, and appreciation, is the idea played with by Klangwisan of syzygy. This idea, of a coming together of two discrete objects in opposition, in God—and reflected in the marriage covenant—speaks to the sense of otherness in God which is vital to a proper understanding of his internal relationality. Otherness in God maintains the distinction between the "persons" in God—the Father, Son, and Spirit—so that when we speak of humans as image of God we are able to maintain the distinction between genders, while also recognising that only together, in their mutual encounter and participation, do they truly image a God who is, in himself, self and other.

Volf argues that in trinitarian theology persons should never be reduced to relations, a flawed view of God's internal relationality usually attributed to Karl Barth.[11] For Barth, God's unity in his "threeness" was grounded in his lordship, in his answering to no other authority than himself. Barth termed this lordship the "one essence of the revealed God,"[12] and subsequently spoke of the Father, Son, and Spirit as three

---

8. Ibid., 173.
9. Klangwisan, "Divine Masculine and Feminine."
10. Ibid., 182.
11. Ibid., 177.
12. Karl Barth, *Church Dogmatics* I/1. Translated by G. W. Bromiley (Edinburgh: T. & T. Clark, 1975) 360.

modes of being (Seinsweise) of this one divine essence. In grounding God's triunity in an "essence" Barth blurred the distinctions between the "persons" of the triune God. But his understanding of God's triunity was based in a valid concern—he argued that the term "person" had become so laden with notions of individualism that to use it of God would open the door to tritheism—multiple gods. Nevertheless, Moltmann has taken issue with Barth and argued that it is precisely the personal characteristics of the Father, Son, and Spirit which both differentiate and bring them together, in what he terms the "circulation" of the eternal divine life.[13] Moltmann's concern is to preserve what I have called the otherness within God—the very clear distinction between the "I" of the Father and the "Thou" of the Son, an encounter that occurs in the Spirit. Moltmann himself has been challenged on this point, however. Alan Torrance has taken issue both with Moltmann's use of person and Barth's reticence to use the term. Torrance argues that Moltmann sails close to tritheism because of his "projection of anthropological categories into God and the generic (non-analogical) application of the terms 'person,' 'social,' and 'community' to both the divine and human realms."[14] In other words, Moltmann is accused of projecting his own definition of personhood onto God, much as I have accused Kabbalistic thought of doing with gender distinction. Similarly, Torrance challenges Barth's use, or non-use, of the term person, since in describing as "hopeless" the task of defining personhood in the doctrine of the Trinity, Barth also seems to have bowed to an anthropological, generic understanding of the term, rather than redefine the term in light of revelation, the very process of thinking-after (nachdenken) which is Barth's main concern throughout this particular discussion of the revelation of God. The consequences of losing the distinction of the three persons in God is significant when it comes to crafting an anthropology based on our theological understanding. The negative implications are usually seen, for example, in the attempt to find equality between genders by either transforming one gender into another, or by synthesising the two.[15] As Volf expresses it,

---

13. Jürgen Moltmann, *The Trinity and the Kingdom*, translated by Margaret Kohl (Minneapolis: Fortress, 1993).

14. Alan J. Torrance, *Persons in Communion: Trinitarian Description and Human Participation* (Edinburgh: T. & T. Clark, 1996).

15. Volf, *Exclusion and Embrace*, 184.

"not surprisingly, those who strive to achieve equality sometimes seek refuge in sameness."[16]

This is not the case in Jewish mystical thought, however, where "unity to diversity to unity is the crucial concept."[17] The idea that the syzygy of the masculine and feminine is a precondition of all the worlds is also a nice idea, and has echoes even in Torrance's trinitarian thought: "The gospel does not eliminate our gender identity. But as men and women we find our masculine and feminine identity and fulfilment in Christ, our true being in mutual communion."[18]

I would argue that the idea of otherness is key to Barth's anthropology, despite the apt critique of his modalism by Volf and others. While Barth speaks of the triune God in terms of the "participation of each mode of being in the other modes of being"—essentially Barth's perichoretic circle—he also speaks, in the very same paragraph, of a difference in which there is also fellowship;[19] in other words, a syzygy. Barth's concern with the term person was that, in its ancient conceptualisation, the idea of relativity, or relationality, was not expressed. But, for Barth, person is only complete when there is relationship, communion, and fellowship. So, God is person because there is otherness and fellowship in God, whereas the human needs another in order to be person. When Barth extends this idea to develop an anthropology around the imago Dei, he again stresses otherness—God creates a counterpart in the human, a "Thou," whom he can encounter as an "I."[20] The "image of God" in the human is "simply the existence of the I and the Thou in confrontation."[21] This confrontation is also imaged in the confrontation between man and woman. The gender distinction enables an encounter between human and human that resonates with the encounter between the human and God: "In this way he repeats in his confrontation of God and himself the confrontation in God."[22] The differentiation of gender is the only differentiation in humanity that images the otherness between God and humanity, according to Barth's reading of Gen 1. It is an act

16. Ibid. 185.
17. Klangwisan, "Divine Masculine and Feminine," 5.
18. Torrance, *Worship, Community and the Triune God of Grace*, 105.
19. *CD* I/1, 370.
20. *CD* III/1. (Edinburgh: T. & T. Clark, 1958) 184.
21. Ibid., 185.
22. Ibid., 186.

of special grace towards humanity, the gift of differentiation and relationship that is the "true creaturely image of God."[23] That humanity was created as man and woman is "the great paradigm of everything that is to take place between him and God, and also of everything that is to take place between him and his fellows. The fact that he was created and exists as male and female will also prove to be not only a copy and imitation of his Creator as such, but at the same time a type of the history of the covenant and salvation which will take place between him and his Creator."[24] In other words, the gender differentiation and relationship that we see in human persons does not directly image gender in God as such. But it does image the "I-Thou" encounter within God, as well as the "I-Thou" encounter between God and God's human counterpart. The idea of syzygy speaks nicely to this encounter, in which the coming together of two objects in opposition preserves both differentiation and relationship.

Volf picks up on this idea in the thought of Joseph Ratzinger, who builds his doctrine of the Trinity on the phenomenon of dialogue within God.[25] This idea has promise, but Volf accuses Ratzinger of, ultimately, dissolving the persons of Father and Son into one another with his assertions of self-giving and the presence of the other in the self. The only way around it, argues Volf, is to "affirm self-giving without losing the self and hold on to the presence of the other in the self without slipping into inequality."[26] In other words, we need to maintain the distinctions between the persons of the Godhead, while also asserting their mutual indwelling in love. Says Volf, "this indwelling presupposes that the otherness of the other—the other's identity—has been preserved, not as self-enclosed and static 'pure identity' but as open and dynamic 'identity-with-non-identity.'"[27] Despite Volf's critique of Ratzinger, the latter's use of the category of dialogue should not be set aside too quickly, since dialogism provides a very useful category for which to understand the dynamics of otherness and participation. However, it is not the thought of a theologian but that of a Russian literary philosopher, Mikhail Bakhtin, that, I argue, gives dialogism its greatest clarity.

23. Ibid.
24. Ibid., 186–87.
25. Volf, *Exclusion and Embrace*, 177.
26. Ibid., 179.
27. Ibid., 180.

Bakhtin's theories were concerned with the worlds, and utterances, of both fictional characters, and flesh and blood people. Bakhtin did not use his thought to illuminate literature, but used literature, "quite selectively, to illustrate the course of his thought."[28] Bakhtin saw himself primarily not as a literary theorist but as a "thinker," a philosophical anthropologist[29] whose fundamental principle was that "it is impossible to conceive of any being outside of the relations that link it to the other."[30] As Emerson summarises, Bakhtin's assumption was that "genuine knowledge and enablement can begin only when my 'I' consults another 'I' and then returns to its own place, humbled and enhanced."[31] How this idea impacts the relations between authors and characters, and between readers and characters, can be seen taking shape in Bakhtin's early essay (c. 1920-1923) "Author and Hero in Aesthetic Activity."[32]

One idea is said to undergird much of Bakhtin's thought—that of simultaneity, that identity encompasses differences not through a process of homogenisation, or by being the same as, but by being simultaneous with, thereby allowing for difference, variety, freedom, and unpredictability. Clark and Holquist[33] see simultaneity as the larger category behind Bakhtin's theories of polyphony in *Problems of Dostoevsky's Poetics*,[34] and heteroglossia in *The Dialogic Imagination*.[35] Heteroglossia (other voices) is Bakhtin's way of describing how every utterance is shot through with other, alien voices. It is "another's speech in another's language, serving to express authorial intentions but in a refracted way."[36] Polyphony is the

28. Caryl Emerson, *The First Hundred Years of Mikhail Bakhtin* (Princeton: Princeton University Press, 1997) 74.

29. Katherine Clark and Michael Holquist, *Mikhail Bakhtin* (Cambridge, MA: Belknap, 1984) 3.

30. Tzvetan Todorov, *Mikhail Bakhtin: The Dialogical Principle,* Translated by Wlad Godzich, Theory and History of Literature 13 (Manchester: Manchester University Press, 1984) 94.

31. Emerson, "First Hundred Years of Mikhail Bakhtin," 26.

32. Mikhail M. Bakhtin, "Author and Hero in Aesthetic Activity (c. 1920-1923)," in *Art and Answerability: Early Philosophical Essays by M. M. Bakhtin*, edited by Michael Holquist and Vadim Liapunov (Austin: University of Texas, 1990) 81-87.

33. Clark and Holquist, "Mikhail Bakhtin," 9.

34. Mikhail Bakhtin, *Problems of Dostoevsky's Poetics*, translated by C. Emerson (Minneapolis: University of Minnesota Press, 1984).

35. Mikhail M. Bakhtin, *The Dialogic Imagination,* translated by Caryl Emerson and Michael Holquist (Austin: University of Texas, 1981).

36. Ibid., 324.

word used by Bakhtin to describe a literary design unique to the novels of Fyodor Dostoevsky. For a work to be polyphonic it must be comprised of a dialogic conception of truth, and the author must assume a position relative to the novel's characters that enables a faithful expression of that sense of truth through the characters' individuality and unique perspectives on the world. These two concepts require further explanation.

Dialogical truth is best encapsulated by the conversation, in which several voices come together to create something that is quite separate from each of them but, nevertheless, requires their participation. In the process their voices do not merge—they do not surrender their individuality. Indeed, a multiplicity of distinct voices is essential for a conversation to take place. Even when those voices are competing with one another the dialogue retains its integrity. Likewise, a multiplicity of voices is essential for dialogical truth to be generated, since dialogism reflects multiple and distinct perspectives (ideologies) on the world. Another way of saying this is that dialogical truth requires a "plurality of unmerged consciousnesses."[37] Bakhtin characterises the monologic world as "Ptolemaic": the earth, representing the author's consciousness, is the centre around which all other consciousnesses revolve. The polyphonic world is "Copernican"; as the earth is but one of many planets, the author's consciousness is but one of many consciousnesses.[38] A polyphonic work is one in which the author has intentionally created such a multivoiced environment.

Dialogical truth has a personal, embodied and unrepeatable quality, since the utterances which comprise it are unique to the people who have made them. Indeed, for words to become an utterance, Bakhtin argues—to move beyond the logical and semantic relationships that constitute simple statements—they must be embodied, they must be uttered: "They must enter another sphere of existence: they must become discourse, that is, an utterance, and receive an author, that is, a creator of the given utterance whose position it expresses."[39] Bakhtin calls these utterances "voice-ideas," since they express a unique idea of the world. Voice-ideas represent "a unity of idea and personality: the idea represents a person's integral point of view on the world, which cannot be

---

37. Bakhtin, "Problems of Dostoevsky's Poetics," 9.

38. Gary S. Morson and Caryl Emerson, *Mikhail Bakhtin: Creation of a Prosaics* (Stanford, CA: Stanford University, 1990) 240.

39. Bakhtin, "Problems of Dostoevsky's Poetics," 184, emphases original.

abstracted from the person voicing it."[40] Each voice-idea is ideologically independent. Propositional statements are not voice-ideas, since they are monologic in nature. They are not embodied, since they mean the same whether spoken by one person or by another. Neither do they require a plurality of voices to "mean"; they can be understood and expressed fully by a single consciousness. A conversation, on the other hand, can never fully be comprehended by a single mind. When "monologic thinkers" overhear a dialogue between voice-ideas they "usually try to extract just such a finalising proposition, but in doing so they are false to the dialogic process itself."[41] So, dialogic truth cannot be systematised, since a system requires finalised propositions. What emerges from the dialogue is not a system but an event, the event of distinct voices interacting dialogically.

There are clear parallels between the idea of distinct voices dialoguing—of two or more voice-ideas encountering one another and generating a dialogue that means beyond both of them—and the "I-Thou" encounter that we have discussed in Barth, as well as Volf's dynamic "identity-with-non-identity," and Klangwisan's syzygy. These are helpful categories not only for our understanding of the triune God's inner relationality and dialogical engagement with humanity, but also for describing the dynamic imaging of God that occurs in the encounter between male and female. I suggest that Bakhtin's dialogism is a far more apt way of describing the relationality between Father and Son in the Spirit than the Kabbalist view of gender syzygy in God. I also suggest that it provides a much broader, and more intriguing place to begin our consideration of the relational dynamics between male and female than the idea of the female as "an integral equal force."[42] I suggest that Bakhtin's thought, in particular, provides an opportunity to speak about the dynamics of gender engagement without talking about equality in a way that veers toward sameness. Bakhtin emphasised variety, difference, heterogeneity, dialogue, performance, actuality, the carnivalization of authority, unpredictability, uncertainty, unfinalizability, and the centrifugal forces of existence, which "compel movement, becoming, and history" and "long for change and new life."[43] Bakhtin viewed existence as a struggle between these forces and the centripetal forces of stasis, homogenisation,

---

40. Morson and Emerson, "Mikhail Bakhtin: Creation of a Prosaics," 237.
41. Ibid., 237.
42. Klangwisan, "Divine Masculine and Feminine," 15.
43. Clark and Holquist, "Mikhail Bakhtin," 8.

sameness, and death. He denounced monologism—the idea that truth can be contained in a single belief system, god, text, or person—because such "truth" can be controlled and manipulated. He located meaning in the community: "My voice can mean, but only with others—at times in chorus, but at the best of times in dialogue."[44]

Bakhtin's development of the idea of dialogism, from within the Soviet system that was committed absolutely to the ideals of monologism, seems to have been both a reaction against that system, but was achieved also in response to the uncertainties and heterogeneity of life. His belief was that these vagaries were not to be feared and managed, but acknowledged and celebrated. It is this last thought that I would argue is the perfect place to begin a fresh discussion gender distinctions and dynamics—without fear and the impulse to manage the social construction of gender but in a spirit that acknowledges the differences, and celebrates them.

---

44. Ibid., 12.

Contributors

IRENE ALEXANDER (BSc, MPhil, PhD) is a spiritual director, psychologist, and Dean of Social Sciences at Christian Heritage College, Brisbane; lecturing in counselling and personal development. She has recently published *Dancing with God: Transformation through Relationship* (SPCK); *You Can't Play the Game if You Don't Know the Rules: How Relationships Work* (Lion Hudson); *Interweavings: Conversations between Narrative Therapy and Christian Faith*, edited with Richard Cook (CreateSpace). Irene is the mother of two adult sons.

MIRIAM J. BIER (BA, Dip Tchg, MTh, PhD cand.) is a PhD student in Biblical Studies, currently working on a theological reading of Lamentations. She completed her Masters of Theology at LCGS in 2007 and in a previous life was a teacher of mathematics. Miriam has a particular interest in how difficult Old Testament texts may continue to have life as God's word to the church today, especially in light of valid critique from feminist (and other) voices. Miriam loves being godmother and aunt; and enjoys being part of the vibrant questioning and worshipping community at Ponsonby Baptist Church.

CRAIG BLOMBERG (BA, MA, PhD) is Distinguished Professor of New Testament in Denver Seminary, Littleton, Colorado, USA. Previously he taught at Palm Beach Atlantic College in West Palm Beach, Florida, and has been guest professor at more than a dozen colleges and universities around the world. He has authored twelve books, and co-authored or co-edited five others. His books include commentaries on Matthew, 1 Corinthians, and James, and works on the historical reliability of the New Testament, wealth and poverty, the parables of Jesus, and a New Testament introduction and survey. He has written more than eighty journal articles or chapters in multi-author works. Craig is married and they have two grown children.

Tim Bulkeley (BSc, MA, PhD) lectures at Carey Baptist College in Old Testament and is a faculty member of LCGS. He has lectured in the University of Auckland and the Université protestante du Congo. He has also been visiting lecturer in the University of Sheffield, Colombo Theological Seminary, Sri Lanka, and in a refugee camp. His PhD thesis concerned the use of motherly language and imagery for God in the Bible and Christian tradition. He developed a prototype of a new type of biblical commentary in *Amos: Hypertext Bible Commentary*, and is editing a companion *Hypertext Bible Dictionary*.

Joyce Carswell (BA, MA (Hons), MTh, NZAC, NZCCA) is the Clinical Co-ordinator of Counselling at Laidlaw College where she was initially responsible for developing the Diploma of Counselling. Joyce completed her Counselling training at the University of Auckland and has worked as a Counsellor in both community-based and church-based settings. Her particular interest lies in integrative approach to counselling and theology with relationality as an underlying focus. Joyce is widowed and has two adult children and five grand children.

Kevin Giles (MA, BD, ThD) is a graduate of Moore Theological College Sydney. He has been an ordained Anglican minster for over forty years and has led a number of parishes. He has published widely on Lucan theology, the church, church health, ministry in the apostolic age, and the Trinity. In 1977 he published his first book, *Women and their Ministry: A Case for Equal Ministries in the Church Today*. Since then he has published other books and numerous articles on the Bible's teaching on the status and ministry of women. In recent years he has led the opposition by some evangelicals to ground women's subordination in the immanent Trinity—see his *Jesus and the Father: Modern Evangelicals Reinvent the Doctrine of the Trinity* (Zondervan, 2006). He is married to Lynley and they have four grown up children and nine grandchildren.

Myk Habets (BMin, MTh, Grad Dip Tert Tchg, PhD) lecturers in Systematic Theology, and is the Director of the R. J. Thompson Centre for Theological Studies, Carey Baptist College and Graduate School, Auckland, New Zealand. His publications include: *Theosis in the Theology of Thomas Torrance* (Ashgate, 2009), *The Anointed Son* (Pickwick, 2010), *The Spirit of Truth*, editor (Pickwick, 2010); and *Trinitarian Theology after Barth,* editor (Pickwick, 2010). He is currently working on a series of edited books to do with Calvinism, culture, and the *filioque.* Myk is married and they have two children.

NICOLA HOGGARD-CREEGAN (BA (Hons), MATS, MPhil, PhD) lectures in systematic theology at Laidlaw College and LCGS. She studied mathematics at Victoria, biology in Australia, and theology at Gordon Conwell and Drew University, New Jersey. She co-authored *Living on the Boundaries: Evangelical Women, Feminism and the Theological Academy* (IVP, 2005). Nicola was a participant in the 2003–2005 Templeton Oxford Seminars in Science and Christian Faith. She chairs a Local Society Initiative in theology and the natural sciences (TANSA), and writes a column on science and faith issues for the NZ Journal *Stimulus.* She has a book on *Animal Suffering and the Problem of Evil* coming out with Macmillan in early 2011. Nicola is married and they have two University aged sons.

MARK KEOWN (BTh (Hons), Dip Tch, ThD) is a senior lecturer in theology specialising in New Testament at Laidlaw College in Auckland NZ and is an LCGS faculty member. He has previously been a school teacher, a minister in Presbyterian and Baptist contexts and has lectured at World Gospel College and Carey Baptist College. He has published a number of articles and recently published his ThD as *Congregational Evangelism in Philippians* (Paternoster, 2008). Mark's wife is a Presbyterian Minister and they have three daughters.

YAEL KLANGWISAN (BAppSci, MEd, MTh, PhD cand.) lectures in Education at Laidlaw College. She has worked in a number of fields including exploration geology, science research, and science teaching in Australia and the USA. Yael has also studied linguistics and worked in language education in New Zealand and Asia. Yael is a life-long student of Hebrew language and Hebrew sacred literature and is currently writing a PhD that explores ancient Hebrew poetry using existential philosophy. Her research interests lie in areas of socio-linguistics, Jewish thought, the phenomenon of faith and faith-science dialogue. Yael is married and she and her husband have two children.

IMMANUEL KOKS (BSc, Grad Dip Sc, Grad Dip Theol), upon graduating in mathematics and computer science, worked as a scientific software engineer and web developer for a Crown Research Institute. After going on an OE, Immanuel returned to education in 2005 when he completed a Graduate Diploma in Theology at Laidlaw College. He is continuing studies with a Master of Christian Studies at Regent College, Vancouver Canada. Immanuel's research is in the way the hope of the gospel impacts the lives of people who have disabilities or who suffer in other ways.

PETER LINEHAM (MA (Hons), BD, Dphil), Associate Professor, is a scholar in aspects of history and religion. He teaches history at Massey University's Albany campus, NZ, having previously taught in the History Department at Massey's Palmerston North campus. He now serves also as Head of the School of Social and Cultural Studies. Peter has written articles on many aspects of English and New Zealand religious history and his books include *There We Found Brethren, No Ordinary Union* and *Bible and Society*. He co-edited the standard text on New Zealand's religious history, *Transplanted Christianity*. His interpretations of trends in religion in New Zealand are also frequently reported by the media. He has long been active in a range of church organisations and is also currently involved in the establishment of a Peace Studies Centre and in Tertiary Chaplaincy co-ordination

CHRIS MARSHALL (BA (Hons), BD, MA, PhD) is St Johns Associate Professor of Christian Theology, Religious Studies Department, Victoria University of Wellington. Chris' specialities include the study of New Testament theology and ethics, peace theology and practice, and restorative justice—both theory and practice. He is also an expert in the study of contemporary Anabaptist theology. Chris is married and they have two children.

TIM MEADOWCROFT (MA, Dip Tchg, BD, PhD) is a Senior Lecturer in Biblical Studies in the School of Theology at Laidlaw College (Auckland Campus), where he has been since 1994, and is an LCGS faculty member. He has made a particular study of the books of Daniel and Haggai, on which he has published commentaries as well as articles in a range of journals. This reflects his interest in the Second Temple period. He has also published a number of articles on issues in hermeneutics, and is currently working on a volume on "The Message of Scripture" for IVP. He is married and they have four adult children and four grandchildren.

CATHY ROSS (BA, MA, Dip Tchg, BD, PhD) comes from Aotearoa, NZ and is now based in Oxford. She manages the Crowther Centre for Mission Education for CMS and is the J. V. Taylor Fellow in Missiology at the University of Oxford. Cathy has published in the area of missiology. Her current research interests are in contextual theology, hospitality, and women in mission. She is also General Secretary of the International Association for Mission Studies. She is married and she and her husband have three children.

DAVID WILLIAMS (BMin, BTh (Hons), PhD) is lecturer in theology of Laidlaw College and former Dean of the LCGS. He lectures in theology and has developed a new Bachelor of Counselling programme founded on a relational approach that has deep roots in trinitarian theology. David is a former investigative journalist and newspaper editor who has published a book on the mafia in Western Australia. His research interests are theological anthropology, trinitarian theology, and the interface of theology and culture. David is married and he and his wife have four daughters.

BEULAH WOOD (BA, BD, DMin) makes her base at South Asia Institute of Advanced Christian Studies in Bangalore, India, and in Auckland, NZ. A lecturer in preaching, communication, and a biblical view of family and gender, she is also an editor, and author or co-author of over thirty books and booklets.